LULLABY OF BIRDLAND

Also available from Continuum:

John Chilton: Roy Eldridge
Isabelle Leymarie: Cuban Fire
Richard Palmer: Sonny Rollins
Oscar Peterson: A Jazz Odyssey
Alyn Shipton: A New History of Jazz
Alyn Shipton: Fats Waller
John White: Artie Shaw

LULLABY OF BIRDLAND

GEORGE SHEARING
WITH ALYN SHIPTON

continuum
NEW YORK • LONDON

2004

The Continuum International Publishing Group Inc
15 E 26 Street, New York, NY 10017

The Continuum International Publishing Group Ltd
The Tower Building, 11 York Road, London SE1 7NX

www.continuumbooks.com

This edition first published 2004 in hardcover in the United States by Continuum by
arrangement with Bayou Press Ltd.

Printed in the United States of America

Library of Congress Cataloging-in-Publication Data

Shearing, George.
    Lullaby of birdland / George Shearing with Alyn Shipton.
      p.   cm.
    Includes index.
    Discography: p.
    ISBN 0-8264-6015-1 (hardcover : alk. paper)
      1. Shearing, George.   2. Pianists—Great Britain—Biography.   3. Jazz
musicians—Great Britain—Biography.   I. Shipton, Alyn.   II. Title.
    ML417.S57A3   2004
    786.2'165'092—dc22
                                                    2004001218

CONTENTS

To Ellie,
who patiently waited 20 years for this . . .

ACKNOWLEDGEMENTS

The authors would like to acknowledge the help of several people whose contributions behind the scenes have greatly assisted in the preparation of this book. We were first introduced by BBC producer Terry Carter, while making a radio program to celebrate George's 80th birthday. That on-air conversation at the piano in the BBC's Pebble Mill studios eventually led to our collaboration in print, and some aspects of our subsequent broadcasts, produced both by Terry Carter and Oliver Jones, have also found their way into the text. We are grateful to the late Dean Jennings, whose interviews from the 1960s provided a backdrop to the present text, and to June Knox-Mawer whose radio interviews with George also opened up several areas for us to cover in more detail. Fiona Cairns gave us useful assistance in preparing the manuscript, and Peter Symes was invaluable in researching pictures. Both the authors and publishers have made every effort to acknowledge all copyright photographs used in the book, and apologise to anyone whose name may have inadvertently been omitted from the credits that are included in the captions to each picture. We would like to pass on our thanks to Alan Siegel for his help in matters contractual, and also to George's manager Dale Sheets.

Finally, and above all, we would like to acknowledge the consistent support of Ellie Shearing without whom this book would not have been possible.

LIST OF ILLUSTRATIONS

Q. *Where were you born?*

A. London, England.

Q. *When were you born?*

A. August 13, 1919

Q. *Why?*

(please turn page)

≡ I ≡

THE HOUSE IN ARTHUR STREET

Being born blind, there was nothing for me to get used to about blindness, because it was there from the start. I didn't know, and still don't, what having sight is like, but from earliest childhood I've also been aware that there isn't such a thing as a blind world. There's a sighted world to which all blind people have to adapt and adjust. This book is about my path through that sighted world, a world perceived mainly through sound, as well as touch, taste, and smell. In due course, as an adult, I eventually came to the conclusion that even if I were offered the chance of sight, I would refuse it, because it would be so shattering to see everything around me that I had only known as sounds up until that point. I'd have to go through a whole new process of education, because everything from reading to writing is entirely different. I'm used to hearing cars go by, not to seeing them flash in front of my eyes.

There are things I'd love to be able to do, such as to get up from a group of friends and say, "I'll see you guys later on," and mean exactly that. Then to be able to move off, totally on my own, to go somewhere else. Of course, all blind people can move with a degree of independence, but not with the ease of a sighted person, and on strange territory it's hard to do it at all—we wait for somebody to be with us. Maybe we miss a lot, but for the most part that's more than made up for by what we have to replace sight— the ability to conceptualize the world through sound, or our other senses, and the close connection with all those other people who help us get our bearings in unfamiliar surroundings, whatever they may be.

Living in a world in which sound plays the most important role has always been a great stimulus to me as a musician.

There were no other musicians in our family, to the best of my knowledge, and I'm the youngest of a family of nine. When I was born, at our house in Battersea, in South London, the oldest ones had already left home, so I remember only four of my sisters, Margaret, Dorothy (whom we called Dolly), Mary, and Lily, and my brother, Jim.

Dolly did domestic work somewhere. Margaret worked in a grocery store. Lily and Mary seemed to have been married forever. Both Mary and Dolly were primarily in the business of raising children, and it seemed that their main preoccupation was to try their damnedest to populate the entire neighborhood. Certainly Dolly, who is over ninety years of age and still living as I write this, had a raft of children—eleven or twelve—and grandchildren to match, so she had a really huge family. Margaret, who was younger, although she's also in her nineties now, was the one who tended to look out for me.

Jim worked on the buses. He was a bus conductor, the character who went around saying, "Fares please!" The passengers would give him a penny or twopence or however much the fare was. Although he did the kind of conducting where a baton was absolutely useless, I kid people quite a bit about him when the topic of conversation turns to the performances of figures like Daniel Barenboim or André Previn.

I say, "My brother was a conductor, you know."

They say, "Really?"

"Yes, on a number 49 bus."

To be honest, I'm not sure at this distance in time whether he worked on a bus or a tram, but he was most certainly a conductor.

If pressed, Jim could probably have cranked out a chorus of *Just a Song At Twilight* on the clarinet. Actually, although I've said there were no other musicians in the family, at a very early age my sisters would come down on Sunday morning and try to play *Chopsticks*. Then I would try to play it after them, while we were waiting for the eggs and bacon to be cooked. I've always referred to them as Sunday morning piano players. Just as we have Sunday drivers now, back in the 1920s there were Sunday morning pianists in Battersea. Sometimes the piano, as ancient and as much of a relic as it was, was all that the player deserved and sometimes it was even more than the player deserved!

We lived in a two-storey house at 67 Arthur Street in Battersea. I can still remember every step of the way to it. You'd turn right off Battersea Park Road, coming from Latchmere Road, into Alfred Street, and then a little twist to the right before heading left into Arthur Street. It's still there today, but sometime after I left, the name was changed to Rawson Street. The whole area was a reasonably poor district and there was a railroad line running right along the bottom of our little street, which was almost a cul-de-sac. The houses were very close together and there was really no garden at all, just a little backyard, the total extent of which was only a few feet. Over the back wall was the next backyard, which was part of Alfred Street. And it would be that way on all sides.

Upstairs was Mum and Dad's bedroom, and two other bedrooms. Downstairs were the kitchen, the dining room, and the living room or "parlor," as it was known in those days. One of the bedrooms became my room as we got older, and it remained my room alone until I finally left home. I had my gramophone and piano in the parlor. We had a piano in the house from my early childhood—or rather we had something which had the hallmarks of a piano in that there were keys on it (85 rather than 88). I believe it was either a Broadwood or a Schlitz. The make didn't matter. What really mattered was the number of keys which were, to all intents and purposes, "unemployed." My parents bought that piano for me.

I seem to remember my Dad saying something about paying five pounds for it and paying three pounds to have me taught to play it. So, it looks like the total sum of my parents' investment into the music business was eight pounds, which in those days was equivalent to about $32. I would say that the reward, although they weren't around, unfortunately, to reap too many of the benefits, was rather handsome.

As I said, Arthur Street was almost a cul-de-sac. The houses were close by to the street and the toilet was in the back garden. That wasn't too bad in the summer. It had a chain to pull, the proper plumbing and everything, but it was in the garden nevertheless, so in the winter it wasn't the most pleasant thing in the world to have to go out there in the middle of the night. The house had no bathroom. We would put a round tin tub in front of a coal fire to take our weekly bath, whether we needed it or not. It was one of those tubs with two handles that you put the washing in, and you kept filling it from the kettle.

My father, James Philip Shearing, was born in Westminster, London, in 1872. The Shearing family originally came from Winterbourne Earls in Wiltshire, where my great-grandfather, Philip George Shearing, was born in 1815. There had been Shearings in that village since the sixteenth century, but my great-grandfather Philip and his young wife Charlotte, whom he had married in Wiltshire, came to London, where he worked in the Artillery Brewery in Westminster, until he was carried off by the great cholera epidemic of 1854. My grandfather was twelve at the time, but he remained in London, so mine was the third generation of Shearings to be Londoners.

In some of the things that have been written about me, my father has been called a coal miner. He's also been called a coal porter, but America already had one of those! Actually, he was a coal man, which meant he put coal into hundredweight or two hundredweight sacks and delivered them to wealthy homes and places of business. I always said jokingly that for his trademark he should have had a question printed on the back of his cart that read, "Do you prefer your coal *à la cart* or *coal de sack?*"

He would get up at somewhere between four thirty and five o'clock in the morning. I don't remember if he got his own breakfast or whether my mother got breakfast for him, but he would leave the house about six, get to the firm, probably between six thirty or quarter to seven and he would come home about five thirty or six at night. For his job, he would wear corduroy pants. Of course, they'd be covered in coal dust and just as he'd go to sit down on a chair at the end of the day, and God knows the chairs in our house were not luxurious in any way, shape, or form, my mother's voice would be heard saying, "Now, Jim, go and change your trousers before you sit down." So he had to go into the bedroom and change his pants, and then come back in, sit down, and have a little bit of dinner.

Later, when I started working at the pub at the age of sixteen, shortly after dinner we would leave the house and go to the pub and get there about seven thirty at night. I would work there until ten. We'd come home, go to bed, and then the next day Dad would be up about four thirty again, and the same routine would be repeated. This happened six days a week. It's amusing to me nowadays to listen to people talking about their three-day-a-week jobs and their holiday for this and sick-pay and sick-time—all of which I feel is a human right—but the discontent that happens when it doesn't appear automatically is something to behold when you come from a family like mine where there was a very hard day's work six days a week.

Regarding my Dad's salary, for all those hours, he would make three pounds a week. When I first came to the United States in the 1940s, there were four dollars to the pound, so that's a weekly salary of twelve dollars. And when he retired he received a pension from the firm of one pound a week. Of course, at 65 he qualified for an additional old-age pension from the state that came to about five shillings—that's much less than a pound, and worked out at about a dollar. However, if he earned any more money on top, that would be taxed. It was calculated by what was called the "means test." In other words, if you had the means to live or even to buy a few crusts of bread above and beyond what you were given as an old-age pension (which you couldn't live on, anyway), you'd be taxed on it.

This came about because, in the 1930s, during the worldwide Depression, economic conditions were so bad that steady work was difficult to find and keep. So the Government of the day decided they had to help the unemployed on a national basis and in 1931 introduced a statutory test of an applicant's income—what was known as his or her "means"—in order to calculate the amount of assistance that they were to receive. But what was originally introduced to help working people eventually became a hindrance, and by the time my father retired, the test was being applied for pensions as well as for unemployment allowances, so the resources of the entire household had to be disclosed, to work out what tax (or occasionally, benefit) was due. This "means test" was always a bug to the working-class people because they weren't even allowed to enjoy their old-age pension without the Government claiming some of it back again.

Dad worked for the same firm—Cockerell's—for close on half a century, and he had a fierce pride. After my mother's death he went to live with my brother, Jim, and his wife, Dora. If you could get by Jim's clumsiness, you could probably find a joke in what Jim was saying somewhere. And I think he tried to show it to my father when he went into the bedroom one morning and said, "Come on, you lazy old man, it's time to get out of bed."

Most people would take that as a joke, but Daddy cried to me about that. He said, "I worked fifty years, all but three months, for the same firm, and your brother called me a lazy old man."

The thing about the Shearing family is that there is a degree of fragility in the make-up of their personality. If you knock it in the wrong place, it chips or breaks, just like my father did when my brother tried to crack that joke with him.

Instead of laughing and saying, "Well, why should a man work when he has the health and strength to lie in bed?" or passing it off in a similar way, it hurt him very, very badly and he cried.

Through all this apparent strength and bravado, we break down quite easily. Say the wrong thing, and there will be a very deep hurt as if you intended to hurt us, and while we know that most thinking and caring and feeling human beings don't want to hurt anybody unless they have a deep hatred, that doesn't lessen the possibility of being hurt by the wrong thing said at the wrong time.

When I was about eleven or twelve, my father would always enter the horse that his firm gave him to use for the coal delivery into the annual horse show in Regent's Park. I used to go on the cart and sit up with him all night long and help polish the harness and make the little rosettes and things to put on the cart and around the horse. It was very exciting. We'd set off about six o'clock in the morning, taking our food with us to go around Regent's Park for the show.

I'd have a little harmonium and I'd sit up and play on the cart while we were driving around to get to where the judge was.

Sometimes it could be quite a heart-breaking thing. You'd spend days on preparing the horse, the little rosettes and so on, until everything would be shiny and polished. All kinds of elbow grease went into shining up the harness and the brasses, so you'd get there and you'd know that the horse is going to win. You'd just know it. My father had fifteen first prizes, so he got to know when he thought he was in the market for first prize or second prize or whatever. But occasionally, you'd get to about fifteen yards from the judge, and the unpredictable would happen—the horse would shy, or become unruly.

And you'd hear: "Disqualified!"

Just like that!

All that work down the drain.

My mother was born Ellen Amelia Brightman, on January 14, 1874, at 8 Rockingham Street, Trinity Newington, London. Her family came originally from Daventry in Northamptonshire. For much of her adult life, she cleaned railroad trains at night and tended the family in the daytime. Until around the time I was born, she worked on the main line trains at a depot not too far from where we lived in Battersea. She actually had a tremendously hard life. Having nine children to care for and with me being blind, it was very rough on her and she really wasn't strong enough to take it. Regrettably, early in life, she turned rather heavily to the bottle and became an alcoholic. I think it was because of her drink problem that I never touched alcohol until I was about forty-five years of age. I can remember walking along the street in Battersea, with my sister and I each holding on to one of my mother's arms, and she'd say, "I need a drink!"

And we'd say, "No! No!"

We could tell she didn't need any more, but she'd insist, "I need a drink!" And she wouldn't be satisfied until she went into the pub and got one. Mainly she just drank beer, but occasionally she turned to whisky.

And yet, through all that, and goaded by the pride of the working class, if anybody came to visit who earned a pound more than Dad, my mother would see to it that there would be a clean, starched, white tablecloth (something we rarely got as a family)

With my mother, late 1920s. (Author's collection)

on the table for that man or woman when they came over. Regardless of whether she drank a lot or not, the presentation that my mother endeavored to make and the way she brought us up was a tremendous credit to her. She was fighting to do the right thing—losing most of the time—but always more than deserving of an "A" for effort.

One curious result of my childhood is that even today when I hear a mother talking to a baby or a toddler, patting it on the head, or singing to it until it goes to sleep, I will start to cry. I connect to all those feelings of calm, warmth, and security. It's just that as a child I have no memory of experiencing them myself.

I never felt close to my mother. In fact, I didn't feel that I was close to either of my parents. That's borne out by the fact that I did not go back to England for their funerals. I stayed in the United States. Mother died of a heart attack in the late 1940s, and I'm not sure of what Daddy died of, but he lived on to the end of the 1950s. I suspect that his death was because of very hard work and premature wearing out of the body.

Nobody really had anything in common with me in the family, and that gulf between us grew during my teenage years, when I went to the residential school for the blind at Linden Lodge. My parents and my sisters were relatively uneducated, and during the time I was receiving a full-time education, I was finding out about a world that had little to do with them and their lives. It's an amazing thing, almost as if I were from another family altogether.

My father, in what I suppose he thought was an attempt to help me and to advise me to do the right thing, would forever be discouraging me. He was one of the old school who believed everybody had his place in society and that you should keep to your own place. If you were a working man, you'd say, "Yes, sir," to your superiors. Such traits are very good in their own way, and I often wish that many more people had a similar level of respect today. For example, I still bristle instinctively when anyone calls me "George" at first meeting. But while one side of me looks back on some of the attitudes of those days with a tinge of regret, I realized long ago that such ideas also carry with them plenty of unnecessary stagnation and stick-in-the-mud thinking, and I have no time for either.

A good instance of my father's discouraging attitude came about after I left school at sixteen to take a job in a pub, the equivalent of a tavern in the United States. When I eventually left that job to go to work for a semi-professional band, he said, "Why are you leaving your job? The landlord's been good to you."

"What do you mean, he's been good to me?" I replied. "He's been paying my salary every week."

I got the princely sum of one pound and five shillings, the equivalent of about five dollars, each week, and there was a box on top of the piano for any extra gratuities the customers cared to donate. You'd be surprised how many times one has to play *Melancholy Baby* under those circumstances!

Every time I left one job to go to another, my father would say the same thing. "Why are you leaving? The boss has been good to you."

Even when I came to America, and after I'd proved that I could have a series of broadcasts and a number of recordings, he just didn't understand that I had achieved everything I wanted to in England and was ready to start my career across the Atlantic. My father would still ask, "Why are you going to the States? You're making enough money over here. What are you trying to prove?"

Frankly, if I had taken notice of him, I would probably still be in that pub today earning five dollars a week. I say this with all due respect to a man who, I'm sure, gave every bit of advice with the best of intentions,

This is the downfall of that generation's "everybody in his place" business. Dad felt my place was there in Battersea. One day when I was writing to the BBC, he came over, looked at the letter on my typewriter and said, "Son, what are you doing?"

I said, "Writing a letter to the BBC, trying to get an audition."

He said, "Son, you know, those jobs are for the nobs. These jobs are not for the likes of us."

He always had this attitude. It was consistent throughout his life. And I suppose that's why he worked fifty years for the same firm—"fifty years all but three months"—and wound up with a princely pension of around a pound a week.

Fifty years! It is incredible that someone could have that tenacity and that loyalty for so long a period of time and then be so poorly remunerated at the end of it.

2

SHILLINGTON STREET SCHOOL

When I was small, my day-to-day life in Battersea fell into a regular pattern. In the morning, my mother, or someone else, would take me to school, which was about a mile from where I lived. I would be there all day and then someone would pick me up at about four o'clock in the afternoon. When I say school, I mean Shillington Street School, located quite close to the Latchmere pub.

About the only thing I remember from that first school took place at the end of each afternoon, when all the kids would get together and sing,

> *Now the day is over;*
> *Night is drawing nigh.*
> *Shadows of the evening*
> *Steal across the sky.*

There was a beauty and a peacefulness about that song which, of course, in my case was not to be followed up by a lot of peacefulness at home.

In those days, I used to go biking in the street with some sighted kids. Being with them, I'd be very envious of those who had mothers who were teetotalers. How lucky they were to be able to go home and communicate with their mothers. If my mother wasn't already drunk by the time I arrived home, then many's the night she would leave and go out to the pub after I'd been to school all day.

It was curious, the way that some working-class people lived in the 1920s, especially if you dared to live to the full extent of your income or beyond. In our family, for instance, the only money we had to live on was generated by my parents' jobs. So to bring in occasional extra cash, we would make a small down payment and use credit to buy in excess of what we needed—extra blankets, extra china, extra tableware—anything that could be pawned for more than the initial amount we had spent on it. This was called "buying on the YP," in other words, "Yours Perhaps."

Every Saturday the tally man would come to the door and want his weekly payment towards what was owed. "Tally man" is a good name—he would tally up the weekly indebtedness. By the time he appeared on your doorstep, the money received from the pawnbroker had usually been spent on food, drink, or clothes, and the upshot was that you neither had the things you'd bought nor the money to pay the installments. It was always the unpleasant task of one of us children to go to the door and say, "Mother will see you next week."

We would each hope that when next week came round there would be a different tally man, to whom we could say the same thing.

The first investigation into why I was blind revealed that there were, apparently, "no backs to the eyes"—whatever that meant. Much later in life, I learned that blindness is often hereditary and that one out of four boys is likely to be born blind if they have a blind parent. But neither of my parents was blind and there was no history of the condition among the Shearings or Brightmans.

One theory in the family, about which I have always wondered, is that having already produced eight other children, my mother tried to abort me herself and failed, leaving me without sight. Another possibility has to do with my actual birth and delivery. The little boy who lived next door to us was also blind, and his mother and mine were attended by the same midwife. Perhaps with medical education not being what it is today, she used the wrong eyedrops on us both?

I will never know the answer.

All I can say to those who ask when I first realized that I was blind is that I don't honestly know exactly when it was, except that it must have been very early in my life, because my blindness was diagnosed soon after I was born.

Regrets or maladjustment among the blind tend to come for the most part from reflections on "I used to remember when it was so-and-so." But having no such barometer to go back to, no experience of ever having been sighted, I have no regrets.

Discounting theories about my mother attempting to abort me, the doctors eventually concurred that I have what is supposed to be a very unusual case of hereditary blindness, even though I was the first one in the family to have it. I have a slight sensitivity to light, but no way at all to visualize color. Of course, I have verbal descriptions of it from other people, and I have tried to translate them into terms I can relate to. For example, if someone said, "Describe blue to me," I would play them a calm Delius piece or something similar. I think Delius is very blue and very calm most of the time. Blue as applied to the blues is just too obvious, and slightly ridiculous. To my mind that's not really the meaning of "blues" at all. If somebody said play something black, I would probably get all kinds of low instruments to create somber sounds. For something white, I would probably have an English soprano and a harp.

I don't know whether I ever thought, "I'm different from other children," although from early in my life I played with most of the others in our immediate neighborhood. Nevertheless it was obvious that if I was going to go out in the street to play cricket with a bunch of sighted kids, I was going to have to have somebody to help me.

The main person who did so was a boy called Freddy, who was one of my older sister Mary's children. Going out with me to play cricket involved Freddy and me holding the bat together. Just holding the bat together is, of course, no guarantee that there's going to be a smooth contact with the ball, because Freddy has to move his arms when he sees which way the ball is coming. He sees it and I don't. So I try to anticipate the way Freddy moves his arms and move mine in the same way. However, once in a while my anticipation is wrong. On one famous occasion, I remember an incident that—if it ever happened in a real game of cricket—would probably be described as "Jaw Before Wicket."

Now, most of us know about Leg Before Wicket, but Jaw Before Wicket is virtually unknown. In just the same way that a cricketer would make an unconscious move, for some reason I stood there fully conscious after this ball had hit me smack on the jaw—I repeat, *fully conscious*—and said, "I'm out!"

In retrospect, I'm not sure if that meant I was out as a batsman or I was out physically!

Cricket was just one of the normal things that kids did, in which I took part. You'll find that a blind person who realizes that he or she has got the rest of life to live, whether they consider the alternative or not, will do as many normal things as they possibly can. If they take too many—or too few—chances, generally it's because they're not well adjusted.

Among the other normal things I did was to ride a bicycle. I got it after my mother said to me, "If you pass your first musical exams, you can have whatever you want as a present, within reason."

Having passed the exam, I said, "I'd like a bike."

She'd promised it to me, so she went out and bought me a big two-wheeled bike. I used to ride it around the block by myself because the noise made by the chain was usually enough for me to hear whether there was anything in front of me or not. One day, it seemed as if I had rather smooth sailing ahead of me, so I started to pedal quite vigorously. Suddenly, the noise I was listening to changed—I knew immediately that there was something ahead of me.

I was told later on that it was a stationary car. At the time, I didn't discover exactly what it was myself, even though I pulled on the brake right away. I had been going at a pretty good clip, and as I braked I almost pushed myself over the top of the bike. I don't know if most American bikes have front and back brakes worked by little levers on the handlebars, but I suspect some of them do. The idea is that the lever on one side works the front brake, and the one on the other operates the rear brake. In my case, it was the front brake that I pulled, rather than the back, which sent the saddle forward and upward. Curiously enough, despite my weight, the back seemed to rise more than the front. If I could have gotten the front to rise, I would have been the first flying cyclist in the world. But by some good fortune or through not pulling too hard on the brake, I did not turn a somersault, and stopped just short of hitting the car.

What did happen was that the front lamp left the bicycle and came splattering onto the ground. The glass broke and the lamp became redundant. But, of course, a fat lot of difference that makes to a blind guy!

There were times when a "good Samaritan," like my brother-in-law, Bert, my sister Lily's husband, would be glad to run along beside the bike while I was cycling. This way, we could leave the limitations of the block and cycle through Battersea Park until poor old Bert gave up, gasping for breath.

Of course, things are better in adult life because today my wife Ellie and I have a tandem. I ride on the back, naturally, for safety reasons and insurance purposes. However, whenever the need arises to pedal more vigorously because of an approaching hill (and being a creature wishing not to overexert myself), I thought I had found a ploy to save energy by entering into the joy of the moment through telling one of my (as I thought) exceedingly funny jokes . . . only to be cut down in mid-sentence by the succinct request from the front seat, "Shut up, George . . . and pedal!"

Which brings to mind another cycling experience. It was in the late 1950s and I was in Los Angeles at the time. I received a call from Ian Bernard, Dick Haymes's music director, asking me if I'd like to go tandem cycling with him.

I was delighted, so we met, rented a bike and just before we started off, we received some helpful advice from the man renting us the bike. He advised, "The tall fella should be in the front."

Since I was the "tall fella," Ian, pointing tactfully to his eyes, firmly rejected the advice. But our renter was rather slow in catching on, so the advice was repeated. This time, Ian pointed to *my* eyes and the lights went on in the guy's head.

Approximately five minutes after we were underway, Ian asked me if I'd like an ice-cream cone. Being delighted with the offer, we pulled up at what Ian thought was the ice-cream stand. You can imagine my surprise and sudden concern when Ian said, "Oh no, that's a gasoline pump!"

The only thing I could summon up in reply was, "You know, Ian, that guy is right. The tall fella *should* be in the front!"

I said earlier on that the Latchmere pub was on Shillington Street. Many times I would walk home alone from the Latchmere. It was over a mile. But I used no cane, no dog, no anything. I had many bruises and scars to prove how daring I was. I always thought it was a shame that I wasn't christened George Spanner instead of George Shearing because if you were to take a look at my shins, legs, or arms where these scars appeared, you would know immediately that I was the "scar-spangled Spanner"!

One time I was walking back home when I heard two cockney ladies, real Londoners, talking loudly together as I came along. One said to the other, "Look, watch 'im; watch that poor boy! Look! Look at 'im! He's gonna hit that board!"

I felt like a sideshow, and I hadn't even sold any tickets!

Again she said, "Look, look! He's gonna hit that board."

And then she shouted, "Mind that board on your right! There's a board on your right."

Well, in fact the information had been conveyed to me several seconds before that admonition because once I overheard one telling the other I was going to hit the board, I took evasive action. And so I didn't hit the board.

I've frequently been asked for a description of how we know if we're going to hit something or not. Well, of course, if something is at the level of your knees, you're not going to know. But if something's over your head, it covers a fair area, and you'll know about it. For a sighted person, it's like the difference between walking into a completely empty room and then a room filled with books, drapes, and every other kind of sound deadener there may be. You can easily tell the difference in sound, and for us it's the same only more acute. I could almost always tell if there was something in my way in the streets of Battersea, as long as it was large and high enough.

My present wife, Ellie, took a long time working out some of the things that still cause me problems today. For example, she'll never leave a door open or half open. I won't necessarily know that a piece of material or a half-open door is in my way, and the only certainty is if the door is shut. Then I can hear an acoustical difference. To make the point, try putting your hands up in front of your face and see if you hear the room around you with the same clarity as if they are by your side.

When it came to crossing roads, you'd either ask someone, or take a chance. One thing I learned during the short period of my adult life when I had a guide dog was that even a guide dog doesn't have a sense of color. He won't know when the light's green at traffic lights, for instance. But he always knows when there's traffic coming. You're supposed to be listening for traffic as well, for example, if the traffic is going across you, from side to side, you can't cross, but once you hear the cars moving in the same direction as you are facing, then it's possible to cross with care. That's an over-simplification, because very few junctions, specially in London, are simple two-way intersections. The real trick is to know how to cross when traffic is moving in five or six different directions, like Cambridge Circus in London's West End. That's a tough one! Oh boy!

There are other things I found out about as well. Such as how to recognize people. Obviously, blind people can't recognize others by their faces. So, we grab on to the next best thing—the voice. If our ears are acute enough, we can remember a person's identity by a distinctive voice pattern or sound. In fact, of course, plenty of sighted people know who is talking to them by this method, as well. I learned to recognize many of the people in and around Battersea from their voices, and once you learn how to do this, the technique stays with you. In the 1960s and 70s, the West Coast jazz writer Grover Sales was always astonished that I could recognize him within a couple of syllables, even if we hadn't met for several months.

We can also remember people by the perfume they wear. Other methods are to identify their preferred topics of conversation or the way they introduce themselves. In later life, I got to know a friend by the name of Ed LeVesconte, who would always greet me in the same manner, with a low, deep "Friend." It's so slow and drawn out, I'd know him at once. Charles DeForest, a New York-based singer and pianist, is an example of what you might call catch-phrase identification, as his greeting would always include the words "Absolutely stinking," which was a phrase he'd picked up from a Noel Coward play.

One thing I've tried to achieve ever since those early years in Battersea is to do everything in my power to prevent a sighted person from being afraid to talk to a blind person. Because even today I might go into a restaurant, where nobody knows me, and the waiter or waitress will turn to Ellie, and say, "Does he take sugar in his coffee?"

She'll say, "I don't know. Ask him."

This has happened so often, we've thought about taking the mickey out of them by having a couple of pieces of paper in my pockets. The one in the left would say, "Yes, he does." The other would say, "No, he doesn't." And then according to how I'm feeling about having sugar or sweetener in my coffee, I could hand the correct note to Ellie, and she'd pass it to the waiter or waitress.

I don't want to dwell on blindness, but I do want to ensure that sighted people have as much information about blindness as possible, so that they have some idea what we can and can't do. There's so much misinformation and ignorance around, I'm keen for everyone to realize that each of us is just another human being, who perhaps doesn't look straight into your eyes while we are talking. That's really the only difference.

Today, there are probably more opportunities than there were when I was young for the blind child to get a sense of how the outside world appears to the sighted person. For example, we had nothing else to learn from but rather basic Braille books, but recently I have discovered a collection of Braille nursery rhymes for children that includes tactile pictures along with the text. So, for example, *Baa-Baa Black Sheep* is accompanied by a three-dimensional picture which includes the sensation of wool and of bags. In fact the bags even have little Braille labels on them in the illustrations so that you know one is for the master, one for the dame, and one for the little boy who lives down the lane. Another rhyme is to do with a wise old owl, which appears in an impression on the page, so again, short of actually handling a model of an owl, you are able to sense the bird's shape and its huge eyes. This is a twenty-first-century approach to overcoming some of the things I had to deal with as a child.

When I was growing up, I amused myself in many of the same ways that sighted children did. For example, I played with yo-yos. I loved to feel the yo-yo hit the bottom and then pull it up and have it come up and hit my hand. And then let it drop again and hit the bottom and then come up and hit my hand again. I used to see how many times I could do it before it would die on me.

We had a game called Bagatelle. Several times since, I've tried to get someone to make that game again for me. I had one at one time from the Royal National Institute for the Blind. Somehow or another, it got damaged and it became unplayable. Eventually, when I was living in Toluca Lake, California in 1961, I gave it to my carpenter, who promised to make a new one for me and I never saw that Bagatelle again.

It was a game which involved a board sloping on a 45-degree angle towards you, and the object was to hit a little ball (about the size of a marble and made of brass, I think) with a cue with enough force to overcome the slope but not so forceful that it goes off the board. The idea was to get the ball into little cups made of pins to score points. I loved this game, and enjoyed playing it for hours.

At the age of three or four, one of my more humorous and macabre indulgences allowed me to enjoy rather primitive musical sounds. I threw bottles from the upstairs bedroom window— without ever thinking that I could hit anyone, I should add. The bottles would crash down on the pavement unless anything or any-body was in their way. Even then I showed some class, though. If I wanted a classical sound, I would use a milk bottle and if I wanted a jazz sound, I would use a beer bottle.

Where did I get these bottles from?

Sometimes, when I'd break one, my mother would say to one of the others in the family, "Oh, go and buy him another one!" And they'd have to go out and get me another bottle to break in the street.

But also, in those days, the milk was delivered to all the houses in the area in one-pint glass bottles, and that's how I came by several of the ones I broke. Which leads me on to another story.

One of the games we played—sighted and blind alike—was to go around to the neighbors whose milk bottles were standing just outside their doors. On the top of the bottle was a flat cardboard lid with a small tab. We'd creep up to the door, take a bottle in hand, lift the tab off the milk bottle, drink the cream, put the tab back and move on to the next house.

That was fun!

Did we get caught?

No—that's not the aim, is it?

Another "toy" that gave me great pleasure, because of its nois-iness, was the head of a hammer on a piece of string. It used to rattle over the cobblestones. That made an interesting sound as I dragged it along behind me. I also used to have a big iron replica of John Bull—the fat English symbol of a statesman—and I dragged that over the cobbles as well. Most of the sounds that I made were not just dead banging—I never just crashed two pieces of tin together. I preferred the noise of a milk bottle which would perhaps make a sound which would not terminate in one second, but would clank around for a while. Equally, the hammer on the end of a string produced a continuous clang, the more noise the more cobblestones you went over. So I was interested in sounds with a slow decay, or a resonance, even at that age.

At three or four years of age, I would be listening to the old crystal radio set, hearing programs such as Roy Fox's show. I was told that I used to wander over to the piano and, with one finger, play the tune I had just heard. So I guess that even at that age I would "connect" one form of music to another.

Nevertheless, I don't remember my early childhood being pleasant at all in any way, shape, or form. A party, to me, based upon those days—and I was later to find out that that's not really the way it goes—a party to me contained two factions: those of us who never drank at all and those who drank to excess. Even dur-ing a party, those who drank to excess would leave the house, even though there was plenty of drink, go to the pub and stay there for two or three hours. We would be home hoping that they would return in a condition to enjoy the rest of the party . . . which they seldom were. That was my memory of a party as a child.

I received my first general music lessons at the age of four at Shillington Street School. It was a school for blind children of primary-school age. It was also where I first learned to read Braille, by the time I was five. The majority of children at Shillington Street School were either totally blind or myopic. In those days, blind children were not put in sighted schools. I thought later on that maybe they should be, because there isn't a blind world—there is a sighted world to which blind people must adapt and adjust. So you ought not to cushion a blind person by bringing them up to believe that there is a blind world and they never have to enter the sighted world. In those days, as a blind person, you were brought up to make baskets or hairbrushes, or you tuned pianos, or wove mats. There was much more prejudicial categorization then.

There was a lady who came to the house named Miss Dearsley, and she gave me my first two or three piano lessons at the age of five, or so, and she said it wasn't really worth my parents wasting the money because I was a bit too advanced, even for her. It was because of those lessons that my father always boasted that it cost him three quid to teach me to play the piano.

Nowadays, the other main thing I remember about Shillington Street was one of the teachers, a Miss Brautigan. I remember her because of her loving ways of coming round and clouting you on the back of the head with the flat of her hand if you did anything wrong—I mean hard, really hard. For some reason, that and the song at the end of each day are almost all I can recall of that first school.

3

LINDEN LODGE

The greatest boon to me, as far as learning to be blind and to live with blindness, was the four years I spent at the Linden Lodge residential school between the ages of twelve and sixteen, an education that was compulsory for all blind people of that age in England at that time. The school wasn't too far from home, being only a couple of miles away on Wandsworth Common, at 26 Bolingbroke Grove.

I always got the feeling that the place was an old house, with balconies and things on the outside, and there seemed to be a lot of glass in the internal decorations. Around the main building there was plenty of playground space, where we used to scurry from one class to another. Some of the older guys knew where to jump the fence and go down to the shop to buy cigarettes, but if they were caught they got a public flogging for escaping from the school. If you jumped the fence you'd be in Broomwood Road, and you could get to the shops from there.

The locker room had Braille markings on all the lockers, and I remember my number was 26. The numbers were hammered into the locker doors using tacks to give the configuration of each character, and the reason I recall my number so well is that, in Braille, 26 is equivalent to "BF", which, to me, stood for "Bloody Fool!"

There was a big garden, which seemed to us to cover quite a lot of ground. There was a gardener, and he'd be there on a Friday when we had our weekly bath. I can recall his voice saying, "Come on Shearing! Scrub those knees!" Like all young boys who wore short trousers, my knees took the brunt of a rough-and-tumble life.

I don't recall there being any particular school uniform, but I do remember that when we went to church on a Sunday, we had to put our ties on. Each of us kept our tie in a tin—an oblong-shaped tin—that we kept in our lockers or up in our bedrooms. There were seventeen boys in one dormitory. We weren't exactly kind to everyone who we shared with. For example, there was a guy who snored all the time, very heavily, so a couple of the others lifted him out of his bed, turned him and his mattress over into a laundry hamper, and rolled him down the fire escape. I think he woke up by the end of the roll. There was another chap there with no sense of direction at all. He was very blind, in the sense that he'd go around scuffling with his hands in front of him, with almost no ability to walk naturally, so that he was rather a pathetic kid. He was from an orphanage and his name was Arthur Wood. One night a couple of the fellows in our dormitory decided they were going to move his bed out onto the porch. So when he came up, he said plaintively, "Where's my bed?"

They directed him to someone else's bed and he climbed into that, not knowing it wasn't his. Then the guy whose bed he'd gotten into came around and said, "Oy! Get out of my bed."

Eventually I suppose he got up enough nerve to go down to the duty master and report to him that they were playing around with him and he couldn't find his bed. I sometimes think that the master must have been in on the gag, because he came up and helped lift the bed back into position. And then Arthur Wood got into bed.

Another guy was very interested in electricity. His name was William Webb, and he would set up a battery with some wires and a switch and wait for a chap to get into bed. As soon as he did, there'd be a buzz, and he'd get a little shock. What a bunch of cards!

We were terrors, as all children are. We specialized in apple-pie beds, stacking our tie tins under the sheet, so when you got in you thought you were on a bed of rocks or something. Other times we'd put hairbrushes or toothpaste into somebody's bed, so they'd have to get out and remake it before they could go to sleep. If it seems harsh to do this to a person who couldn't see what they were doing, remember nobody else could see either.

There were some great handball players and cricket players at school. By handball I mean a kind of game devised for blind lads to play, using a football. It was played in the gymnasium, with eleven on each side. It was much the same kind of thing as soccer, except that all the dribbling, the passing, and everything would be done with the hands. Some of my fellow students were really amazing at it.

Cricket was also played in the gymnasium, and instead of the regular stumps, we'd have two long blocks of wood and a piece of three-ply screwed in between them sandwich style. We'd play with a ball made of some rubbery inner-tube type of substance that was more or less like a great big thick balloon, but it would have a bell in it. They bowled this thing underhand, and the reason for the plywood was that we could tell if it hit the plywood instead of the player's bat, because it had a different sound. That way we could tell when someone was out.

In trying to make runs I'd attempt to hit the side wall of the gymnasium for one run. If you managed to reach the wall at the opposite end of the room with your shot, that was two runs. Four runs were scored if that same opposite wall was hit without a bounce, but if the light or overmantle were hit and broken, it would mean two weeks' suspension from cricket. Such things were only to be expected, and we'd never get seriously punished for anything like that. It was just a natural action while you were playing to see if you could score as many runs as possible.

Although in some respects life at Linden Lodge was really rather rough, we were nevertheless taught to make our own beds, clean silverware, and clean our own shoes. We would be quite severely punished if we didn't do as we were told. For instance, if we failed to clean our shoes, we would have to write a hundred Braille sheets of the sentence, "I must remember to clean my shoes."

Not write it a hundred times, but write a hundred sheets.

And of course, they'd give us newspaper to write it on instead of the usual thick Braille paper—that was more economical. So what we would do was to put five or ten sheets of paper in the frame at one time and press a little harder, so when we got through writing, we would have ten sheets done at once, and then we'd pull them apart. Of course, when you do that, the dots have a thick, rough feeling, so the master would know immediately that you had done this and he would say, "What do you think I am? A blithering fool or something?"

Often he would be very annoyed because you had done it this way, and he would say, "I'm going to give you a hundred different sentences. You sit there and you write a hundred different sentences and then I want one sheet of each sentence."

So you couldn't go through your frame with the duplication process. You had to do every sheet.

As far as the teachers themselves were concerned, the headmaster's name was Reginald Peppit. Some of the other teachers in school were Mr. John, Mr. Emory, and Mr. Vaughan. William Plear used to teach French and geography. The woodwork teacher was Arthur Greenley, and he was very good. We would have wooden rulers—measures—marked up in Braille. We didn't have much to do with tape measures, but we used good solid measuring devices. What we would do if we were going to hammer in a nail, say three-quarters of an inch from a line, was first to draw the line, using a marking knife or scriber, so that we could feel it, then measure the point for the nail, and put it in so that all the time we could feel exactly where it was. We got to be quite proficient with nails and screws. We also used glue, which came in great big slabs like toffee. We'd melt these down and after preparing the wood, we got to be quite good at gluing together joints, with grooves for one piece to fit into another. I wasn't very good at carpentry myself, but there was one boy in my year who made a chest of drawers. It was perhaps a quarter of the size of the kind that most people have in their bedrooms or closets, but it was a real functioning piece of furniture. And this lad was incredible—I think he was a born carpenter.

His name was Sidney Howe, and he had a little sight. He always dreamed that he and I would leave school and find an apartment somewhere together. He was a funny guy, but most of the time he was really nice. We would go for long walks together or go and sit down on the bank and talk together. Yet, other times, he'd go through a mood where he'd have to have what he wanted. He'd make you give him your Sunday cake or there'd be some kind of punishment, like opening medicine (in other words the school laxative potion) heated up, or in a double dose. Otherwise perhaps you'd get a beating from him. He went through a period where he was a brute.

As far as the other teachers went, well, I wasn't literarily minded in those days. Later on I ended up setting the works of Shakespeare to music, and so far I've completed two sets of such pieces for singers, but to be honest that interest didn't arise until well into adulthood, after I heard some arrangements that my friend, Steve Race, had done. But in terms of my life overall that was pretty recent.

Despite not taking an interest in reading great works of literature, the whole experience of Linden Lodge was good for me. It really was good. For example, I had learned to type. My brother-in-law, Bert Couzens, had got my first typewriter for me, back in the days when he used to run with me in Battersea Park, and he taught me a good deal about how to use it, but it was at school that I really mastered the art of typing. By the time I came out of school at sixteen and entered into the seeing world—the world of sight—I felt that I was a well-adjusted blind person, and that blindness was really no handicap at all. In fact, in some cases, it is an advantage in that we are blessed with an extra degree of concentration. If somebody comes in the room, we don't look around to see how their hair is fixed or what color dress they're wearing. If we're involved in something, we couldn't care less about anything else because we're not distracted.

Music lessons had begun for me when I was about five years of age, at the Shillington Street School, as part of the regular course with the rest of the students. But I started really serious piano lessons when I was about twelve.

At Linden Lodge, I would try to get in at least an hour's practice a day, and I would often ask whether I could play the piano outside formal practice times. You could get permission to play the piano in the sitting room, usually during the evening. So I often played for an hour or two during the evening, usually doing some of the tunes of the day rather than too much classical stuff. Between the ages of twelve and sixteen, I went through a period of learning classical pieces, or diligently practicing scales and exercises, which I continued to do while I was at home. Then, after I'd left school, I would practice for four hours a day. In the Lodge itself, most days it was more play than practice.

At school, I was already experimenting with playing jazz—things I'd heard on discs or on the radio. What touched me most about it from the very start was the spirit of the music. It wasn't the sweetest sound this side of heaven—to our ears the British bandleader Maurice Winnick was—but I loved the "American" sound of jazz: bands with no smooth vibrato, whose brass and reeds cut right through the ensemble.

By the time I was sixteen, the music teacher, George Newell, had said to my parents, "It is obvious that this boy is going to become a jazz pianist and any further study of classical music would be a waste of time."

He used to hand out, say, a sixteen-bar section of a piece to learn between one lesson and the next. I would learn maybe four bars of it during the course of the week. Then it would be time for the next week's lesson and he'd say, "Have you learned that section I gave you?"

I'd say, "I've done part of it."

Then I'd play the four bars that I'd learned and he'd say "Go on."

"This is all I've done."

At which point he'd say, "You silly ass, it goes this way."

Then he'd play the whole section for me. Immediately I would have the remaining twelve bars in my head, just as soon as he'd played it, and I could play it right after him. I've always had that kind of an ear.

Once he had said to my parents that any further study of classical music would be a waste of time, it was about all my sixteen-year-old self needed to resort to laziness and take the easy way out. As a result, not long after I left Linden Lodge, I took a job playing in a pub, becoming a professional popular pianist and then eventually a jazz pianist. And I make that distinction quite clear. There is a distinct difference between playing anything that people want you to play, *Nellie Dean* and *Melancholy Baby* and whatnot, to actually becoming a jazz pianist with some direction about what your style is going to be. That involves thinking about who you're going to follow or how you're going to develop a style of your own, and from what grounds. My jazz style was developed from a pretty complete study of Teddy Wilson, Art Tatum, Fats Waller, Bob Zurke, Albert Ammons, Pete Johnson, and Meade "Lux" Lewis. So it's well grounded. I'm sorry for those people who come into jazz and know little further back than say, three, four, or five years and have no real background. It's like a classical musician who professes to be well rounded, but has never heard of Johann Sebastian Bach.

Of course, I was soon to find that this advice about giving up Braille music was a big mistake because I found many jazz musicians in England who were quite conversant with, and in many cases quite proficient at, classical music. And I suppose it was to maintain an intellectual level with them that I felt it necessary to go back to classical music again. So I got one of my friends to re-teach me Braille music. I could have continued to learn classical music by ear, since my music teacher had taught me the Liszt piano transcription of the *Rákóczy March* in three lessons, simply by playing it through for me to remember. I suppose that means I could do more or less anything classical by ear, because that's a pretty difficult piece of music. But I prefer to read. I think it's more of a brainwashing and I think it's better from the point of view of getting the correct phrasing and tie signs between one bar and another and so on. So that explains why I took up Braille music again.

Funnily enough, there's a postscript to this story. I went back to Linden Lodge in 1962, and that same music teacher, Mr. Newell, was still there. I thought to myself, "Aha! Here we go. The old smart Leo personality is coming out . . ." and I went over and said to him, "Mr. Newell, do you remember the advice you gave my parents when I was sixteen?"

He said, "Yes, I do."

I said, "Has it come to your attention that in the interim I must have learned enough about classical music to have learned some full-length concertos by Bach and Mozart, and to be playing them with symphony orchestras across the United States?"

"Yes, it has," he told me.

"So, armed with that knowledge," I went on, "were you to be asked the same question today, what would you say?"

"I suspect your main dollar still comes from playing jazz, does it not?"

"Yes, it does."

"Then my answer would be the same."

He was a very wise man, that Mr. Newell. And he was a very accomplished musician, because as a blind musician you are obliged to develop your memory and study skills. If a sighted player is any good as a sight reader, then he or she can just sit at the piano and play, but we have to learn a piece from Braille music a phrase at a time. You learn a section, play it in the left hand, then the right, and finally put the two together. But Mr. Newell could read through a short piece of Braille music on the bus on the way home, and play it when he got there. That's a seemingly impossible feat, but you develop those kinds of skills as a blind pianist.

Of course in much of jazz you don't need all that academic approach. I suppose my own musical memory has always been pretty good. I don't hold with the theory that blind people actually hear more or have the ability to memorize more than sighted players, but I do believe, as I have already said, that by lacking one sense we learn to develop greater concentration in the others.

There weren't any other particularly talented musicians among my exact contemporaries at school as I was growing up. Another well-known English jazz pianist, Eddie Thompson, was also educated at Linden Lodge, but as he was some years younger than I, our paths barely crossed at school. There was, however, one boy in my class named Derek White, who was quite a chum of mine. I could play him off the stage, but he could run rings around me when it came to music theory, and I think the way he was able to get this complex subject into his head at such a young age proves my point about concentration.

A very graphic illustration of the limitations of Braille is the ordinary pocket dictionary. A sighted person can just pick up a relatively slim book and pop it into a brief case or an overnight bag. But a Braille dictionary with the same information might run to several volumes, each the size of a New York telephone directory. Nowadays a lot of that inconvenience has been overcome with the advent of computers—for example, I have the complete works of Shakespeare on five floppy discs that I can load into my computer in order to read the plays in Braille. That's made access to long and complex literature much easier.

Although it took me some years and the arrival of modern technology to get to grips with the works of Shakespeare and some other major authors, nevertheless, I've loved to read all my life. I like to read Braille whenever I can—after all I've been doing it since I was five! I don't profess to read as fast as a sighted reader— for a start we can't read as far ahead in advance of the phrase we're actually on, but I've never read AT—THIS—KIND—OF— PACE, I read at about my ordinary conversational speed.

I would suppose that if you were asked what you didn't like about George Shearing, some of you may have a problem about where to start. But a good place, as far as I'm concerned, would be with the limitations on my diet, which are something fierce to deal with, particularly from the point of view of whoever is catering for me, including my wife Ellie.

She has always said that if one looked up "picky eater" in the dictionary, my picture would be there. And I guess many of the reasons for this go back to my childhood, both before and during my time at Linden Lodge.

Let's start with the food groups: I don't like fish of any kind. I don't like cheese of any kind. No garlic. Very few sauces. Vegetables that are out are squash, mushrooms, eggplant, cabbage, and turnips. And I'm not a great person for game—pheasant, rabbit, venison. So, with me it's lamb, beef, veal, chicken, omelettes. Some desserts are fine but not many. Forget the ones that are sloppy or filled with lots of whipped cream. Save those for someone else.

I wouldn't say that this list of "don't likes" has plagued my life because if somebody prefers not to limit their dinner to my requirements, I prefer not to be there. Ellie and I were once invited to a dinner party in Los Angeles at the house of a friend of Les Brown, the bandleader. The hostess wanted to show off her newly acquired knowledge of Chinese cooking—another of my dislikes. Normally, Ellie asks discreetly what is being served but this particular dinner invitation came suddenly and we decided not to make the enquiry.

I'm sure that the hostess and her Chinese houseboy had worked very hard on the multi-course Chinese menu. Anyway, I passed up one course after another. I didn't want this, I didn't want that. It was all Chinese so I, obviously, didn't want anything to do with it. The hostess was furious.

A few months later, another friend in San Francisco revealed to us that the hostess was so annoyed at my refusing to eat anything that she announced to the world she would never again ask me to dinner. That was the best news I had had in a long time! In fact, I even check the menu at the White House! I can usually get a very good steak and baked potato while the rest of the guests dine on whatever is going. So, everybody's happy. I can just imagine the chef at the White House getting the order for 120 poached salmon dinners and one steak, charred rare, with a plain baked potato. "Good grief," he thinks, "Shearing's coming again!"

This whole diet business started when my mother realized that I refused to eat anything I thought I didn't like. I suppose this is the wont of childish behavior. Perhaps, more prudent parents would have said, "You have a choice for dinner, George. It's either ham or no ham."

But my mother didn't. She decided that she would pander to my likes and dislikes. In fact, it really began when I went to hospital when I was about six years old. I had the croup and the resulting tracheotomy. When my mother came to visit me, she found out that these naughty people in the hospital were trying to force some perfectly good chicken down my throat.

Didn't they know, after all, that I lived on sausage and mash? From then on, my sister had "the sausage and mash duty" every day for little Georgie. So, you see, I got a very good beginning on dietary limitations. But, for the most part, I do enjoy the things that I eat and while I'm not quite sure whether we eat to live or live to eat, I would think off the top of my head—and bear in mind I'm not a doctor—that the enjoyment of food does do wonders for the digestive juices. Very rarely do I have indigestion problems. The only way I can enjoy what I eat is to eat what I enjoy.

I'm also being told how much I miss out on the wonderful tastes of certain foods and it's true in that wherever I am and whatever country I'm in, I look for a good steak and a good steak is not always to be had. I think America has the best steaks anywhere.

This parental indulgence went on through the time that I was in boarding school at Linden Lodge. My parents used to bring me jam tarts and sponge cakes, pots of jam and stuff that we did not have in school. Now, the problem with really liking something is that you tend to OD on it. I did that on more than one occasion.

One day, I was in class and I put my hand up. The teacher, who was a Welshman, said, "Yes, Shearing?"

I said, "Sir, I feel sick."

He said, "Well, you know how to be sick, don't you?"

I said, "Yessir . . . BRAHCHCHCHCH!!!!!!!" This constitutes my best effort to describe the sound of some impurities attempting to depart the body through the uppermost exit in hopes of landing in the shortest time on any landing place that happens to be available.

Yes, I knew how to be sick! It was the result of overindulgence—but it sure was fun while I was eating it.

As quite a young child I realized that by digging my heels in I could get what I wanted. Once I was very keen to have a paper bird on a stick that made a very distinctive noise. I cried until my parents gave in and got me one, so by the time I was at Linden Lodge I knew the value of willpower.

I was still at the school when I met my first girlfriend, in Battersea Park, listening to the band. She came over to me, introduced herself, said, "Excuse me, aren't you George Shearing?"

I said, "Yes, I am."

To my surprise, she said, "We have staying with us one of the lads who goes to school with you."

The funny thing is, they were housing Arthur Wood—the chap who used to stutter all the time, who had no kind of sense of direction, and whose bed had been lifted out on to the porch. Because her family were housing him, we immediately had quite a number of things in common, and in addition to that, she was learning Braille.

She was perfectly sighted, and her name was Patricia Pitcher. We all knew her as Poppy. Maybe that's not a very romantic name—Poppy Pitcher—but we became very friendly and she used to take me skating at the Brixton Skating Rink. We went there practically every Saturday for a while, and I remember they played the *Skater's Waltz*. I got so good at it that on the first beat of the first bar I'd put the left foot down and let it carry me along for the other two beats, and then on the first beat of the second bar I'd put the right foot down, so it would be "SHHHHhhhh, Shhhh, Shhhh, SHHHHhhhh, Shhhh, Shhhh." I can still feel this sensation now, I have such a vivid recollection of it. It was a good feeling.

In fact roller skating got to be quite popular at my school. In the 1950s, I went back to Linden Lodge, and as I was walking around the grounds, I experienced a sound this fast: "Whshht!" It was a blind guy going by on skates at absolutely top speed. I heard lots of them using roller skates on the asphalt, and they'd know just how far to go before they turned a corner. Any of them would know where to turn if they'd been walking, but to know when you're skating and going along at that speed was pretty impressive. Then they'd turn around and whizz around those grounds like it was going out of style.

As well as our visits to Brixton Skating Rink, Poppy and I would exchange Braille letters and go to hear the band in the park.

I remember the thing that made me stop writing to her for good and all. I was supposed to go skating with her one Saturday and although I didn't understand at that time, I later realized she had a sighted guy on the string too.

I overheard her saying to her mother, "Where are my skates?" after she'd told me how she couldn't go this particular Saturday because she was going to get her hair fixed.

Realizing her mistake, she said to her mother, "Where are my skates? I want to clean them."

To which her mother said, "Are you going skating?"

To which Poppy mumbled, "I don't know."

I could tell as she said this she must have been pointing at me. I could sense this.

This was the reason I stopped writing after that. It's a funny thing. A sighted person will often think that if they want to do something that a blind person will not observe, that all they have to do is just point. If they just point their finger without moving their arm, that's fine. But, you see, most people don't consider it that carefully. If they want to point, they just move their whole arm.

Frankly, in most cases, and particularly with a girl, she will be wearing something that will rustle, and you can hear the rustle of that dress when they're pointing. So nothing really gets by you unless they're extremely careful.

I realized what was going on, and that she was seeing someone else. And to be honest, I don't really look down upon it because I think at our age—what were we? fifteen, sixteen?—I think it behooves people to go out with a number of different people. It's just that I wish there'd been a little more forthrightness and a little more honesty, saying something along the lines of "Look, I have a number of friends, and this week I think I should go out with so-and-so. Do you mind if we could leave our arrangement 'til next week."

That's all. Of course, I don't know if I'd actually have understood it then. I guess I wouldn't, and I suppose she knew I wouldn't have understood it, which is why she covered up in that way.

So after that it just settled down to an even more platonic friendship than it had been up til then.

My parents didn't like her anyway. I guess they very rarely do like the people their children go out with, but they said she was kind of sarcastic. One day I asked my mother, "What happened to my watch and my ring?"

She said, "They're upstairs in your drawer. Did you think I'd pawned them or something?"

Poppy said, "Well, I wouldn't be surprised."

I'm sure she was probably being humorous or endeavoring to be humorous, as she came from a very sarcastic family. I expect she thought it was funny, but my mother didn't like it. In fact, my mother didn't want her to come to the house any more because of that remark, and so we just drifted apart.

4

MIGHTY LIKE THE BLUES

The time I really got started playing in the pub was about 1935 or '36. The place I began my professional career was not the Latchmere, near at hand, but the Mason's Arms in Lambeth Walk, which was a little farther away, about fifteen minutes on the tram. I don't remember the exact details of how it came about, but it was my parents who found the job for me. They got to hear about it through a friend called Alfred Thripp, who had played there for a while and, I think, had previously attended Shillington Street School.

Dad said, "If you don't want to go to college or anything, there's a job here waiting for you in this pub." So I chose to take it because, in any case, the family budget really wouldn't have allowed me to go to college, although I suppose I could have gone supported by the Government one way or another if I had really wanted to.

The first night I worked there, I just sat down and played. Most English neighborhood pubs at that time had two bars. There'd be a four-ale bar—the regular working man's beer bar with sawdust on the floor—and then they'd have the saloon, which generally meant advancing to linoleum on the floor. At the Mason's Arms, I was playing in the saloon, and as I played, between eight and ten people would come and sit round the piano. Once I'd been there for a while, oftentimes I'd have a couple of friends sitting on the couch beside me, and they would ask for certain tunes. Then, more people would come over and ask me to play particular songs. Some of them knew what they were talking about and others just wanted regular tripe. But in those days I was very conscious of playing everything they wanted that I knew I could play, because it would mean that, in most cases, the box would jingle on the top of the piano.

I guess I felt a little strange coming out of school and going into this new environment. However, over the period of the years I had been at Linden Lodge, being a pianist, I would often wind up at a party somewhere, and I suppose this primed me, in some respects, for the pub. It was also something that, even more than the occasional party at home or in the neighborhood, turned me against alcohol. The stupidity and the clumsiness of people under its influence really got to me.

I was playing for a party once at someone's house, and there was a group of people dancing. If they had just been shuffling their feet and dancing, that would be one thing, but this was a real old drunken English dance, *Knees Up Mother Brown*. And they really did. They put their knees up and they jumped in some way or other while dancing, and you could feel it vibrating through the floorboards. You can imagine if you had a rickety old piano with anything on top, and the vibrations were strong enough, then the stuff on the top would probably come off.

On this particular occasion, there was a glass jar of salmon on the top of the piano. I went on playing and they went on dancing and suddenly this salmon just came down and went all over the keys. I suppose anybody with any responsibility would probably have come over and started to wipe it up and perhaps inquired, "Did you get hurt?" and all this kind of thing. But the general attitude at that party was, "Play on, sonny!"—fish and all!

At parties and at the pub, I would play things like *Some of These Days, We'll All Go Riding on a Rainbow*, in fact just about anything. There was no kind of taste at all in the repertoire. Nothing. No real discretion. If they wanted *Nellie Dean*, I played *Nellie Dean*.

I guess I picked up the basic repertoire from just growing up in and around Battersea. You could walk around the local neighborhood there, and particularly on a Saturday night, my Dad and I might go for a walk and stop at a store to get a glass of lemonade, and en route we'd pass one of the local pubs, and there'd be a few drunkards in there singing songs such as *Nellie Dean*. My friend Chappie D'Amato, who was later my bandleader at Hatchett's club, used to have a mock Latin name for this kind of song. He called it *"Pro Bono Public Houso."*

So I'd hear these things one way or another. Some of them, of course, were broadcast on the air, sung by people like Denny Dennis or Little Mary Lee, who were the vocalists with Roy Fox. I had no real difficulty in learning them from the BBC or from records. We'd crank the old phonograph up and put on a record of Sophie Tucker or Sir Harry Lauder, or one of these guys. That's how I learned a whole host of standards, and once I had a tune in my head, if somebody asked for it, I could play it.

The job paid twenty-five shillings a week, plus what I collected from the box on top of the piano. On Christmas week, which was an exceptionally good week, I made six pounds, three shillings, which figuring four dollars to a pound, was twenty-four dollars, and added to that, the three shillings would be about seventy-five cents. Twenty-four dollars and seventy-five cents for a sixteen-year-old kid in 1935 wasn't bad, not least when that sixteen-year-old kid came from a poor family.

Around the time that I started at the pub, some of my family went to one of the local dances, where there was a bandleader called Matthew Lark. Not long afterwards, his son Willie Lark started a band of his own, and by this time, Willie had got to know our family, so he said that he'd like to try me out on a few jobs. To start with, I went round and listened, but before long I was playing with his band. Gradually Willie began to give me a few shillings here and there for playing a job. In due course, he would give me a few more shillings and the jobs would get better. Finally, somebody said, "You know, you should have a dinner jacket—a tuxedo." So Willie loaned me one of his tuxedos, which fitted pretty well, and eventually I earned enough to buy my own tuxedo and then tails.

Quite often, I used to go down to the pub in full dress suit—tails, white waistcoat, white tie, winged collar and all. Now, obviously, in the ordinary local pub, this was somewhat incongruous, but the reason I would turn up in this get-up was because when I got through there at ten-thirty at night, I would have to go on to somewhere else, like the Mayfair Hotel or the Park Lane Hotel, where I'd play a big Masonic dance or something with Willie's semi-professional band with whom I would be featured on accordion.

The band would be considerably enlarged for such an occasion and as part of the floor show, I would play something like the *Light Cavalry* overture, or one of these well-tried and tested classics. One hesitates to call them classics because they're so hackneyed. Then, more often than not, I'd play for dancing later on.

One night, Lou Jaffa, the owner of the pub, said to me, "You know, George, this is just a neighborhood bar. I don't know why you're coming in dressed like this."

So I said, "Well, the reason is that I've got other jobs to go to when I get through here, and I don't have time to go home and change."

"Well," he said, "I think you should choose between them and me."

So I did. I chose them, because I could make as much money doing a better class of work for three nights a week as I would at the pub for six nights a week—having to be largely dependent on the generosity of the public.

As a result, I was with the semi-professional band for about a year. Willie Lark sprayed cars during the day, and at night he played drums in this band, which varied in size according to the nature of the gig. He'd have a big band for playing some of the hotels, a mid-sized band for Masonic dinners, and for the Greyhound Racing Association from Wimbledon, it would be somewhere between the two, with strings in the first half of the evening, and then during the second half, three saxes and a trumpet for dancing. The music was different in each half as well—in the first we'd be playing semi-classical selections, from *The Student Prince* or *Glamorous Night*, and afterwards it would be popular jazz numbers like *Bugle Call Rag*.

Not long ago, I was playing a concert at Cheltenham Town Hall in England, and I thought the place seemed vaguely familiar, until I realized, by gosh, I'd played here with Willie Lark back in the thirties, doing one of those split programs of light classics and jazz I've just described. The place had hardly changed at all!

Because a lot of the arrangements needed reading, they actually employed another pianist in the group and I played accordion all the time. In fact there were two pianists who used to work with Willie Lark. One's name was Bob Harvey, and the other's name was Joe Kidd. If Willie had only classical or light classical music to play, he'd get Bob Harvey, but if he had one of these Masonics or the Wimbledon Greyhound Racing Association where we'd play both, he'd use Joe Kidd.

I quickly learned the main parts of the arrangements, say the trumpet or violin lines, and then came in when I could, or played solos. I had been playing accordion for quite a bit of the time I'd been at Linden Lodge, and when I joined Willie, I had a twelve bass accordion for a while. During my time with the band I graduated to a hundred and twenty bass accordion. Willie used to count off the numbers from the drums, or on some arrangements the pianist would start us off.

I don't play the accordion any more, and I got rid of the instrument many years ago, having come to the conclusion that the definition of a gentleman is someone who knows how to play the accordion and doesn't.

In due course I left Willie Lark's group, because I had an offer to go with an all-blind band, under the leadership of a fellow named Claude Bampton. I almost didn't get into this band at all, not for any lack of talent, but because of the attitude of my family. When I first heard that the band was going to be formed, I went along to my teacher at Linden Lodge, Mr. Newell, and asked him if he could secure me an audition.

"Certainly," he said.

Well, I didn't hear, and I didn't hear, until one day I bumped into him and said, "Mr. Newell, I never heard from them."

He said, "Yes, you did. You got an application for an audition and it was turned down."

I went home ready to hit the roof, and asked, "Who did this?"

My father said, "Your brother and I did it between us."

"Why?"

"Because I work, your brother works, your mother is suffering from an ulcerated leg, and we have no idea how to get you up there."

One of my first professional photographs, in the clothes that lost me the job at the Mason's Arms. (Author's collection)

The definition of a gentleman . . . (Author's collection)

To which I replied, "If you ever do this again, I'll leave home." Quite a pronouncement from a seventeen-year-old blind kid.

I found—and still find—that lack of ambition and imagination staggering. But eventually I did get an audition for the band, and they offered me the job.

Fifteen blind musicians were taught to play instruments. They became full-time musicians instead of being basket-makers, chair-caners, and the like. They were all taught to read Braille music and a couple of the guys in the band would take down tunes off records from the Jimmie Lunceford band and Duke Ellington's orchestra and transcribe the arrangements into Braille. It was quite an achievement, because some of the arrangements they took down were really complex—the part-writing was extremely busy, and some of the harmonies quite advanced. In fact, when I first joined, knowing that I was a fairly slow reader of Braille music, the bassist Alfred Heckman said to me, "George, if you need any help with chords or anything, just let me know." But in fact—and I don't like blowing my own trumpet, but this was the case—at the end of the first rehearsal he came over and said, "After I'd heard your first sixteen bars, I knew you didn't need any help." I've just always had that kind of ear, I can hear harmonies almost immediately, and once I've actually heard a piece right through, I can almost always play it straight back.

Braille music, just like written text, is a series of dots that are raised on paper, and you have to read it with your fingers in the same way. You read it and memorize it, and it has to be memorized because there's no way we can read it at the same time as playing. There are no staves and clefs or anything of that nature. It's just a series of dots—a certain number of dots represent particular notes or octave marks or finger marks or whatever. So, in the band, the Braille parts would be handed out to the guys—they would memorize the music and go down to rehearsal and play it, taking their parts with them.

From time to time, Claude or one of the arrangers would say, "Shouldn't this be an A-natural?"

Whoever it was would play it again and say, "Maybe. But I have an A-flat in my part."

Then he'd start rubbing a dot out on the paper. And we'd all mark it as an A-natural. Not that he would really need it, but just in case he forgot the part, he'd be able to re-read it and know that it was an A-natural, and so would the rest of us.

So we toured all over England with this band, and as usual my father said, "Why are you leaving Willie Lark's semi-pro band? The guy's been good to you, paying your salary all this time. This new thing'll break up in nine months."

Which, of course, it did. But in the meantime I had nine months of very good experience on the road. We traveled through all of the major cities of England and Scotland, and played a couple of cities in Wales. For the majority of those shows we played what was considered to be some very advanced stuff for the time. I remember an arrangement of Jimmie Lunceford's *Stratosphere*, as well as Benny Carter's *Nightfall* and his *Swinging at Maida Vale*, which he'd written and recorded during his stay in Britain, shortly before this band was formed. To digress for a minute, when I went over for dinner at Benny's house in California, many years later, I took with me a recording of a broadcast by the All Blind Band playing *Nightfall*. He listened to it for a minute, and he said, "That's not my band."

"No," I said. "It's Claude Bampton's band of blind musicians, and we took a chart down from your recording." Benny was really surprised.

With Claude Bampton I was no longer an accordionist, but playing piano full time.

As a matter of fact, looking back on it, I think this band was really a fantastic thing. It was sponsored by the National Institution for the Blind, which has since become known as the Royal National Institution for the Blind, now being patronized or endorsed by the royal family. The Institution provided the money with which to get the band rolling. Mind you, people had expensive tastes in the band, especially those who were involved in running it—there were at least a couple of costly drinking habits among the management.

The band lasted, as my father predicted, exactly nine months.

The Claude Bampton Orchestra. (Lebrecht Library)

THREEPENCE Vol. XIII. No. 218 JULY 24, 1937

CARLO KRAHMER—Drums SAM KERRY—Sub-Leader BARRY HODGES—2nd Alto ALF HECKMAN—Bass GEORGE SHEARING—Piano

PHENOMENAL VENTURE WITH BLIND STAGE ORCHESTRA

CLAUDE BAMPTON'S ROMANTIC AND ARRESTING CHALLENGE

THIS week the "Melody Maker" is happy to unfold one of the most romantic stories ever told about dance bands. It concerns the formation of a stage orchestra of eighteen blind artists got together, coached, directed and presented by Claude Bampton, undertaker of queer jobs.

In his amazing project he is assisted by one sighted player only, the leader of the brass section. The venture is under the aegis of the National Institute for the Blind and is particularly inspired by Dr. Ernest Whitfield, the famous virtuoso of the violin, who is one of the treasurers of the Institute.

The story starts eighteen months ago, when Dr. Whitfield, who takes a deep interest in all matters musical pertaining to the N.I.B., conceived the idea that some of the younger blind musicians, naturally

THE BAND WILL MAKE ITS BOW IN PUBLIC WITHIN THE NEXT FOUR WEEKS, AND WILL IT? GO TO IT, CLAUDE BYRON. THE SHOWMANSHIP AT THERE IS A METER, LEGS STAGE I GET T.
FOR IT.

Press cutting showing how Claude Bampton's band was 'sold' to the public. (Frank Driggs Collection)

Even during rehearsal time, the guys were paid full salary, or at any rate close to full salary. Six of us in the band played piano, so we carried our own "six piano symphony" around with us, with a specially made rostrum, on which all six grand pianos would roll out for one or two numbers every night. Our uniform suits were made by Hawes and Curtis, a very exclusive men's tailor, if you please. They were not off the peg, but individually made by the custom department. I'm sure that the band was actually far more expensive to run than Ambrose or Roy Fox or any of the other well-known bands of that day, which is why it didn't last for very long.

To start with, it received what I regarded as some very undesirable publicity about how it was marvelous when the blind people groped their way to the stand, and similar nauseating phrases. I've always tried to steer clear of this aspect of blindness. It doesn't do anybody any good.

I prefer to remember the humorous side of the thing. Imagine, if you can, a band with five brass, four saxophones, three fiddles, piano, drums, bass, and guitar. I guess there were fifteen or sixteen musicians, plus three girl singers and one male singer, not to mention about seven or eight chaperones. So it was a big feat of organization. Picture what it took to get a band of that size set up on the stage before the curtain opened.

Somebody had the humorous idea, which actually went into practice, that our theme song should be *I'll See You in My Dreams*. And the leader—the only guy, along with the first trumpet player to have complete sight, although some of the others were myopic cases—had a big baton that we could hear swishing or whistling through the air.

So every time someone would announce, "Ladies and gentlemen," we'd hear, "Swish, swish, swish . . ." giving us the tempo. Wherever we were, on air, in a concert, or a theater, we'd hear this thing whistling through the air. Of course, if he'd not had such a baton, he could have been waving his hands around all day long and we'd still be sitting there waiting to start playing.

One night we were in a theater, all ready for the curtain to go up, and the manager said, "Okay, fellows, are you ready?"

One of the singers—the guy—said, "No, wait a minute. Lost my eye!"

His glass eye had fallen out and rolled across the stage. And suddenly there were fifteen blind guys down on the floor looking for his glass eye.

Another time, during my period with Claude Bampton's All Blind Band, that same singer, the one who lost his eye, was staying with me. We were coming home from somewhere, I don't remember exactly where it was, but probably one of the engagements we were playing. We got off the train and were walking along the platform when suddenly I felt the ground leave me. I let him go and I just fell right down on the railroad line. Right on the track.

I just missed the live electric rail by a couple of inches. So he, in his broad Birmingham accent, said, "George, where are you, fellow?"

And I said, "I'm down here."

"Give us your hand," he called down. "Let me help you up!"

So I gave him my hand. He pulled and I jumped, but then I fell down again. He pulled again and I jumped. It seemed impossible to get back up, because the darned platform was up to my chest. Anyway he pulled and I jumped again, almost pulling him down with me. And the third time I cleared it.

Just then a train came along.

It seemed no more than about ten seconds before that train appeared. And pretty quickly word got around the station as to what had happened, and soon afterwards a law was passed in England that no blind person must travel on the railroad without a sighted person or without special permission.

That's the closest call I ever had.

Another time I fell down an open beer cellar. In the streets of London, outside almost every pub, they used to have a wooden board—a kind of a trapdoor thing that you lifted up so you could roll the barrels of beer down into the cellar. I was walking along, and one of these things had been left open, so I fell down there, and I felt all kinds of crates and barrels and things all round me. It was a bit of a shock when it happened, but I seemed not to have broken anything, or to have cut myself, so I got up from that and walked away with no trouble.

I've had plenty of similar kinds of scrapes. For example, I've fallen off my bike and broken my arm. Another time, we were doing some gardening in school and I was running down to the plot with a partially sighted guy, arm in arm, when my left foot caught behind his right and I went forward on my face. I slid forward a few yards, and I still have the piece missing out of my front tooth to prove it.

This kind of thing can happen to anybody. Anybody can fall off a bike and break their arm. You don't have to be blind to do that. You don't have to be blind to catch one foot behind another. People have fallen like that every day.

You do have to be blind to fall down a beer cellar or onto a railroad track!

So that band lasted, as I said, for about nine months. I still have very fond memories of those days, and many, many years later, the bassist, Alfred Heckman, used to come over and tune my piano when I came to stay in England during the summer, and we'd talk for ages about those times. Later, Alfred moved to Australia, but we stayed in touch.

Looking back on it, I guess it's true that my real introduction to American jazz came through the Claude Bampton band, both from the charts that we played, and also through my friendships with two people who were in the line-up—the first trumpet player, Ben Dudley, who was the only fully sighted person in the band apart from Claude, and particularly Carlo Krahmer, the drummer. I used to go over and spend hours and hours at Carlo's house in Walthamstow, listening to records. He'd play things for me that introduced me to the styles of many great players. He had big cupboards with glass doors. I remember putting my hands on these glass doors, opening them up and finding albums upon albums of records. They were all 78's of course, and over 90 percent were American jazz. Carlo later went on to be a producer and to found the Esquire record company, but he had three or four thousand discs, even in those days, and that was exceptional by any standard.

He seemed to have everything there from the early jazz of players like Johnny Dodds, to all the things by Bob Zurke, a favorite pianist of mine. But he also had discs by pianists like Joe Sullivan, Pete Johnson, and Albert Ammons, as well as by singers who played their own accompaniment, like Cleo Brown. As it turns out, I later got to hear Cleo Brown play in the United States, and she still had the qualities I admired in those early records, including a really first-rate jazz feeling in everything she did. Another pianist whose playing I knew well from Carlo's records of the Andy Kirk band was Mary Lou Williams, and I loved a lot of what she did on those big band sides. In fact, Carlo had discs by just about anybody you could mention. It was a real education to go over there and listen to these records day after day.

Sometimes we'd come out of a club after an all-night jam session, and it would be broad daylight. Then Carlo would say, "Do you want to come back for some coffee?"

So instead of going to my house, which was three or four miles away, I would go to his, which was about eight or nine miles away, and we'd have coffee before spending most of the day listening to discs. More often than not, he'd say, "If you're not doing anything, why don't you stay on?" And I'd stay over, probably go to sleep for a little while in the afternoon until the early evening, get up and eat dinner before we went out again to the club.

I would be away from home quite a bit, spending days with Carlo listening to music—going from clubs to records and from records to clubs. But all the time I was really getting a good grounding in American jazz, getting to know the differences between players and styles.

It affected my own playing too. As a matter of fact, I cut some acetates which are probably still around somewhere, where I tried playing in several styles, everything from Dixieland style to Bob Zurke's style. I had a go at playing boogie-woogie and trying to play like Earl Hines. I remember Carlo played me one amazing record called *Chimes in Blues* by Earl Hines, made in 1926, which was most impressive and had a big effect on me. Carlo was a real walking jazz discography. He really knew his business, and it was he who introduced me to the critic, pianist, and producer, Leonard Feather.

Leonard used to run something called the "Leonard Feather Jazz Club," which wasn't a bricks-and-mortar venue but what was known at the time as a "rhythm club"—a group of people who got together to listen to records and analyze them. Leonard would talk knowledgeably about the discs, and then everyone had a chance to chip in with their ideas about music. Sometimes after the records had been played, there'd be a jam session by a group of live musicians, people like trumpeter Dave Wilkins, or Ambrose's former pianist Eddie Macauley, and Carlo. It was through attending many of those that the ball really started rolling between Leonard and me. We became good friends, and in due course he got me a broadcast and a recording session.

I first recorded together with Leonard in 1939, with him playing piano and me on the accordion in *Squeezing the Blues*. He wrote another song called *Mighty Like the Blues* which became my theme tune for a while. Even in those early titles you could see evidence of our mutual fondness for awful puns. Most musicians can think of dozens of alternative titles for songs that exist already, like "I've thrown a custard in her face," but we liked to come up with similar jokes for the new songs we wrote. Leonard in particular had no shame when it came to punning titles and his numbers include *Bebop's Fables* and *Life With Feather*, which was a pun on the Broadway play (and later a film) *Life With Father*. When I came to make a couple more accordion discs for MGM quite a few years later, I kept the idea of puns going, because one was called *Good to the Last Bop*. Particularly when bop was in vogue, I used to try to get a play on words about it into my titles—another favorite was *Bop, Look and Listen*. I later found a kindred spirit in my drummer Denzil Best, who wrote a pseudo-Latin thing called *Nothing but D. Best*, but he always resisted my suggestion to go one stage further and write a tune called *A Denzil in Distress*.

My first discs with Leonard were made for Decca, and this began a relationship with the label that went on for quite a few years. After the war broke out, I did a number of sessions for them, which must amount, I suppose, to a couple of dozen solo sides.

One that I remember to this day was a piece called *Delayed Action*—named after the kind of bombs that fell during the Blitz—it had a kind of suspension in the left hand that I held onto for a very long time until suddenly it resolved and the tempo picked up again, and that was the "delayed action" of the title.

My very first broadcast on the BBC was actually a little earlier than my initial recording session with Leonard, and it took place in 1938. The announcer introduced me by saying in his very pukka BBC tones: "For the next fifteen minutes, you'll be hearing the music of George Shearing."

I opened up with *Mighty Like The Blues*, and then went on to play a medley of other current numbers. In those days, I still spoke like a real cockney, with a broad London accent, and after I'd finished playing, I said: "G'mornin' ev'rybody, we jus' played a medley of commercial pop'lar nummers, includin' *Tears On Me Piller, Le' me Whisper I Love Yer, Magyar Melody*, and *Jeepers Creepers*." And then the announcer came back—ever so precise: "For the past fifteen minutes, we've been hearing the music of George Shearing."

That taught me to dispense with the cockney accent. Funnily enough, around the same time, when she first started broadcasting, the actress Jessie Matthews—who went on to have one of the best-known voices on radio—had an equally strong London accent, but I reckon in due course she and I ducked it pretty well!

Following my first time on air for the BBC, I went on to do a series of broadcasts, largely as a result of Leonard's help.

One thing that was a really important part of the London jazz scene in the late 1930s was the chance to jam with other musicians—including some visitors from America. I think we learned a lot from such American musicians because, after all, jazz was born in the United States, even though we picked up on it rather quickly in England. In due course, a number of very well-known musicians came over. I well remember sitting in at a club with the great saxophonist Coleman Hawkins, and playing right through the night until about seven the next morning.

That was at the Nest, a small basement club in Kingly Street, parallel with Regent Street and just below Oxford Circus. You entered by going downstairs from the street level, just the way some of the 52nd Street clubs were in New York, and it was a very sincere jazz club. It was the antithesis of today's venues, where you have a cover charge of $60 and a minimum of $40. As I remember it, you just went in and ordered your drink, and there was no other charge of any kind. The Nest was where we all went after we'd finished our gigs in the West End. It opened after the pubs cleared, and the music went on until the sun came up the following morning.

Even if there weren't any American musicians in town, that was always the place to find the best British players. Trumpeters Dave Wilkins and Jiver Hutchinson, and the alto saxophonist Bertie King, played there a lot. They were all members of Ken "Snakehips" Johnson's band, from the Café de Paris, and had arrived in England from the Caribbean, but all of us thought of them as local British musicians, which of course they were, because they'd all lived in London for some years. Although they weren't American musicians as such, most of the Caribbean players on the London scene at that time had a fantastic, extrovert sense of rhythm, which was a really noticeable characteristic in their playing. It's hard to express exactly the difference between their sound and that of several of the musicians who were English born and bred. It's partly a question of upbringing, but that's not the whole thing.

A really interesting example of the difference between refinement and that kind of extrovert playing comes in the 1950s Basie orchestra. Listening to that band playing a number like *Moten Swing*, for example, many groups would just go into the opening riff swinging hard and loud. But Basie takes it very, very gently, with a fantastic sense of restraint and refinement—and then, BAM!, the whole band opens up for the second chorus, swinging as hard as you like. It's almost as if it had two personalities, the perfect, refined one of the opening, and the wild abandonment of the second, anything but refined. What very few British bands had in the 1930s was that emotional range, but Ken Johnson's musicians got close to a similarly full gamut of expression.

It was at the Nest that I first met the wonderful Fats Waller. The first time I heard him, I couldn't believe my ears. We were used to Jack Hylton, Ambrose, and some of the other better British bands, but Fats Waller! He covered enough piano for two normal pianists, and he had a tremendous ability to stride with the left hand. Now I don't want to get too technical here in terms of piano playing, but stride is when the left hand comes down on a bass note and alternates that with a three- or four-note chord. The hand is constantly moving up and down, or "striding," on the keys. I was taught to avoid a particular bad habit, which is that it's easy to turn your hand on its side to hit those bass notes. It adds strength, but it gives birth to inaccuracy in terms of hitting precisely the right note. What you have to do is to keep your hand flat, and not to turn it at all as it moves between the lower notes and the upper chords. I remember Claude Bampton telling me I should be able to balance a penny on the back of my left hand and keep it there while I was striding. I know from placing my own hands over Claude's, while he was demonstrating this, that he never deviated to the side at all. And Fats had just that kind of perfect control—absolutely precise placement of every note.

What I hated about him—I was so jealous—was his reach. He could stretch thirteen notes with one hand. If he put the little finger of his left hand on the C below middle C, he could play the A above middle C with his thumb. Incredible! His stretch was so big he could play a countermelody above his stride patterns with the thumb of his left hand, something that most of us can only do with two hands.

I remember the first time I met him I acted very blind. So when I shook hands with him, I extended my hand as far back as I could, but I could feel those giant fingers of his, which seemed just to go on and on. They were like a huge bunch of bananas, they were so large.

I knew lots of his records very well, and I can't hear a song such as *Keeping Out Of Mischief Now* without immediately thinking of Fats. It has such memories for me that when anyone simply mentions the title, I can't hear anyone else in my mind playing or singing it except him. His piano solos were also incredible—there's one called *Handful of Keys* that ought to be called *Two Hands Full of Keys*. I learned that and several more of his solos off the records, ranging from well-known songs like *I'm Going To Sit Right Down and Write Myself a Letter*, to the more specialized piano numbers like *Viper's Drag* with its little quotation from Grieg in the left hand—typical of Fats's marvelous sense of humor. One of the other things I liked about Fats was the way he used to talk at the end of a record. At the end of *Paswonky*, for example, he says "Paswonky! I love it! I love it!" and there are similar endings on many of his other discs. It was so typical of him, and his voice was just as big and raspy in the flesh as it sounded on those records. I remember him coming into the Nest and calling out my name, "George!" in that huge voice of his.

He made some discs in London that were produced by Leonard Feather. On trombone there was a great player, George Chisholm. Even back in those days, George was so versatile that he was busy in the studios as a freelance session man. He worked with some of the big bands of the day like Ambrose's orchestra, but he had the mental and physical toughness to do studio stuff in the daytime as well as playing jazz in the evening and after hours. One thing I enjoyed about playing with him was that he would see a cadence coming three or four bars before he played it, and build up his phrases accordingly. He was a wonderful improviser.

One of the other musicians with whom Fats recorded was the singer Adelaide Hall. I knew her very well, as there used to be a regular program on the BBC in the late thirties called *To Town on Two Pianos*, and I often played on it as one of the two pianists. At the other piano would be either Arthur Young or Reginald Forsythe. Addie was frequently the guest singer on the show, and I have very fond recollections of working with her, around the same time as she cut those discs with Fats. There's another connection that springs to mind there, of course, in that Fats once made a record of Reginald Forsythe's *Serenade for a Wealthy Widow*, which I think must have been his best-known composition at the time. Reginald and I both later appeared on an American radio show in the late 1940s called *Piano Playhouse*, which was produced by Maggie Fisher, and which featured pianists in all styles from the light classics to jazz.

With Adelaide Hall in London, 1939. (Frank Driggs Collection)

The tragedy of Fats's life was that he died a relatively young man. He used to drink a bottle of gin or bourbon every day. That's a hard pace of life for anyone to keep up, and I never met him again after his second visit to England, which took place a month or two before the start of World War Two.

5

DELAYED ACTION

The war broke out in the fall of 1939. Rather than ruin my career, it actually helped, because many London musicians were called up to the armed services pretty quickly and I had the field pretty much to myself. Actually, immediately after war was declared, I took the family down to Porthcawl in South Wales, away from the threat of bombs. My mum and dad stayed in a hotel there until we all realized how quiet it was in London—so we came back to the city, and that's when it started for real. Eventually, my mother was bombed out three times. (When he heard this, Mel Tormé used to say to me, "George, I knew she drank . . .") Being bombed out was really no laughing matter, and I still have graphic memories of feeling debris under my feet, of broken laths sticking out of shattered walls, and people sitting crying in the street surrounded by the few possessions they had managed to save.

I started to get even more recording sessions and broadcasts and to work at a place called Hatchett's, a restaurant in the West End of London. I loved it there because the Hatchett's band was first rate. One unusual piece it used to play was written by the leader, Denis Moonan, called *Let Me Call You Sweetheart*—not the song that became very well known, but an entirely different, more romantic number that I think is much nicer. As well as directing the Hatchett's band at the time I first played there, Denis actually played viola, but the most memorable thing about him was that he spoke in a very old Etonian manner, and he used to greet you as "My dear old horse," or "My dear old thing!"—rather the same as the cricket commentator Henry Blofeld does to this day.

Because I was doing an increasing amount of playing around the West End, I moved away from my parents' home to be closer to where I worked. It was actually only about four or five miles away, but there I began to live with a song-plugger that I'd met through my various activities in the business. His name was John Franz, and he worked for the publishers Francis Day and Hunter.

We used to go to a place called the YWCA Air Raid Shelter in Scotland Court Road every night during this phase of the war. John and I used to play four hands on one piano, to entertain the people down there. It was a funny thing to end up living with a song-plugger. Most of the time, musicians do their best to try and duck them!

John had a girlfriend. I don't remember her last name, but her first name was Nina. She would come around to the piano and she was trying to get another girl named Trixie Bayes, who was also down in the shelter, to come over to the piano with her and talk to us. At the same time, Trixie's mother was trying to get her to come around by the piano as well, but Trixie was always pretty shy and wouldn't do it.

One day, John and I were playing *All The Things You Are*. Trixie finally took her eyes off the book she was reading—she was always poring into books as a young woman—and came over to the piano, where she was introduced to John and me.

Sooner or later, Frank Thornton, a trumpet player friend of mine asked Trixie out for me, because I was pretty shy, too, I suppose.

The way he put it to her was, "Say, do you ever go out on dates?"

She said, "I don't know. Once in a while. Why?"

She thought he was a fairly good-looking boy and that he was asking for himself, but he said, "Well, you know, this pianist here, George Shearing? He would like to go out with you."

"He may be blind," she replied, "but why doesn't he ask me himself? Why does he have to have someone else ask for him?"

I used to stay down at the YWCA Air Raid Shelter quite late at night, right up until it was time for me to go to work at the club, around 9 o'clock. I would get a taxi at the last minute, so as to avoid the the air raids as much as possible. I remember one instance when I was going from one job to another and while the taxi was at a light or stopped somewhere, two bombs came whistling down just a few hundred yards from the cab. It shook like mad. I leaned forward and said to the driver, "Boy! That was a close one, wasn't it?"

No answer.

So again, a bit louder, I said, "That was close, wasn't it?"

Still no answer. The driver had jumped out of the cab and sheltered in a doorway for safety, leaving me sitting there, only to return when the coast was clear.

My nerves were really on edge because early in the war, in the wintertime, the raids would probably last fifteen or sixteen hours. Before we beat the day raiders, we'd have it day and night.

But then we beat the day raiders. They knew they'd catch it cold if they came over in the daytime, but instead they'd come about six o'clock at night and then leave, probably, around eight or nine in the morning, depending on when it got light and when it got dark. They'd use the full extent of the darkness to come over—first blasting with incendiary bombs that would light up the whole town, and then with the big explosives shattering buildings and people and everything.

It was a pretty ghastly experience. I wouldn't want to see it repeated, and if you've been through it, whenever international affairs take a turn for the worse, you're never in any hurry whatsoever to see it start up again.

Anyway, soon after we met, Trixie and I started to go around together fairly regularly. She was working at the city telegraph office at the time, but before long, that was bombed out, so they laid her off with six weeks' pay. Once this happened, I started kidding her about coming around with me because she could do things like find papers for me, sign my name and everything. I was supposed to pay her a salary, but then we became involved with each other to the extent that it didn't matter whether the salary was forthcoming or not. Everything she wanted she had.

We'd go around to the publishers and pick up music for recording and whatnot. The publishers would say, "When are you two going to get married?"

Trixie's temperament was such that the moment anyone tried to suggest anything like that to her, she ran the other way fast.

But finally we did get married, on May 1, 1941, in Bloomsbury where she lived. We were supposed to be married in the registry office, but we found out that it had been bombed out the night before our wedding. Then the strangest thing happened— sometimes it can be such a small world. Next door to her mother's home at 30 Bloomsbury Street lived a registrar, and ironically I had actually been living in the very same house for a while. I had left Johnny Franz's place, and moved into this boardinghouse next to where Trixie lived, in order to be close by. Quite by chance we found out that the woman who lived upstairs from me was a registrar. So we got married as planned, and Frank Thornton, my trumpeter friend who had first asked her out for me, was the best man.

I actually wasn't doing too much, as far as work goes, when Trixie first knew me. So there was never any question of her being a fair-weather friend, because she had known me during a period when I wasn't doing that well. Once you've made something of your life and career, you get a little doubtful sometimes as to who are your real friends and who are opportunistic hangers-on. Of course, half the time you get to live with it and in due course you get to know who your friends are. Many of my very best friends did not meet me until I enjoyed some degree of success in the business, but I know they're my friends, because even if I've been so snowed under with work that there hasn't been time to write, as soon as I call them when I get to town, the door is open.

"Come and have dinner, buddy!"

They never ask for anything. They never want anything. Just want to see me. And I know that these people are my friends and they will still be when the weather changes.

As it turned out, I found out that Trixie had seen me years before we actually met, because she'd been at one of those horse shows in Regent's Park where I was playing the harmonium on the back of my Dad's coal cart.

For our honeymoon, a relative of Trixie's had suggested that if we wanted to get away from the raids, we should go to stay at a farmhouse down in the Southwest of England, in Cornwall. I think the name of the farmer's wife was Mrs. Williams, as I recall. I had recorded a broadcast just before leaving London, and when we got there we asked whether we could listen to it on the radio.

She was one of these old witches, a real country woman from way back, but she said it was all right. So we tuned in to the program, during which we had been playing some jazz, of course. Immediately, she came bustling in and said, "What's that row? Turn that noise off! I can't abide that noise!"

She'd given me permission to listen to it, but, the minute she heard it was jazz, it was turned off immediately.

At that point I hadn't realized what an old superstitious country woman she really was, but I soon did. I had a stye on my eye and the farmhouse turned out to be not at all, really, what we wanted. Sometimes well-intending relatives can misguide you! We had to get a jug of hot water to wash with in the bedroom. It was one of those old places where there was a washstand in the corner. So Trixie went down to ask for a jug of water to bathe the stye on my eye.

The woman said, "Ah, you can have the water if you want, but I tell you what to do. You see that cat over there. You take he upstairs and wipe his tail across Hubbie's eye nine times tonight and it'll be better by morning."

Now, like a lot of blind people, I could not abide cats under any circumstances. I've always had a deathly fear of cats, for a very real and logical reason. When a dog comes around, you can hear it panting, and for the most part you can hear it coming. The first thing a blind person knows about a cat is when it's on your lap.

I've often heard the famous last words: "Oh, this cat never goes near anybody."

But as everyone who knows anything about cats can tell you, if you ignore a cat enough, it goes near you out of pure curiosity, to find out why it's being ignored. My first impulse, when a cat jumps on my lap, is to stand up. The cat's first impulse, when he finds he's no longer on terra firma, is to dig his claws in. And then we have all the threads coming out of the pants and the whole business.

I was washing, barebacked, in my mother-in-law's house, one time. A cat jumped clean on my back. Another time I was in a friend's house and I was sitting in an armchair and apparently a cat, although I didn't know it, was perched on the chairback above my head. In front of me was a table. The cat jumped clean over my head and landed on the table with a spine-chilling "Meow!" The first I knew about it was hearing the thing going over my head like a house on fire. They've haunted me throughout my life, cats. I just can't stand them.

So my wife eventually got the water, and we left the farmhouse a little sooner than anticipated, not just because of the superstitions, the radio, and the cat, but also because the cooking wasn't good and, as I say, it really wasn't what we wanted.

We went back to London, where we moved into a very nice apartment in a new block called Park West on the Edgware Road. I started working again, and, as you can imagine, because of the shortage of musicians, I was soon very busy. It's actually one of the few times in my life that I briefly regretted not having sight, because obviously I couldn't take session work that involved sight-reading. But I was able to take on pretty much everything else, and the moment of regret soon passed. I would be doing recording sessions and broadcasts in the daytime, things like the Radio Rhythm Club with Harry Parry's sextet. Then there'd be two shows for a theater at night, after which I would come back and play a restaurant from around midnight to one thirty or two o'clock. Finally I'd play the last two hours in a nightclub from two until four.

My wife drove me around most of the time, at least, to the theaters.

Of course, during World War Two you can imagine how necessary it was to keep a sense of humor going as much as you possibly could. What with people sitting out on the streets in their last chair, crying, there wasn't much to laugh about in everyday life, with the rest of us knowing that anything up to fifteen hours would be spent in an air-raid shelter almost every night to try to stay away from the devastation of the German bombs. One story that did the rounds was about the fellow who came home one night and said to his wife, "Liza, come on, we've got to get down to the shelter. The siren just went off."

She says, "Wait a minute, Jim, I'm looking for my false teeth,"

And he replies, "Come on, love, they're dropping bombs, not sandwiches."

As well as the stories that did the rounds, there were real-life incidents to laugh about as well. One day during the war, I traveled back to Battersea, to my parents' house. There wasn't too much traffic around, and as I was coming home, this guy patted me on the shoulder and said, "Hey, buddy, will you see me across the street?"

So I said, "Sure. Take my arm."

I took him across the street, and he never found out that it was a case of the blind leading the blind. His name was Mr. Boyd. I don't think I ever learned his first name, but I recognized his voice immediately from all the time I'd spent in the streets in Battersea.

When I know that someone I'm talking to—generally another blind person, or a telephone caller—doesn't know I'm blind, I don't always let on. So back in the days of the war, when they'd ask, "What do you do?" I'd say, "I'm a boiler maker!"

As well as the wisecracks, there were practical jokes.

In 1941, while I was playing at Hatchett's Restaurant in central London, Chappie D'Amato, the leader of the house band, knew that I really disliked cheese. He was also aware that while I played, I had a habit of bobbing my head back and forth over the piano keys. One night while playing with the band, I noticed that there was an awful smell that was emanating from in front of me. It seemed that the more I bobbed my head the closer I would come to this smell. So, for the rest of the evening I tried hard to play without bobbing my head at all, never suspecting that Chappie had set a piece of the most terribly pungent cheese he could find on the music rack!

But it didn't stop there. The next night, somebody decided that they were going to put garlic on the mouthpieces of all the front-line musicians in the band. I think the culprit was Charlie Pude, the other pianist and novachord player.

Chappie went to beat off the first number and he said, "OK, fellas . . . two bars . . . one, two; one, two, three, four . . ." and nobody could play. Charlie Pude was the center of another little joke, common among musicians, which was to re-word the lyrics of a well-known song, so that in this case they went, "I gazed at a picture of Hatchett's, and Pude was there . . ."

So, I had some early experience of the practical-joke business, which has been going on for quite a while in the music world.

Then from about July of 1941, I began doing a series of broadcasts with the Ambrose Octette, and I also went on tour with the band. Bert Ambrose had been a very famous bandleader back in the mid-thirties. He was quite the darling of English society, who appeared in movies and on the radio. In many ways, I like to think that he really gave me my first real start in the business, by bringing my name to a wide public in Britain for the year or so that I played for him. One solo feature I used to do with Ambrose was a piece called *Midnight In Mayfair*. It had quite a dramatic opening, with lots of little runs and flourishes, but the central section was a contrasting slow theme. To play it involved crossing my hands, and one night I was concentrating hard on getting this right technically, when I realized that all the other members of the Ambrose Octette were singing along quietly with the bridge section: "George-Shearing-plays-like-Charlie-Kunz . . ." Well, I broke up immediately—I couldn't play for laughing, not least because Charlie was a pianist who specialized in this crossed-hands technique.

Other novelty features I used to play were Billy Mayerl numbers, like *Hollyhock*. I began playing this kind of solo routine during our broadcasts. There'd be Ambrose's Octette, which had its own pianist, and then I'd do a solo piece, which got a great audience response. Then I went on tour with the Octette, but I was always featured in a solo as well, just as I had been on the radio.

Traveling during that period of the war was absolute murder. Rationing made it impossible to get fuel to travel by road, so all our tours were done by rail. There were no restaurant cars on the trains, and to get from London to Scotland normally took about ten hours for the five-hundred-mile trip. But if a troop train came along you'd be shunted into a siding for another two or three hours. Once Trixie realized this, she always used to save rations and take sandwiches. But on the first tour we didn't know any better, so we suffered terribly.

The second tour I went out with was called the Ambrose Merry-Go-Round. It was a larger show, and we'd learned our lesson, and this time for the outward train journey we took a flask of coffee and sandwiches. On our way to Scotland, I was starving, so we broke out the sandwiches and coffee, only to find that nobody else in the show had anything and they were all starving as well. Two sandwiches and a flask of coffee split between twenty people doesn't go far!

We said, "Why don't you bring something next time?"

But nobody did, and the same thing kept happening for the first few weeks. Finally Trixie said, "This is ridiculous. It's just as if we had nothing." So before we set off the next time, we scoured every shop and filled a bag with sandwiches and loaves—anything in the way of food that wasn't rationed. And we took along two flasks of coffee. So finally somebody said, "We're getting hungry."

We said, "Fine! We have food." So everybody on that trip had something to eat and drink.

We had a lot of fun though. Sometimes we'd have to travel in baggage cars loaded with soldiers. One time, we played a theater in Birmingham and it was so bitterly cold that everybody was freezing. I put on a long-sleeved sweater under my white evening shirt and white jacket. With a great big sweater under it, I felt absolutely bloated, but not for long. There was no heating in the theater and there was a big hole in the roof where it had been bombed the week before. Just as I sat down to play, what little heat there was in the theater started to melt the snow on the roof, and it began dropping through the hole onto my hands while I was playing. Melting snow is really cold, and I came off absolutely blue. Several of the girl dancers went on stage and just fainted with the cold, so they had to drag them off.

Often, when you'd arrive at a town, you couldn't get into a hotel because they were taken over by the American forces, which meant you just had to get into what we called "digs"— boardinghouses that took theatrical folks. Usually they were way out on the outskirts of town and bitterly cold, although maybe, if you were lucky, you'd have a room with an electric heater. But whoever had that room, everybody else would stay there until the last possible minute.

On one occasion we checked into a hotel somewhere on the road, and I overheard two women talking nonstop about me. "Oh, that poor blind boy, it must have happened to him because of the war."

I didn't know any better, so I decided to put their minds at rest. I said, "No. I was blind before the war—but at least when you're blind you're saved having to go out there and use guns and fight."

Immediately these two women turned on me. "You should be ashamed of yourself! You ought to be glad to go out and fight for your country."

In one town we got to, we reached the theater and I asked the doorman for digs. Nothing. Everything was full up. It was a very small town and the American forces had completely taken it over. He said, "Sorry, old chap, I have nothing left."

We wandered around for a bit, but after a while we'd tried everywhere and so we came back to the theater.

I was getting ready to play, but Trixie said to the doorman, "Please. The show goes on in an hour. I don't care what it is. Just get us in anywhere."

So the doorman looked at her for a long time and then he said, "Well, if you really don't mind, I'll give you an address."

So we went to this place and there was a charming woman there who took one look at us and said, "All right. I do have a room."

She gave us a room on the ground floor, but loads of people were coming and going, and the door kept banging all night long. So when we got to the theater the next day, during the morning rehearsal I talked to a comedian on the bill and said, "How did you manage for digs?"

And he said, "Oh, I have a pretty nice place."

I told him, "We're in a terrible place. I couldn't get any sleep."

"Where are you?"

I said, "In this place the stage doorman told us about."

"What address are you at?"

So I told him, and he said, "My God! That's a brothel!"

So he got us in with him and that was it. We talked his land-lady into giving us a room in her sitting room. I'll never forget that night, but we were grateful to her because we had nowhere else to stay in the town.

There were several other well-known musicians involved in the Ambrose tours. I particularly remember trumpeter and singer Teddy Foster, the young vocalist Anne Shelton, and of course, Al Bowlly, a fine singer and a very nice fellow, who was killed soon afterwards in an air raid when a bomb fell right outside his Jermyn Street apartment.

Back in London, I was even busier than I had been earlier in the year with Harry Parry and Radio Rhythm Club Sextet, because now I was doing the Ambrose broadcast which went out live from ten to ten thirty every morning. Then I was rehearsing in the after-noons for the next broadcast the following day. Then, around about four o'clock we'd leave, as we were playing theaters all around London with Ambrose—places within a half-hour range of the center of town. Now, as I mentioned, we'd bought a car and because I was blind we were allowed a little extra fuel allowance, so Trixie would drive me out to whichever theater we were play-ing. On the way, she would have to note every landmark on the curb. You'd have to watch the curb all the way and know every inch of the road because we had to come back in the blackout and find our way back. Wartime cars had a little tiny light which shone onto the road through slits in the headlamp covers, which gave less visibility than your average parking light.

We'd get to the theater and play two shows, which by this stage in the war would have to be be finished at nine thirty because of the air raids. Then I'd have to get changed and back to the West End of London, and because of the blackout and everything, that was never less than a half an hour ride at the best of times, so that I reached Hatchett's by ten thirty. Then it was the same routine as before—play there until two in the morning, then get a cab and go to the Embassy nightclub and play from two til four.

Finally we'd dash home, get some sleep and be up in time to be at the studio again by ten the next morning. I did this for a number of weeks, getting about two or three hours of sleep a night.

A little later, I went on the road with Stephane Grappelli. He used to be with the Quintet of the Hot Club of France, which featured Django Reinhardt on guitar and Stephane on violin. They'd been touring England at the very moment that war broke out, and although Django fled back to Paris, Stephane stayed on in London right through the hostilities. We first worked together at Hatchett's in a quartet, and later in a slightly larger group that went on the road, which often featured the singer Beryl Davis who was famous for the version of *Undecided* she had recorded with the Hot Club Quintet just a matter of days before the war began. Stephane and I also made several discs together, and a short film, which featured guitarist Dave Goldberg, bassist Coleridge Goode, and drummer Ray Ellington who also sang on one of the numbers. Ray's singing used to break me up, because of his natural comic timing. He might sing a ballad with lines like:

> *It's not just sentimental,*
> *She has her grief and her cares,*
> *And a word that's soft and gentle*
> *Makes it easier to bear . . . D'you hear!*

And he'd shout the last words, ruining the romantic effect, but making everybody laugh.

At one point later on in the war, Stephane's group even had an offer to come over to the United States. He turned it down, because he didn't think it was good enough for him.

He was a tremendous fiddle player and a good classical pianist, with a real talent on the keyboard for the French impressionist composers such as Debussy and Ravel. He was very quick at writing music, too, so the way we used to do our arrangements for the band was that Stephane would stand or sit by the piano, I would play something and he would jot it down. For example, I would play a bass line almost in tempo, and he'd be taking it down just about as fast as any secretary could take down shorthand. What he wrote could be used as a finished copy, so that the bass part would then be ready for the bass player to play. I think Stephane actually played in a much looser, more wide-ranging way when he was backed up by a piano than he had done with the string Quintet. Partly this was just because Django laid down such a strong rhythmic foundation that you just had to go along with his approach—indeed Django's personality was so strong that he imposed it on everything they played. If Django felt like taking a couple of solo choruses, he just went ahead and did so, but for the rest of us who played with Stephane, the general rule was that one took just a single chorus on each number.

Stephane used to pretend, during the war, that he didn't speak nearly as much English as he actually did. He'd do it with the musicians just as a gag, but he'd do it with other people to benefit himself. For example, someone would say to him: "Get back into the queue, buddy!"

He'd say, "I no understand. What is the queue?"

He understood all right, but he'd give a very good impression that he didn't. Essentially, though, he was a very nice person. I worked off and on with Stephane, on recording sessions, on tour and so on, for seven years.

One event that really sticks in my mind from those years with Stephane was the first time I visited a real country house. It was down in Devonshire, at Bovey Tracey, just north of Newton Abbot, and it belonged to a doctor, who was a musical enthusiast, but who was also one of these really stuffy guys who would get quite upset if the locals didn't doff their hats to him when he passed. He was rather a snob, and employed a maidservant and all that kind of thing. But he was quite knowledgeable about jazz, and Stephane and I used to go down there from time to time to play for him, over a long weekend.

There was a disc by Teddy Wilson which had been issued not long before the war, that I was very keen on. It was a quartet recording called *Just a Mood*, or *Blue Mood*, and it went over both sides of a 78-rpm disc. Teddy's band included himself on piano, John Simmons on bass, Red Norvo on vibes, and Harry James on trumpet. Teddy played a solo on that record that was just magnificent, and I really admired it. In due course, it came out in print form, and the doctor used to try to play this thing on the piano, reading it off the sheet music. He'd say to me, as he struggled through it, "I say, George. D'you think I'm getting more of a beat, now?"

Teddy was so relaxed and fluent, with lovely spaces between the phrases, and unfortunately Jack Harrison, the doctor, was exactly the opposite—very stiff and metronomic. What was I to answer?

One time when we were down there, Stephane and Jack both drank quite a skinful, and Stephane became quite loquacious. He turned to Jack and said, "You know, you and I, we are good friends, now. You invite me down here for the weekend to have fun, does it mean I still have to play?"

Well, of course it did mean he had to play—that's why he was there. But he managed to use his French charm and innocence to try and break out of the rigid social code that applied to us as musicians when, although we were treated as guests, we were really there as employees of the doctor.

Being down in the country was a marvelous contrast from the tensions of living and working in London during the Blitz. I noticed it very acutely in Stephane's behavior, because not long after one of those weekends in Devon, we were back working at a theater in the West End, and there had been some very heavy raids.

"We should not play the show," said Stephane. "Look over there at that girl singer—she's very nervous!"

The stage manager glanced across, then he said, "She seems fine to me, Mr. Grappelli."

Then Stephane tried again. "You know, I'm not sure it is good for us to go on—after all, our pianist, he is blind. What if something were to happen?"

Finally, the stage manager killed all this stuff by looking him straight in the eye and saying: "Now then, you know who's nervous? It's a man named Stephane Grappelli. Now be a good boy and go out there and play your show!"

As I've said, it could be extremely nerve-wracking to be in London during those years, and one thing I realized when I arrived in the United States was that very few Americans had any idea what Londoners went through during World War Two, because, thank God, nothing similar has ever happened to America. This devastation was not just limited to London, either. Stephane and I traveled to Coventry to play in the theater there for a week. The city had been so severely bombed that not much was left standing in parts of the center, and the closest hotel we could find was five miles out of town. Owing to the severe food shortages at that stage of the war, we were offered a choice for dinner of either rabbit or cheese. I can't stand either, so I spent the week living on bread and butter. Another thing I came to realize that few Americans understood was what Britain had experienced in terms of rationing. I well remember when the meat ration was cut to three-quarters of a pound per person per week, at a time when Americans were still able to enjoy their usual big steaks.

During the years that I worked with Stephane, although the war was still going on, Trixie and I moved out of central London to a house in Pinner in the Middlesex suburbs. It was recommended to us by a man called David Miller, who was a producer at the BBC. He lived nearby and had seen a house in a road called East Towers that was for rent at a fairly modest price.

Our married life together had helped to make me much more independent on the domestic level. To start with, my mother accused Trixie of ill-treating me. When I had lived at home, my shirts and so forth would be put out for me, but Trixie just told me where everything was and said, "Now you're on your own."

Mother was horrified. She'd come to visit us and ask, "Where's George's shirt?"

Trixie would say, "He knows where his shirt is."

"I'll get it. Where is it?" But my wife would never tell her and she'd get annoyed until she was more or less forced to sit down. Despite her fondness for the bottle, mother was used to being on the go all the time. So after a while, she'd come to our house and we'd make her go into the garden and sit down in a deck chair. One day she said this was the first real vacation she ever had in her life, and she liked nothing better than spending the weekend with us, just being waited on, because she'd never known that before. She'd known nothing but hard work. Our house was about fifteen miles out of central London, and like most of the houses in the area, it had a small garden.

Although I had been quite accustomed to using public transport in and around Battersea and the West End, life was a bit different where we now lived. When Trixie became pregnant, and couldn't drive me into town, my mother was horrified to find out that I was setting off for work on the bus. I'd walk to the end of the road and then down a little hill to catch the bus to the station, and get on the tube—the subway—to London. Then I was supposed to get a cab from the station to wherever I was working.

In fact it got to the point where I walked to the end of our road and as soon as the bus came along and the driver saw me, he would stop and wait. I'd cross the road and get into the bus. The minute I'd hear the bus, I used to wave like mad and the bus would stop. Then it was on to the Metropolitan Line to London, but instead of always getting a cab, I'd usually change at Baker Street, and get on the Underground to Piccadilly Circus. After all, this was wartime and there weren't that many cabs. And from Piccadilly, I'd walk the several blocks to the club.

Generally, I'd get home about five or six in the morning. The first train went about five thirty, so I'd either hang around the night clubs and talk to the barflies and prostitutes, or settle down with a drummer friend over a cup of tea at the Lyons' Corner House, until it was time to catch the first train home. Sometimes I used to forget my key and Trixie would have to come downstairs half asleep, open the door, and just walk upstairs again, leaving me to come in and sort myself out.

So one morning, I rang the bell. Trixie came downstairs, opened the door, and started back upstairs. I guess she was subconsciously aware that I hadn't followed her in, because halfway upstairs she turned around sleepily, took a look at me and realized I was standing there, wringing wet and covered in mud from the waist down. She took one look at me and just broke up.

Once she'd stopped laughing, she finally caught her breath long enough to ask, "Whatever happened to you?"

So then I confessed. It was a beautiful morning and I'd decided to walk home. And I knew from doing the journey countless times on the bus that you walked down the hill from the station, turned left, walked as far as Eastcote Road. Then you turned right, and as you started to go up the next hill, there was a left turn and that was our road.

So I was walking along and I heard footsteps—a workman. I thought, "Well, I'd better make sure."

I said, "Where's Eastcote Road?"

And the fellow said, "Turn right. Next turn right, mate."

As a result, I walked along until I came to the end of the pavement—ah, this must be the road. So I turned right, and it didn't quite feel right. I thought I should be on the pavement, and that perhaps I shouldn't have got off the pavement at the corner. But then I found that there was a step and I thought, "Well, maybe I just slightly got off the track."

So I stepped up, and immediately tipped over and rolled down a bank. It wasn't a road at all, but a petrol filling station I'd turned into, and behind it was a steep slope. I rolled right down into the river—luckily the water wasn't deep but it was awfully muddy.

I tried and tried to scramble up and eventually I caught hold of a couple of twigs. If they could talk, I'm sure they'd have said "Sucker!" because they broke in my hands. So I went back down again. Finally, somehow or other, I scrambled up, found a policeman who put me on the Eastcote Road, and I made it back home.

Many years later, in the 1990s, I decided to go back there with my second wife, Ellie. We took the Metropolitan Line from Baker Street, and the names of all the stops came back to me as if it were yesterday. Finchley Road, Wembley Park, Harrow-on-the-Hill, North Harrow, and eventually, Pinner. We got out, and turned right at the exit from the station. Careful not to make the same mistake I'd made that long-ago morning, I led Ellie into Eastcote Road, and after we'd been walking for quite a while, I said, "Now, East Towers should be coming up soon." We stopped a passerby who said it was the very next turning, and soon I was able to walk right up to the house itself.

I turned to Ellie and said, "This is where I used to ring on the doorbell for Trixie to let me in when I forgot my key."

She said, "Do you want to try it?"

So I pressed the bell. A man answered the door, and I said to him, "Excuse me, I don't mean to intrude, but I lived in this house during the war. My name's George Shearing."

"George Shearing!" he replied. "They told me you used to live here when I bought the house twenty-seven years ago. My wife would love to meet you—why not come in and have a cup of tea?"

So we found ourselves back in the house once more, all those years after Trixie and I had our family there.

Our daughter, Wendy, was born in the middle of the war, on October 28, 1942, while we were living in the Pinner house. Almost two years later, we had a son, David George, who tragically died before his first birthday. Unlike Wendy, who was born sighted, David was blind, which goes back to my earlier observation that one out of every four children born to someone with my particular form of blindness is likely to inherit it. Blindness apart, he was a beautiful child in every respect, always very healthy, but towards the end of 1944, he caught a cold. We put him to bed and called a doctor who turned out to be a lady doctor as there weren't many male doctors around at that stage of the war. They were all in the forces.

This lady came and said it was just a cold and we should keep him in bed, which we did. Now, our house, like most of the homes in England at that time, was heated with coal fireplaces. We practically used up all our ration of coal keeping the fire going in the bedroom, but a week later, the boy was still unwell, and nothing seemed to make him any better.

The doctor kept coming every day, and Trixie finally said, "Can't you give him anything?"

But she said, "No, he's too young."

By that time, there was no coal left, but we got a ration permit from the doctor, so Trixie went down to the local borough council offices and said, "I have a baby who is very sick. I've got a special permit for coal. Can you help?"

They said, "Very well."

"When can we get it?"

"Two weeks."

She said, "But my baby is ill! I must have it now."

They said, "Sorry. We have a waiting list. Two weeks."

So we had no heating.

Later that day, Trixie went all over London and spent the whole day trying to find some way to keep the little boy warm. Finally, she managed to get a little tiny electric heater at a fabulous price, and we kept this in his bedroom. It didn't work too well, but at least it took the chill off. It wasn't a matter of money. In wartime London, in December, you just couldn't get coal or any other fuel.

The next time the doctor came, we said, "Look, he's not getting any better."

Again, she said, "There's nothing else we can do."

With no help from the doctor, we tried everything, even rigging up a steam kettle for him. And next day she said he was a little better.

Then Christmas came and both sets of parents, mine and Trixie's, were staying at the house.

Now as it happened, I had a broadcast to do on Christmas morning. Normally, I was quite able to go into London on the train myself and someone would meet me. But because it was Christmas, all the train times were different, and so I asked Trixie to go with me. She really didn't want to come, because of the baby, but in the end she agreed because both grandmothers were there—they'd both brought several children into the world, and were very experienced in dealing with childhood illnesses. Meanwhile the doctor came by early on Christmas morning and told us she'd be away for two days.

We asked, "Can you give us the name of another doctor while you're gone?"

She said, "That's not necessary."

"Supposing he gets worse?"

But she repeated, "No, it won't be necessary. I'll be back within two days."

So, we felt quite reassured, and leaving the poor boy with our mothers, we went up to town to do the broadcast. Afterwards, the producer said, "Come and have lunch with me." So, partly because we were reassured that the boy was being well looked after, we stayed on and had lunch.

When we got home, the first thing we asked was, "How's the baby?"

My mother said that he'd had convulsions, but he was all right now and was sleeping. Trixie's mother was up in the room with him when he suddenly had another attack of convulsions.

Finally we got a doctor to come and he said, "If this child isn't in a hospital within an hour there's nothing we can do." But he couldn't get an ambulance, and we had no fuel for the car. In the end it was nearly two hours before they got him to the hospital. Meanwhile, my mother said, "Put him in a hot bath."

So they stripped him and put him in a hot bath to ease the convulsions and then wrapped him in a blanket. Anyway, we got him to the hospital. The doctor who examined him in the receiving ward said, "This child is neglected. He should have been in a hospital weeks ago. He'll die."

We were absolutely stunned, and we said, "We've had a doctor every day for this child."

The man asked, "Who's the doctor?" And we gave him the details.

They put our son in an oxygen tent. He had pneumonia, and during the night he died. I'll never forget when the nurse told us that he had died. I think she thought she was easing the pain when she said to Trixie that he would probably have been blind all his life, and that his death was a blessing.

Then the next day our doctor came home. She arrived, cheerful as anything, and said, "Well, how's the baby?"

We told her, "The baby's dead."

She said, "Oh no. I am sorry."

It was a real blow, particularly coming at what was normally a festive time of year, and Trixie took it very hard indeed. I think she blamed me for taking her into London for that Christmas-morning broadcast, and it wasn't until we finally moved to America that she was able to put the whole thing into some kind of perspective.

In the short term, however, life had to go on, and about three weeks later Trixie said to me, "George, that lady doctor. Call her up. Let's get her bill settled. I never want to see that woman again."

So I called up and to my surprise, I discovered she was no longer in practice. At first, I wanted to sue her, but Trixie said it wouldn't have brought our boy back and she didn't want to go through all the business of a court case on top of the tragedy. So we gradually picked up our lives and I went back to work.

Immediately after the war, in 1946, I was playing regularly with the saxophonist Harry Hayes. In fact we swapped round some of the same musicians between his band and mine, because I had had a group a little earlier that made some records, with Kenny Baker on trumpet, Aubrey Franks and Harry Hayes on saxes, Tommy Bromley on bass, and Carlo Krahmer on drums. I wrote a bunch of numbers for that group including pieces like *Riff Up Them Stairs*, which we recorded in February 1944. The general style of the band was very much in the contemporary swing idiom, and we'd actually got hold of some arrangements that had been done in the States for the John Kirby Sextet, things like *Undecided*, and on live gigs we played them straight off the published charts. Most of what we recorded, on the other hand, was original material by me or other members of the band, and as ever, we chose some puns for the titles, of which my favorite was *Cymbal Simon*.

In fact that's the first band I led on record, because my original quintet never made it on to disc, on account of the Blitz. It was back in 1940, and I was leading my own group at the St. Regis Hotel in the West End, with trumpet, clarinet, piano, bass, and drums—not the quintet line-up I later became well known for, but a quintet nonetheless. Basically what happened was that a bomb hit the building. We had gone out to get something to eat, and we made our way back through a great gushing spray of water, but they wouldn't let us back in because there was a time bomb in the lift shaft. We went back the next day, but they still weren't letting anyone in because of the unexploded bomb, and that was the end of the first George Shearing Quintet.

It was a funny thing how I got to join Harry Hayes. He called me and said that he was working at a place called Churchill's on Bond Street. They wanted me to join the band and he told me that the boss of the club wanted to see me. Well, at this time I had taken on a number of pupils and I was doing a couple of arrangements a week for various bands, so I thought I had a nice little job going. Not long before, I had been working at Fisher's Restaurant with Frank Weir, until for a while I just gave up the nightclub and restaurant gigs, and concentrated on arranging, on the pupils and doing the occasional recording with Stephane or with Frank. After the frantic pace I had kept up a year or two earlier, I had a very nice thing going, to the point where I could sit in my garden quite a bit in the daytime and not have to work too much at nights.

I was making somewhere between thirty-five and fifty pounds a week doing this—which was somewhere between $150 and $200, given that the rate of exchange at that time was far greater than it is today.

So, earning this kind of money, when I went to see the owner of Churchill's with a view to joining the Harry Hayes band, I was armed with a pretty good weapon to refuse their meager offer. I think the union scale at the time was about twelve pounds a week, and since musicians were in short supply, they were offering fourteen or fifteen, according to the standard of the musician. The manager offered me eighteen.

I said that if I was going to work until three or four o'clock in the morning with the band, that I would want thirty.

The guy said, "This is an outrageous figure! But I do want to feature you with the band, so what I'd really like to do is have you come in for two or three weeks at eighteen and then if we find that you're drawing well and bringing people in, we'll give you a raise."

I said, "Well, I frankly don't need the work for audition prices. I think that it's worth thirty pounds for the job. I have a number of things going that are netting me quite a good salary. I don't want to break friends with you, but really and truly, I don't need your job."

He came back with, "Well, some of the sessions and some of the clubs and some of the other things that you've been doing may not be here in ten years, but Churchill's will be here for twenty years or more."

So I said, "Who even said anything about me even being here in ten years? I hope in ten years time to be well and truly settled in the United States!"

So then he turned to Harry Hayes and said, "Can't you give him some extra money out of what I'm paying the rest of the band?"

Harry said, "You know what I'm working for—that's quite impossible."

Finally the guy had me stand up and shake hands with him and he said, "You start on Monday."

I secured the job for thirty pounds a week when they were paying fourteen and had offered me eighteen. The guy's name, I recall, was Harry Meadows.

When I got outside, after a minute or two Harry Hayes came up and said to me, "You know, while you waited out here for me to say good-bye to him, he said to me, 'I intended on giving it to him anyway. I just didn't want to be too easy and agree his price right away.'"

Then he said, "George, I'll tell you, you're one of the first people who has ever really beaten this man down and got what he wants from him. I want to congratulate you because nobody beats this man down and gets what he wants!"

Actually I shouldn't really take that much credit for it, because when you go there armed with a weapon of ample supply of cash and goodly connections, such as the one I had with the arranging and the teaching, you don't need the job and so it's not difficult then to get up your nerve and say so. When you're down to your last hundred bucks, then it's difficult to say to anybody, "Look, I don't need it."

If you have the guts to do it then, it's rather like having the guts to put all your money, or a good part of it, into the stock market when the shares are really falling down low. This is really the time to buy, but who has the nerve to do it? As you'll see, I was in a very different position myself once I'd made the decision to move to America, but that was still some way off when I joined Harry Hayes.

Churchill's was one of the really top nightclubs in London. A very particular memory of my time there was that it was where I met the famous English comedian, Oliver Wakefield. His nickname was "the Voice of Inexperience," and his act involved very rarely finishing a sentence. He would say things like: "To be standing once again in front of a . . . makes me feel . . . It strikes me more forcibly . . . more so perhaps because during my entire service career nothing struck me. No shot was fired at me in anger or in Burma. And as I sit and look at your simple faces, I feel simply . . ."

When I came over to America, I heard a Pet Milk commercial and you can imagine my surprise when I recognized the voice-over—Oliver Wakefield. It was the only commercial I heard him do in the States, but if my memory serves me correctly, he had been kicked off the BBC for being a little bit near the bone.

He said, "Really, ladies and gentlemen, if you have an earnest desire to try some of this Pet Milk, you should really get up off your . . . and buy some."

6

SWING STREET

I first came over to the United States, just on a vacation, in November 1946, and I stayed for about three months. Before the war, I'd gotten to know a number of American musicians, bandleaders, and personalities who visited Britain, and I met several more in the latter stages of the war. The seeds of the idea that I should move to America were sown by Fats Waller's manager, Ed Kirkeby, who said as far back as 1938 that I should make the move. Other American visitors whom I met in London said much the same, from Coleman Hawkins during those after-hours jams at the Nest in the late 1930s, to Glenn Miller, who was in Britain with his Army Air Force band during the war. Glenn's sidemen, players like Mel Powell and Peanuts Hucko, were even more enthusiastic. Encouraged by them, and through listening to American records and musical movies, I just thought that as soon as you set foot in the United States, if you could play jazz, everybody would just swallow you up and your career would take off. Well, of course, I have no complaint about the way things eventually turned out, but it certainly wasn't like that in the beginning.

I organized my first trip through Leonard Feather. He had spent time over in New York on and off since 1935. I just missed him when he returned briefly to Europe in 1939. He went to Switzerland or Sweden or somewhere for a vacation, and when war broke out, he returned directly to the United States, where he stayed all during the war.

By the time hostilities ended, I was beginning to have the feeling that I had gone about as far as it was possible to go with my career in England, and that perhaps Ed Kirkeby had been right. If there was a single event that prompted my decision, it was when I was coming out of a tube station one day, and somebody stopped me and said, "I know you! You're Stephane Grappelli's pianist, aren't you?"

In many respects I don't have much of an ego, but that really was a blow to me, because I didn't want to go through life being the piano player who belonged to another jazz musician. I might have found it a bit more verbally digestible if he'd said, "You play *with* Stephane Grappelli, don't you?" Anyhow, in the wake of that, I called Leonard, a few months after the war had ended, and said that I was planning on coming over. Could he do anything?

He was very helpful, and when I arrived, he took me around and introduced me to a number of club owners. Of course, by this time, I'd got a car, a house, a big grand piano and everything in England, because during the war years I really had built up quite a reputation, although in a different way than I subsequently did in the States. In Britain, I was a sort of general freelance musician, arranger, teacher, and whatnot. I had no manager, or agent, or any of those things, and perhaps I was not as well known as some other musicians who did have managers and agents, but you'd be surprised at how much money I was making because of my low overheads!

For that first visit to America, I traveled with my wife, and we left our young daughter Wendy behind in England with my sister. When we came back, my sister told us that when Wendy saw my brother-in-law reading the paper, she said, "Uncle Wally, why do you read like that? Why don't you read with your fingers like my daddy?" It's amazing how children's minds work even at a young age.

If you were coming to New York from England during the late 1940s in search of jazz either for pleasure or for business, you would have wanted to hit 52nd Street. There was never anything like it, and since it saw its demise, to my mind, there never will be again. After all, since then, musicians have learned that you can play in less stuffy atmospheres, and you can make money at a much faster pace, while still being able to play jazz. This is just one reason why 52nd Street will never again rise to fame.

But it's there to be remembered. When I first hit the American shore, just off the ship, I thought to myself, this is the place of

Benny Goodman, Artie Shaw, Billie Holiday, and Ella Fitzgerald! This is the birthplace of all this stuff and here I am! And it didn't take me very long before I found myself on 52nd Street, where you could hear more people within a block or two than you could hear all over the rest of New York.

As you walked down the street, there was just one club after another. Billie Holiday would be in the first one. Maybe two doors down, Art Tatum would be playing. Across the street, Ella Fitzgerald. A few houses down, a big band—maybe Basie. And then, as things went on, the bebop era was coming into being and so you'd find Dizzy Gillespie and Charlie Parker in one club, and next door would be Lucky Thompson and his quartet. You could go in there and have a few drinks and it wouldn't cost you very much money.

The working conditions were horrible, really. You were on for forty minutes and off for a twenty-minute break from nine at night until two, or two thirty, in the morning. One thing that shocked me, the following year when I got a job playing opposite Sarah Vaughan at the Onyx Club or when I played opposite Ella Fitzgerald at the Three Deuces, was when I noticed that somewhere along the way, my $100 check at the end of the week had become $90. It had nothing to do with tax withholding. It had only to do with the fact that the club had an agreement with the Musicians' Union whereby if they gave us an intermission of an hour instead of the allotted twenty minutes, they would then be permitted to take something off the paycheck. It was rather unfair because you couldn't do very much in an hour. You could go out and get yourself a meal, which you can't do in twenty minutes, but it was rather an unfair decision. But I was the new kid on the block and there was nothing I could say about it.

However, I've never forgotten it, because I still wonder why somebody who was successful enough to own a club would find it necessary to chisel $10 off the musicians who worked there. But, as one goes through life, one finds out such weaknesses and strengths, all of which have to be accepted or rejected and the ability to reject depends upon the amount of power you actually have to change the status quo.

On that first visit, I wasn't working professionally. I sat in with Charlie Shavers and a few other such people on 52nd Street. Charlie was extremely generous and invited me to come up and play with him long before anybody else even had an inkling who I was or what I could play. I also sat in up in Harlem at Minton's Playhouse, with a band that had Big Sid Catlett playing the drums. I got so excited I was literally shaking when I came off the bandstand, because playing with Big Sid was a thrill—he could just tickle those drums when the music called for it, but what a beat, and what power! It was astounding to hear such a big man play so lightly. I had that "Where am I?" feeling while I was playing, because it was one of those wonderful sessions where everything was going right. There was a lot of bebop involved, and I was so excited and so overcome I became covered in perspiration. The standard at Minton's was incredibly high, and I was lucky enough to be called to sit in. You certainly didn't go up and ask to sit in at a place like that, but with the help of Charlie Shavers, Dizzy Gillespie, and one or two others, I was fortunate enough to be invited to join in with some great players.

Another drummer I sat in with on the Street was Gene Krupa, although when that happened, I said a couple of words of thanks at the end of the set, but he just muttered, "Nice to meet you," and walked straight past me and left the club.

I never did figure out what that was about. Otherwise, I was always made welcome to sit in with various groups on the Street. There was a tangible sense of playing jazz for real there, treating it as a serious business, that I hadn't found in Britain.

I didn't do anything else as far as work was concerned, but during my stay I did hear some marvelous music, particularly when I went to a club called the Aquarium, where the Lionel Hampton Orchestra was playing. He had a really fine band— really swinging. We were very excited about it. Back at the hotel, in the middle of the night I woke up startled because someone suddenly sat down on my bed.

I said, "Huh!"

And Trixie's voice answered, "Oh, it's me! I guess the excitement of hearing that band must have made me walk in my sleep!"

That Lionel Hampton band was quite an experience, and it was exactly the kind of thing I had wanted to come over to New York to hear. However, although there was lots to be heard in the small clubs, there was relatively little going on with the great swing bands. By the time I got over to New York, the Jimmie Lunceford Orchestra, which I'd really wanted to experience ever since I played some of its arrangements with Claude Bampton, was about through. In fact Jimmie died out on the West Coast only a few months after I made that first American trip, so although I so much wanted to hear his band, I never did.

Then I heard that another band which I really admired was playing a theater in town. I thought, "This is great! Tommy Dorsey!"

What happens? They open with a number, like *Marie* or *Song of India* or one of Tommy's other popular things, and then they play for all the other acts, before closing with another one of Tommy Dorsey's best-known tunes, and that's the end.

Here was the actual band I'd wanted to hear, but during that show I couldn't really sit there and say to myself, "Wow, I'm listening to Tommy Dorsey!"

It was just a really good band that was accompanying lots of singers and dancers, really cutting the show like crazy, but it wasn't anything like the same experience of hearing it in one of the clubs or one of the hotels. But even there, more often than not they've got the mutes in and they're playing for dancing. What a waste!

Sometimes it could be the same when you went on 52nd Street, to somewhere like the Downbeat, and there was Art Tatum, with nobody paying any attention. He might as well have been a bar-room piano player.

One thing that stood out for me from that first American visit was hearing the sounds of bebop for the first time. I heard Dizzy Gillespie with his big band at the Apollo Theater, and afterwards I went backstage to meet him. He had a little harmonium in his dressing room, and right then and there he began to show me some of the new chords he was using, the "flatted fifths" and so on. I could hear these voicings straight away, and it was great to have that firsthand contact with Dizzy. I took some of his records back with me to England, as well as some discs by the Boyd Raeburn Orchestra which were not exactly bebop, but which contained some really advanced harmonies which I found fascinating. At that stage, hardly anyone in England knew anything about bebop, except for the few of us who had had the opportunity to experience it at firsthand on 52nd Street.

When I went back to the United States a year later, I became part of the 52nd Street scene myself. In the intervening months, I returned to England and cleared up a few things. I did some more arrangements, mainly for a bandleader named Frank Weir. I was with the Frank Weir band long before he recorded his successful version of *The Happy Wanderer*, from which he became quite well known for a time. Frank Weir and the Astor Club Seven is what his group was actually called. There were five front line and three rhythm, so I guess whoever named the band couldn't count! I used to do two or three arrangements a week for Frank. We'd have a guy come over to my house one day and then the next day I would go over to his place and between us we would work on these arrangements, probably two or three days a week. I also had a lot of arranging to do for Ted Heath at the time, and although it was not as profitable for me as it would have been if I had been able to sit at the desk and write them out directly myself—just as I did for Frank, I always had to employ somebody to take them down for me—Heath's band was packed with good musicians and it was marvelous to go along and hear my pieces being played at rehearsal.

I made some good friends in Frank Weir's band, including the drummer, Norman Burns. I remember one night when Frank shook his fist at Norman, and said, "Too bloody loud." I advised Norman to shake his fist back at Frank and answer, "Too bloody late!"

Norman was a great practical joker, and once during that period with Frank's band, he was over at a party at our house. I love watercress sandwiches—in fact even after many years in the United States, I still do. It's one of the really English traits I still have left, liking watercress, with bread and butter. On this particular day, Trixie had made some, and to fool me, Norman had got hold of a couple of extra pieces of bread and butter and filled them with honeysuckle, which has a rather similar feel to watercress.

He handed this to me and said, "George, Trixie asked me to give you this watercress sandwich." I was just about to bite into this darned honeysuckle sandwich when Trixie caught sight of it out of the corner of her eye, and rushed across, saying, "What's Norman giving you over there?"

All he could say was, "Oh Trixie, you always spoil the fun!"

Sometimes Norman was on the receiving end of a similar prank. One day he got a call about a gig in Hyde Park. So, he dutifully arrived with his drums half an hour before the appointed time and set them up on the designated bandstand in the middle of the park. There he sat . . . and sat . . . and waited . . . and waited, and nobody showed. The appointed hour came and went. Finally, he shrugged his shoulders, tore down his drums and went home.

If there were two ways to take me from Point A to Point B, you could bet on it that Norman would choose the path where I would have to climb over piles of coal or mounds of debris— especially if there were anyone else there to enjoy the fun. He would always volunteer to cut up my food when the band would grab a bite at some nearby restaurant or pub. When my meal arrived, I would hear the sound of a knife and fork on the plate, and soon Norman would say, "Okay, George, it's all ready." However, no matter where I put my fork on the plate, all I would find was dry bread where I expected to find meat, potatoes, and vegetables.

When he had had enough of the joke, he would remove the dry bread, and there would be my meal all ready for me to eat.

When I said that practical jokes were so necessary during the war, I also found that musicians' senses of humor were just as much in evidence some thirty years later. In the mid-seventies, I had a drummer in the Quintet by the name of Rusty Jones. He was from Chicago, and was the nephew of the famous bandleader, Isham Jones, but he was also one of the funniest men I have ever met. He could always be relied on to reduce me to tears of laughter with his many voices and accents and he had a joke for every occasion. One of his favorite places to pull a practical joke was at an airport, particularly if he knew that a lot of musicians would be on the premises. A good time was when many bands were headed for the same or different summer jazz festivals.

Walking towards our gate to catch a plane, we would hear over the public address system, "Would Mr. Charlie Parker please pick up the white courtesy phone?" or "Would the person or persons meeting Mr. Art Tatum please come to the Information Desk in the lower lobby?"

Every musician in the airport who heard it would collapse with laughter, knowing that in every case the person being paged was deceased—and their merriment would be much to the puzzlement of the other passengers around them.

Fortunately, I've always enjoyed the company of people who share that kind of sense of humor, and from time to time I've had my own opportunities to play similar jokes. Around the time of the honeysuckle sandwich incident, a bunch of us in England played a practical trick on somebody else. One of us spotted a little car standing outside the film studios, where I had been playing, and from somewhere we got hold of some small bricks, each just about a half-inch thick.

One of the fellows jacked up the car, put the bricks underneath the axles, and then let it down onto the bricks. A bit later the poor guy who owned it came out. He revved up his engine, but nothing happened, although the wheels were spinning like crazy. He wasn't moving anywhere. Finally, he found out what had happened, and then he had to get out of the car, jack it up again, take out the bricks, and then go.

Norman was often at the center of this kind of joke, but he always remained a very loyal and true friend. He eventually moved to Australia. The first time I flew out there, I arrived in Sydney somewhere about four thirty in the morning but despite the time, Norman was there to meet me.

In Frank Weir's band there were two of us playing piano—Ralph Sharon and me. For the most part we played two pianos, but occasionally he played piano and I played accordion, which I was still using from time to time during that period. Ralph had actually been a pupil of mine during the war, so we got on very well playing arrangements for four hands. He'd studied with me at a place called Weekes' Studio, where I used to go along once a week, usually on a Saturday, to give him a lesson. He always played so well I wondered why he needed me, but he obviously thought he did, even though he'd already played with Carlo Krahmer, Harry Lewis, and Victor Feldman.

I mainly worked with him on harmonizing various songs in a more contemporary way, and introducing him to the styles of one or two pianists he might not have been familiar with. I also gave him exercises to improve the way he heard harmony in different keys. We might start with a chord such as a C-seven with a flat nine, a flat five and a thirteen, that's a C, E, B-flat, D-flat, G-flat and A-natural. I'd make him transpose this voicing through all the keys of the chromatic scale, so that starting with C, he'd take it down through B, B-flat, A, and so on. Every one of those chords would have to be correctly transposed and voiced. This was something I'd never really had to think about myself, I could always just hear these voicings, and when I started playing things that involved complex harmonies, when I was sixteen or seventeen, I already knew in my head how what I wanted to play should sound. Of course, Ralph later moved to the United States, around seven years or so after I did, and went on to have a long career in America, in particular with Tony Bennett. I didn't meet up with him too often after I left England myself, but I still have fond memories of our two-piano numbers.

I've always enjoyed playing two pianos, and I still do a concert every other year at the 92nd Street Y in New York with "Mr. Perfect," or Dick Hyman, as most people know him. I've also played or recorded at two pianos with one or two other musicians, Hank Jones and Marian McPartland, for instance, as well as a single track with Gary Burton on piano, during the time he was playing vibes in the Quintet. It's fun as long as you listen to each other and stay out of each other's way, because there are huge registrations in the piano and you don't both have to collide in the middle range. That doesn't happen, of course, if you're playing four hands at one keyboard. You just have to stay clear of one another, or one player's hands are going to land up on top of the other's. But with two pianos you have plenty of room, and the technique is to use as much of it as you can in an area where the other pianist isn't playing.

Before I left England for good, I made more records and broadcasts under my own name.

On the domestic front, we were still renting our house in the London suburbs, with three bedrooms, lounge, dining room, kitchen and bathroom, plus a garage and a little back and front garden. All this was for the exorbitant wartime price of around $10 a week. That might seem cheap by today's prices, but the difference between the cost of living in England and America was really fantastic in those days. Now, of course, England seems to be coming a lot closer to America in the high cost of living, but it's still a lot cheaper to live there than in the United States, except, of course, that salaries are different too.

Anyway, Trixie and I decided to leave all that behind, and the second time round she and my daughter both came with me to America, with the intention of staying for good. Having a brother-in-law who worked for the US Embassy in London was definitely a help with getting the process started, but most of the questions at our interview were to do with my income. I had made literally thousands of pounds from my BBC contracts that ran from the late 1930s and on through the war, but what the immigration people wanted to know was, "What's coming in now? What are your royalties?"

Their final question was, "How do we know you can support yourself over there?"

At this point Trixie spoke up, saying, "I've been married to him since 1941, and I've never had a problem." And out came the papers—it was that simple in the end. I knew that if I went on a short-term visa I would only be allowed to do certain things, and there could be restrictions on my work. So right at the outset I decided that I had to do everything on the basis that this was to be a permanent move, from joining the American musicians' union, to applying for citizenship. It was a slow process, but I intended to see it through and take everything in the right order.

Leonard Feather signed my affidavit of support for immigration. He might not have already become a naturalized citizen of the United States by this stage, but he had married an American girl, and was to all intents and purposes a fully fledged American himself. So once again, Leonard was very instrumental in the progress of my life—just as effective on this new side of the Atlantic as he had been back in England before the war. He was a very influential person, and when he put his weight behind something, it generally took off.

Before long we found ourselves somewhere to live and settled in. The first time I came over, I had stayed at the Roosevelt, quite an expensive hotel. So this time, when the whole family arrived on immigration, to start with we went to the Capitol in midtown on Eighth Avenue. How we wound up there, I don't really remember. Maybe the taxi driver recommended it.

I remember going up into the room and finding that the table tops were all made of some kind of metal. It didn't feel very nice. I'd been used to glass tops, not in my house, of course, but when I was fortunate enough to stay in some of the better hotels in England. Nevertheless, I thought, "This will do for a start, anyway."

A few nights after we arrived, there was a fire in the hotel. Trixie was very calm. She woke me and Wendy. She said, "I want you to get up very quietly and get dressed."

I said, "What?"

She said, "There's no need for any panic or anything, but there's a fire in the hotel, and we should get up, dress quickly and efficiently and leave the room."

We got up, threw some clothes on, went down the fire escape and, I guess, waited outside the hotel or in a nearby restaurant until the fire had been put out, and then we went back to the room and braved the smoke. Smoke hangs in the air in a fire-ridden hotel long after the flames have been put out.

So the next day we moved to the Schuyler Hotel, on 45th, between Fifth and Sixth. I remember the manager's name was Harry Day, and we stayed there for something like a month.

Fortunately, before long, Lennie Tristano helped me to find an apartment in Queens, where my address was 1 Claremont Terrace,

Elmhurst. It was a very nice property, the kind people refer to as a "railroad" apartment. Everything was just one great big long narrow room, and as you came in the back entrance, you'd be on a porch, and from there you'd go into the kitchen/dining-room combination—all in a straight line. Then you'd go into the lounge and then you'd go into the bedroom. Just one room leading off another. You could have thrown a ball right through the whole thing, but each section could be closed off with doors.

Fortunately, there was a piano there already, and it wasn't too bad an instrument. There was also a radio, and before long a representative of London records, the American branch of the English Decca company which I was with at that time, brought round a very nice portable phonograph—so nice I wound up buying the darned thing. Consequently, we had the basic creature comforts, and pretty soon I got a couple of talking books, because when I first arrived jobs were few and far between, so I spent an awful lot of time just sitting around. It was, after all, a strange country. It was not as if I could go up to town as I had done in England, where I would leave the family in the morning, go into town to see people, have lunch and so on, and most importantly, be able to do all this on my own.

I wrote earlier on about the ways in which you get to know who your real friends are, and when I came to the States to live, two people stuck out in my mind as being receptive to George Shearing as a person rather than George Shearing as an artist who had been fortunate enough to come by some degree of success.

I arrived with $2,000, a family, and no real prospects—no contract in my pocket or anything—but these two people gave me a warm and generous reception.

First of all, as I've mentioned, there was Lennie Tristano. He was also a blind pianist, and he was working around New York with a sextet. Not long after we arrived, and were still living at the Schuyler, he said, "Look, George, I don't want you to spend your first Christmas in the United States in a hotel. I want you to come over to our house."

We found out later on that Lennie had used every penny he'd saved up to make sure that we had a decent Christmas.

The other tremendous help when we came over here, to me in particular, was Charlie Parker. I think of him as a gentleman bum. He was a bum because he would as likely as not urinate in a telephone booth. He was a gentleman because he knew that after Trixie had taken our little daughter home to bed, I was usually in whatever club I was working at on my own. Very often when the set was over, the people playing with me would disappear and do their own thing and I would be seated in a corner on a bench with a glass of milk or something. I didn't drink, didn't swear, didn't do anything very much.

Charlie Parker would see me sitting there, and he'd come over and say, "Hey, man, you want to take a walk around the block and get some fresh air?"

Now, this man had become a junkie by the time he was fifteen, and his reputation was that he was always on the scrounge for money to support his habit. I suppose I laid myself open to it, but I said, "Yes, that would be nice."

Never once did that man ask me for a penny.

Later in our friendship, if he had to get himself a fix and he was in the dressing room where my manager, John Levy, and Trixie and I would be, he would say to John, "Take me out of here . . . I don't want to look foolish in front of these people."

It was a strange dichotomy. But "The Street," as 52nd Street was known, encouraged bad habits like that because there were people around who sold the stuff all the time. Some of the best jazz that was ever played was played on the Street, and because of some of the people who overindulged, at the same time some of the worst jazz ever was also played on 52nd Street. You never really knew what you would find and yet some of the best experiences of my life were found right there on 52nd Street.

One of the very first times I was in a club on the Street on my own was when I played the interval at the Three Deuces. I was sitting down when I heard somebody come and sit down next to me. A voice said, "Cigarette?"

"No thanks," I said. I didn't know what kind of cigarette he meant, and I also wasn't sure where the conversation was going from there. As it turned out, that was all the voice said, and a little later I heard whoever it belonged to moving away. Later I discovered it was the voice of Thelonious Monk, who was playing opposite me. Although we quite often worked at the same club, and later on even toured together on one of George Wein's package shows, Monk and I never really talked much. I always liked his writing much more than his piano playing, and I never really thought of him as a pianist, although within his own highly individual style he played his own compositions better than anyone else.

I first met Bud Powell on the Street as well. There was a story going round, told by Jackie McLean, about how Bud "collared" me rather aggressively. What actually happened was that I was resting between sets, and I felt somebody come along and just "bop" me gently on the top of my head. Nothing was said, and I waited, and then a few minutes later, he did it again. Then he must have moved away a short distance, because somebody whispered to me, "That's Bud Powell."

I guess he was a little strange in his behavior, a little off-center, but what a player!

Once I got to know Bud a little better, I had a long conversation with him one night about Johann Sebastian Bach, as we were both very keen on his music, and both of us at one time or another ended up including some aspects of Bach in our performances. We agreed how, even back in the baroque period, Bach would take advantage of syncopation. It wouldn't necessarily swing in the way we understand now, but I think there are many of us who believe that if Bach were alive today, he would be a great jazz musician. I say that because when you think about it, he composed what was practically a new church service every Sunday. All this glorious music just came out of his head, and he must have been a great improviser. To my mind, that's what a jazz musician is made of— not to mention the fact he had two wives and around twenty kids!

My own attempts at playing in a style that owes something to Bach date from a disc I recorded with the Quintet some years ago now in the 1960s called *Out of the Woods*, with Gary Burton on vibes. It was later reissued as *Bright New Dimensions*. In fact all the compositions were Gary's, but they were in a baroque style, and I had a big fight with Capitol records about letting us record them, because they didn't think the album was very commercial. But I think it was a nice piece of artistry for us to be involved with and to reflect back on.

More recently I've played and recorded a solo feature, based on the traditional Irish *Kerry Dance*, which has a story to do with Bach behind it as well, dating from a time a few years ago, when my second wife Ellie was singing with the New York Choral Artists in a performance of Bach's B-Minor Mass.

I'd gone along to hear the first piano rehearsal for the Mass, which Erich Leinsdorf was going to conduct with the New York Philharmonic. I had a Braille copy of the bass vocal part to follow along as they were singing. At the first pause, after the opening *Kyrie*, the contractor came along and asked me if I would play something for the singers during their break. So I agreed, and went over to the piano. Unbeknown to me, Erich Leinsdorf stayed on his podium, making some notes on the score. I started to play the *Kerry Dance*, and after a little while, with my left hand, I began to weave in the theme from the *Kyrie* that I'd just heard. I expanded on both themes, and turned them into a new piece.

While I was playing, Ellie was watching Leinsdorf, and apparently after a few seconds he glanced up from his score, and his eyes became glued to my hands. When I finished, he came over and asked me, "When did you compose that?"

I said, "Now!"

Almost a year later, Ellie was backstage at another New York Philharmonic concert, which was being conducted by Zubin Mehta. I had just been introduced to Zubin, and suddenly the nickel dropped that Ellie was married to me, so Zubin turned to her and said, "Ellie, I have to ask you a question. It has come to my attention at a rehearsal of the B-Minor Mass with Leinsdorf . . ."

She said, "It's all true!"

But the word had gone round on the musicians' grapevine, because so few people in the classical world would—or could— improvise something like that.

But this is jumping ahead with the story. Back on 52nd Street, between late 1947 and 1949, I was to undergo an invaluable part of my musical apprenticeship. It started when I got a job at the Three Deuces playing opposite Ella Fitzgerald, who was backed by Hank Jones on piano, the left-handed drummer Charlie Smith, and Ray Brown on bass. Since then, Hank has become, and remains, my mentor. He's the most unassuming man in the business, and yet everybody who has come into contact with him has learned from him. He had a touch that was very individual, and a marvelous, understated way of introducing technically difficult things such as tenths into his left hand, while keeping everything smooth and flowing. In a way that's a reflection of his whole quiet, understated personality.

We all had to have one night off during the week, and when it was Hank's turn, I would get somebody to take over my intermission job so that I could substitute for him in Ella's band. After sitting around between sets night after night, I knew Ella's show pretty well and she seemed to want me to do it.

Ray would lay down one of his solid bass lines, really dingdonging downstairs, and Ella would start singing "oop-oop-shooby-doop"—then I'd fall in behind her, gently harmonizing her vocal line with another three parts in the right hand of the piano, with Charlie Smith just swooshing away on brushes in the background. Once again, I thought I'd died and gone to heaven. One piece we played was called *The Other Flying Home*, a real kind of walking thing, and we would swing everybody into bad health until three o'clock in the morning.

I have one strong memory of Ella that happened during this time.

My daughter, Wendy, was about five years old, and in order that Trixie could see me to the club, it was necessary for her to bring the little girl with us. After my wife had seen me safely into the club, she would then go home and put Wendy to bed. When I finished work, the same cab driver, Jack Baker, would pick me up every night and take me back home to Elmhurst, where we had settled. It was like having my own personal driver for the price of a cab, and every night, on the way home, we would stop at the White Tower in Queens and buy a glass of freshly squeezed orange juice each. Sometimes he would pay, sometimes I would, but it became a little ritual every night we made the journey, and we'd have a few minutes of conversation about everything under the sun. I remember he took a particular interest in several topics from music to blindness. Then he'd see me right to the door. Things were not all bad then.

But I digress. When Ella Fitzgerald first met Wendy she remarked on what a lovely little child she was and told her that she would have a nice, big doll for her the next day. We cautioned Wendy the next morning not to be disappointed if Miss Fitzgerald forgot about bringing the doll, because in show business a lot of promises are made like that and then the person who makes the promise gets involved in something else and forgets about it. I would venture to say that at one time or another, most of us have been guilty of doing just this. So I told Wendy not to expect it and although it was meant, it might not happen.

Well, it did happen. Ella came in the next night with the biggest doll I've ever known. It was a lovely china doll with a beautiful dress, and back in those days, it must have cost a small fortune. So, Ella was as totally true to this little child whom she had just met as she was to her audiences when she sang. That's quite a wonderful expression of humanity.

During that same period of time, I also worked at the Onyx opposite Sarah Vaughan, who sang with just the piano of Jimmy Jones to accompany her. I never took Jimmy's place for the entire evening as I had done with Hank, but I did sit in with Sarah quite a bit. More than once when I was doing the solo intermission set, I'd hear a loud voice from the crowd calling, "When is Sarah coming on?" Of course, at one level, I agreed—there was nothing I liked more than to hear her at work at the very height of her powers. She and I got to be pretty close. We used to play that old game called "the Dozens" backstage all the time—that's where you trade ever more fanciful insults about your respective mothers. She knew that I was into it, to the extent that many years later the Quintet was playing a big club somewhere out on the road, and there was a phone call for me. It was a thinly disguised Sarah Vaughan's voice telling me, "I've got your mother downstairs in a paper bag!"

Other people I met on the circuit were equally into the Dozens. Billy Eckstine for one, even sent me a telegram once from the UK, when I was in the States, with a carefully worded insult about my mother: "Have watered and fertilized Amelia's grave as promised, your buddy Billy."

Basie was another one. I'd drop into his dressing room when we were on the road, and say, "Hey, Base, how're you doin'?"

He'd turn to me and say, "Now don't start . . ."

I'd say, "No, I won't. How is she?"

After a bit of this, he'd get up and chase me out.

Dizzy was the worst, he would play the Dozens from anywhere, anytime.

Anybody who remembers Sarah Vaughan from those early times when we were at the Onyx, and who has also heard her later recordings, will realize that there were affectations in the later discs that didn't exist in the early ones. My personal preference is for the early recordings, because to hear her sing without the affectations is to hear a very true, artistic Sarah Vaughan without artificial dressing, because the product itself was of such a pure and beautiful nature that it didn't need any rococo effect at all.

I learned a wonderful trick from Jimmy Jones, her accompanist. Sarah used to really think that the song *Tenderly* belonged to her alone, and at the end where the words go something like "You took my heart, you took my love . . ." Jimmy would hit a chord and then Sarah would sing "So ten-der-lee-ey." The way Jimmy hit this chord would create what we call a *sforzando* effect. This was done by catching the chord with the sustaining pedal and holding it until the sound softened naturally. It produced a kind of an echo, and I've used this trick ever since.

Another pianist who played on the Street with his trio was Nat King Cole. I think the first thing I'd ever heard by him was *The Christmas Song*, which had been released at the end of 1946 for the holiday season. Of course that disc had strings, but when Nat's trio left Los Angeles and came to New York, to hear it in the flesh was wonderful, with Oscar Moore on guitar and Johnny Miller on bass. In my opinion, based on how he sounded then, Nat Cole was one of the most underrated jazz pianists who ever existed. I never tire of singing the praises of Fats, Tatum, and Teddy Wilson, but Nat was right up there with them, along with my mentor Hank Jones. So when I say that my apprenticeship on 52nd Street was very valuable, I'm still receiving value from it today. I am truly able to say that I was lucky enough to have probably the toughest, and yet the most rewarding, apprenticeship anybody could ever serve in my business.

A further aspect of it was that I found myself working with one or other of the two very best bass players at that time: Oscar Pettiford and Ray Brown.

Oscar and Ray were absolutely marvelous in their own different respects. I remember at one time I worked with Oscar Pettiford, Kansas Fields on drums, Lucky Thompson on tenor sax, and me on piano. Lucky would play the opening chorus and then play a few bars of improvisation. Then he'd stop and I would take up where he left off, but I would be very worried because I was the new kid on the block and I didn't know if I had done something wrong musically that would upset him. But eventually he came back in again.

I asked people about it, and Oscar Pettiford, who had his own thing going in terms of personality, would tell me that it was "just part of Lucky's temperament." And I'm sure if Oscar ever stopped playing, I'd go to Lucky and he'd say "It's just temperament on Oscar's part."

I soon began to feel very comfortable around them, and I've been fortunate enough to feel that way through my life. I never really experienced racial prejudice in reverse with black people.

I have, however, experienced blind prejudice. In fact, one of the jobs I most wanted on 52nd Street, because it was at a very well-known club, was in a place called the Hickory House. I obtained an audition there because I was told by a press agent that they had changed their minds about being a jazz club and they really wanted to be an East Side cocktail lounge. Well, although I was a jazz pianist, the other side of it was also very familiar to me because I'd played in a number of society-type clubs in England and I knew what they wanted.

So, I went down there and played all my "society" stuff like *I Get a Kick Out of You* and *People Will Say We're in Love*. After listening to me, the owner said, "Gee, I wish I could play like that! But I'm looking more for a jazz pianist."

So I said, "Well, that's my long suit. Can I take my coat off and play some of that for you?"

He said, "No, but would you like to do an off-night for us next Monday?"

I said, "Yes, Okay!" I think I played forty minutes on and twenty minutes off from about nine until three. I don't know whether it was $15 or $25 for one night, but it was reasonable, and the press agent said at the end of the evening, "You're in! You're in!"

I said, "Good. When? How much? How long?"

"We'll call you," he said. Well, they never did call, and I tried to get them on the phone. Of course, the agency really didn't know my name. Why should they?

They said, "He's in a meeting at the moment. Can we tell him who called?"

And I said, "George Shearing."

"Joe Speery? Very well, Mr. Speery, we'll tell him."

And I didn't have the nerve to correct them. I thought if they did call back, I could answer to the name "Joe Speery" just as well. But they never did call back.

Then I was fortunate enough to win the *Arthur Godfrey Talent Scouts* show. It was a radio talent competition, and my entry was organized by a public relations man. This meant that I would be doing three nationwide Chesterfield shows on coast-to-coast radio. This was in 1948—before the Quintet—and at that stage radio was huge in the United States. A coast-to-coast show was a way of reaching an absolutely vast audience, and it wouldn't do any harm to the career of anyone who was successful in such a contest.

A day or two after the contest, wouldn't you know, I'm walking down 52nd Street and by this time I had a job in the Three Deuces. So I went into the Hickory House and I said to the owner, "Mr. Popkin, remember me? I just won the *Arthur Godfrey Talent*

Scouts show and I'm going to be doing three Chesterfield shows. One of the questions they're going to ask me, I'm sure, is, 'Where are you working?' and I would just love to say, 'I'm working at the Hickory House.'"

He said, "Well, where are you working at the moment?"

"The Three Deuces."

"Oh," he said, "we don't take anybody off 52nd Street."

And they were on 52nd Street themselves!

When I mentioned this to Lennie Tristano, he said, "Don't you know what that is?"

I said, "No, I don't."

He said, "It's a very clear case of blind prejudice. They think you're going to get into an accident on the premises and ruin the present status of their insurance policy."

So, I tell you this to point out that although 52nd Street dealt me some of my best hands musically, it was also responsible for one of the worst hands, in that I couldn't crack the club that I most wanted to be in. It had been an ambition, ever since I'd heard broadcasts by Joe Marsala from the Hickory House when I was still in England. Later, when I got to be better known, I told my people, "If the Hickory House ever does come back, whatever my going rate is, just multiply it by three." By that time, of course, I didn't want to work it, but I must be honest and say that they never did come back.

Today, the Hickory House is no more and, sadly, neither is anything else on 52nd Street. You just walk down that street anywhere from 6th Avenue to, maybe, 8th Avenue and you can only dream of the past. It was really and truly a little pocket of jazz unto itself, and I think I'm safe in saying it'll never be repeated again. All of us who knew it will recall it very fondly because of the tremendous amount of music that came out of there. I doubt whether it was possible to visit all the clubs there in one night and hear everybody. But we'll also remember the little niggly things that I've mentioned. But the good part was so good that you truly can and should afford to dismiss the bad from your mind.

7

SEPTEMBER IN THE RAIN

I went over to the States with some ability to play in the styles of Art Tatum, Teddy Wilson, and Fats Waller. I was the "English Art Tatum" or the "English Teddy Wilson," or even "England's number one boogie-woogie pianist." But so what? All the originators of jazz piano were American, and most of them were still playing. What was I doing, taking coals to Newcastle?

The agents to whom I had letters of introduction thought so too. "Very nice, give Joe my best when you see him, and thank him for recommending you to me. Now go back and build yourself into a $10,000-a-week act, come over again, and we'll handle you."

Another one said, "That's very nice. What else can he do?"

Trixie blew up at him: "What do you want him to do? Stand on his head and play? Come on George, we've no business being here."

Most of them had an artist or two about whom they'd say, "I've got a man named such and such, and he's been doing great business . . ." I'd often go into a restaurant with Trixie after such an audition or meeting with an agent and ask, "When are they going to say they've got a man named George Shearing?"

I'd get so worked up I could hardly eat, because it was at moments like this when it came home to me that I'd moved to the States to move my career forward, and here I was in a strange country with nothing happening for me. Trixie would say, "Look, George, if you give up now and go back to England prematurely, you'll never forgive yourself for thinking that you hadn't given it sufficient time. If necessary I'll go out to work, so let's stay here as long as we can."

Although I made a handful of trio discs for Savoy, first with Gene Ramey and Cozy Cole, and later with Curley Russell and

Denzil Best, and despite the fact I was getting work at the Onyx or the Three Deuces on and off throughout 1948, the nest egg of $2,000 I had brought with me began to be eaten away, and the situation got to be pretty rough. With an apartment on Long Island at $150 a month, and a $90-a-week job in the Three Deuces, it's not very hard to work out that the money was going out faster than it was coming in. In England, we were used to living reasonably well, given the constraints of wartime and its aftermath, but America was very different. For example, we would pass shops full of all kinds of beautiful clothes and other things that had been very severely rationed in England for a number of years. The wartime rationing had been pretty rigid. One egg a month. Two pints of milk a week. Something like half a pound of sugar per week per person. In New York, food was plentiful and there were none of the shortages we still had in England. Moreover, Trixie would go by the stores in Manhattan and see all kinds of fashionable nylon stockings or beautiful dresses and say, "Well, maybe one day, huh?"

Even with her natural caution, our savings were still ebbing away, until finally it got to the point where I said to Trixie, "What are we doing here? Let's go back."

She said again, "You have to give it every conceivable chance. You've come here under immigration, which is something you've been dreaming about for years. We spent a lot of time getting rid of our furniture, selling up everything and packing up what was left. This is a once in a lifetime chance. You can't keep immigrating. You do it once and if you don't give it every chance while you're here, you'll never be able to rest easy. You'll always wonder what might have happened if you hadn't given up."

Nevertheless, nagging at the back of my mind was the fact that I still had a contract with Decca back in England, and if I went back, I could do some recording and pick up some other lucrative work pretty quickly. Anyway, Trixie persuaded me to stay, and I hung on for the best part of a year, until the late fall of 1948. It's funny how things worked out, because when I did go back, it was Trixie's initiative, not mine.

One Sunday I'd gone out somewhere, and when I came home, Trixie said, "You're not doing anything this afternoon, are you?"

I said, "No."

"Then I have a little surprise for you."

Within an hour or two, a fellow knocked at the door and came in. Trixie said to me, "I'm wondering if you'll recognize his voice."

At which point, a very polite and proper English accent said, "Hello, George."

It was the last person in the world that I expected to hear—a guy named Denis Preston, who later became a well-known record producer, but who in those days had had quite a lot to do with English rhythm clubs and was an occasional writer for English trade magazines. He was in New York for a few weeks and was going back a day or two after he called to see me.

Now despite Trixie's strong opposition to my suggestion that we should chuck it all in and go back to England for good, the idea they had dreamed up together was that I should go back for a short visit to do some recording and perhaps a couple of concerts, while Trixie continued her efforts to book me with promoters in the States, so that I remained in with a chance to make it in America.

They said that if I went back with Denis, he would fly with me, and that he would recommend me to a big modern block of flats in Dolphin Square where he was living at the time, so that I could get a room in one of the guesthouses there. You couldn't actually just wander in to this rather exclusive address on the north bank of the Thames and get a room. You had to know somebody who was living there, and normally you'd arrange an apartment for a year or so. It was never one of these transit places where you could just book in as if it were a hotel and get a room for a week or so. As it turned out, I decided to go back for a month, paying my own way with almost the last of my capital, and Denis managed to pull some strings to get me into the guesthouse.

So that was all arranged, but I had never flown before, since I had arrived in America by ship on both occasions. I remember vividly how we went out to the airport and I got onto the plane, which I guess was a Constellation. If you think about it, that's a heck of a flight to take as your inaugural trip, crossing the Atlantic. If you decided after you got up there that you didn't like it, in those days it meant you were stuck for about twelve or thirteen hours. Once we got on board, Denis explained to me about the seat belt and how to fasten it and all that business. Then, as we went, he described everything to me in detail.

"We're just starting to taxi now towards the runway. When we get there you'll feel the plane take off with a good amount of speed."

Then he said, "Now we've taken off. Down the runway we were probably going about a hundred or a hundred and fifty miles an hour, but now we're in the air already."

I said, "What?"

He said, "Yes. We're a few hundred feet up already. We're over the ocean now and climbing steadily."

As it happened it was a beautiful trip the whole way, very smooth, with a stop at Gander, and another at Shannon. I was delighted with it and, in due course, I flew back completely alone, with no problems at all. Funnily enough, once I was back in the United States I didn't do a lot of flying again until 1951 when I was on the road with Billy Eckstine, who finally said, "George, what are you doing, driving three or four hundred miles between each gig? I'm going to take a plane. Why don't you?" So from then on, most of the others drove, while Billy and I started taking planes everywhere. Before that, despite the distances you have to cover on tour in the States, I didn't fly for over two years.

During the month I was back in England, just as we had planned, I made some recordings. These became the London album which had *I Only Have Eyes for You*, *The Nearness of You*, *The Fourth Deuce*, *Consternation*, and some my other best-known pieces on it. I did eight numbers altogether, with a trio. I wrote out bass parts, and I got a Canadian bassist called Jack Fallon, together with my old friend from Frank Weir's band, Norman Burns, on drums.

As well as the discs, we did a couple of concerts together. One was on such a foggy night that although we finished about eleven o'clock, we didn't get home until about six or seven in the morning

The London Trio, 1948, with Jack Fallon, bass, and Norman Burns, drums. (Lebrecht Library)

from a distance of no more than ten miles away. Those were the days of the real dense London fogs, known as pea-soupers, where someone would have to walk in front of your car with a flashlight. During the war, more than once Trixie and I left our car in town and took the train home, because driving was just impossible. You just couldn't see to drive. Of course, the blackout didn't help in wartime, but even in 1948 when I went back, the fog could still be terrible.

After the month was almost up, I got a cable from Trixie, saying that she had a contract for me to play at the Clique Club, on Broadway in New York. The place was brand new, and it was to open on the site of the old Ebony Club. Later on, another club at the same address was to have an equally important place in my life when it reopened as Birdland, but in late 1948, the jazz room at 1678 Broadway was called the Clique, and it was run by Sammy Kay and Irving Alexander, who had also run the Three Deuces on 52nd Street. The strategy Trixie had used was to say, "If George is going to do it, I want him to get such and such a price." She was asking $450 or something, but she knew they were used to paying more like $100 to $125. So her negotiating ploy was to come back with, "We'll come down to a lower price if you give him his own trio."

This was because she'd realized that in the long term the money wasn't as important as getting my own group. Finally they said, "Look, okay, we don't mind George having his own trio, but there's a pretty good clarinet player knocking around who's not doing very much, and we wonder whether we can add him to the line-up and call it the George Shearing-Buddy DeFranco quartet?"

Well, to me, Buddy is about the best clarinet player in the business. As far as jazz goes, they don't come any better than Buddy DeFranco. I don't even know if they come as good. So I was delighted with the idea. As soon as I got back, Buddy and I got together and worked out some arrangements, and Buddy took them down. The other two members were bassist John Levy and Denzil Best, the drummer I'd recorded with the previous year, and the quartet ended up working at the Clique for a month or two. Denzil was quite a fixture on the Street, and had played fine drums with several groups, but he had originally been a trumpet player until he contracted TB and was forced to give up playing a brass instrument. Nevertheless, he retained a fine melodic sense, and continued to write tunes, a number of which we later recorded.

We were playing opposite Machito and his Latin orchestra. Talk about being blown off the stand every night, that band's power and rhythmic energy were incredible. Even though we were playing some pretty fast stuff with Buddy and me swapping eights and fours, we found it hard to keep up with them. I'm sure it was that period of working opposite Machito that started my interest in Latin music, which was to become a big part of my own repertoire during the 1950s.

During that time at the Clique, Buddy's wife was looking out for his interests and Trixie was looking out for mine, so that, of course, there was some little bickering among those two as to whether it should be the Buddy DeFranco-George Shearing Quartet or the George Shearing-Buddy DeFranco Quartet. Buddy and I couldn't have cared less. We just wanted to play together, because we enjoyed each other's musicianship so much.

Buddy DeFranco's wife at the time, Nita, was negotiating a Capitol recording contract for him. Meanwhile, I had two approaches, one from Capitol and one from MGM. Buddy finally signed his contract with Capitol, but I didn't sign with them because they weren't offering enough money. MGM were offering more, but before I signed either contract, Buddy and I were destined to part. To some extent this was because we were two musicians starting out on our careers and aiming at something slightly different from togetherness, but the more practical reason was that once he had his Capitol contract, we couldn't really record together. Nevertheless, we've always remained good friends throughout the years.

Before I signed on the line for MGM, Leonard Feather set up an independent session under which I was to do eight sides for Discovery, the label run by Albert Marx. In fact, Albert had heard the quartet at the Clique club, and really wanted to record the band with Buddy DeFranco, but Leonard persuaded him to try something different. As a result, the group that made the discs,

Leonard Feather (Author's Collection)

with Marjorie Hyams on vibes and Chuck Wayne on guitar, plus John and Denzil, was largely instigated by Leonard Feather. We'd heard both Marjorie and Chuck playing with their own trios, and so when we sat down to plan the Discovery session, Leonard suggested the idea of adding their distinctive sounds to what was originally going to have been my trio at the Clique. It was this idea that was the actual birth of the George Shearing Quintet.

It had a lot going for it in the way of novelty, because had we decided to use conventional front-line instruments like trumpet and saxophone, we would have had a tough job competing with the likes of John Kirby and Raymond Scott in the swing arena, or Dizzy Gillespie and Charlie Parker in the more modern territory. By choosing what was seen at the time as a rather outlandish combination of instruments, there was the chance of doing something genuinely new.

This Quintet was formed in the very early part of 1949, in January or so. Before the recording, we rehearsed for a number of days, and I remember saying at our very first rehearsal, "Let's play some *September In The Rain.*" It was a tune I'd originally played with the All Blind Band, with whom one of the girl singers, and maybe even the whole trio, used to sing it as a feature. For reasons that'll become clear, we eventually got rather fed up with playing it all the time, but as it turned out, it wasn't among the tunes that we recorded for Discovery in early February. The session took place shortly before the Quintet went into its first club, which, as I recall, was the Café Society.

Discovery was a reasonably small company. We used to joke that it had distribution from Hollywood and Vine to Sunset Boulevard, which was a gross exaggeration of the distribution it really had. It didn't have nearly the market reach that major labels, such as, say, MGM or Capitol managed. Nevertheless, we were able to kick things off for the Quintet by making a complete jazz album. Several of the titles were Leonard Feather's. We began with a thing he had written called *Midnight on Cloud 69* (a number whose title, by the way, soon got changed to *Midnight on a Cloud* when people woke up to what the original title actually meant), then we did one of those punning titles of his called *Be-Bop's Fables*, plus

The first Quintet, 1949. John Levy (bass), Marjie Hyams (vibes), Chuck Wayne (guitar) and Denzil Best (drums). (Frank Driggs Collection)

another entitled *Sorry Wrong Rhumba*, not to mention his *Life with Feather*.

I'd composed a tune called *Four Bars Short*, which actually was a twelve-bar blues, but after going on for a number of choruses, it ended on the last beat of the eighth bar, so that it was four bars short and that was the reason for the title. We wound up the session with *Cherokee, Moon Over Miami*, and *Cotton Top*.

That first Discovery session was held up for a while because I was shocked to find when we got to the studio in New York that the piano was quite badly out of tune. Not only was it out of tune with itself, but there was a very noticeable discrepancy of pitch between the piano and the vibes. To start with they said, "Well, it was tuned last week."

So I said, "Sure, but it needs tuning now. In fact, I'd rather not do the recording at all unless it's tuned. I'm surprised that a piano is left in this condition for a recording to be made to go out and be permanently on sale to the public."

The Quintet all waited in the studio on Discovery's time while the piano was tuned. Once it had been properly sorted out, we proceeded with the recording. Although it was a complete session of jazz titles—it contained hardly any standards—and because we played mostly originals, there was nothing for the listening public to catch on to and to understand that this was a new sound, a new approach to playing melodies. The sound was there in embryo, in fact the Quintet format was pretty well developed, but it was going to take something else for it really to catch on.

That something occurred not long afterwards, when I finally concluded my long-term record deal and we cut some sides with the same line-up for MGM. The man who signed me to MGM was Billy Shaw, who had also been agent for Dizzy Gillespie and Billy Eckstine, and he handled all of my bookings for quite a while after that. I don't really remember whether I met him through another musician or through one of the other agencies. Whoever it was said they couldn't do anything for me, but that I should go up and see Billy Shaw. He'd been with the William Morris Agency, one of the really big booking firms, and was starting up on his own. Now, I'd hardly heard of Billy Shaw, so I went round to everybody I knew and said, "What do you know about Billy Shaw?"

And everybody answered in the same words, "The most honest man in the business."

So that was good enough for me and we signed with him. Billy certainly did a lot for me. He did a lot more for me than anybody would have had to do a few years later, because I guess when a vehicle is moving it's not too difficult to get it moving faster, but it is really difficult to get it started in the first place. Because to begin with there was no name involved—there was nobody who knew of George Shearing, and Billy had all the fights in the world with people who didn't want to buy a blind act.

The first session with MGM included *September in the Rain*, *You Are Too Beautiful*, *Bop Look and Listen*, and *Good To The Last Bop*. They were all pretty big sellers, but we had very little idea that *September In The Rain* from that first MGM session on February 17, 1949, was going to become such a massive hit, selling over nine hundred thousand copies, which in those days was quite miraculous. More than all the other numbers we recorded at that time, it came to epitomize what became known as "the Shearing sound." For the first time, I had something original to offer the public and the agents. I was no longer just "the English such-and-such"—I had something of my own that set me apart from other pianists and which justified my decision to go to America.

It came about by combining two distinct musical elements— the voicing of the Glenn Miller saxophone section and the so-called "locked hands" piano style of a man named Milt Buckner, whom I had heard playing with Lionel Hampton's big band on my first visit in 1946.

To understand how I combined these elements, let's start with the piano. For the first and last chorus of a song, and occasionally through the entire length of a piece, I'll play chords that lie entirely within the compass of a single octave. For example, if you take a simple chord in the key of C, the left hand plays the C below middle C, the right hand plays the E just above it, the G above that, the A above that and the C above that. My two hands are never any farther away than that when the sound is created, and

Milt Buckner pioneered the idea of playing entire solos with his hands configured the same way. He was most effective doing this on the blues chord sequence—both on piano and organ—but I realized that the style would transfer very easily to numbers that were not just a matter of a simple blues. One of the earliest pieces I tried it on was *Roses of Picardy*, and so I'd already worked out how to adapt locked hands for this, and a few other numbers, as piano solos, a little time before the Quintet began.

The sound that came into my head, as far as the band was concerned, was to combine this piano technique with elements of Glenn Miller's saxophone voicings. On a piece like *Moonlight Serenade*, which is perhaps the best example of all, he'd lay out a chord in a broadly similar manner, distributing it among the various saxes in his reed section, with the clarinet taking the top line. What I did was to give the guitar the notes allocated to the lowest saxophone voice—the baritone—playing the bottom C, and to give the vibes the notes allocated to the clarinet—the top C— above the rest of the section, and I'd play the notes in between, the ones distributed to the other saxes, on the piano.

There have, of course, been hundreds of imitations of the sound since, but one of the reasons they tended to fail was because we did something the imitators generally didn't think of, which was to turn the motor off on the vibes. Between the piano and the guitar, if both instruments are well tuned and played properly, there's little or no vibrato. If you add the vibes as they are normally played, with the motor rotating a set of vanes under the keys and producing a throbbing sound, it's not going to match the other two instruments. So the first thing we did was to switch off that rotating motor and get as close a blend as possible between the three instruments, without any kind of vibrato. Had the band employed a far-better-known vibes player, who had already made a reputation, like Milt Jackson, we probably wouldn't have been able to persuade him to turn off the motor, because that slow, pulsating throb was already an established part of his sound. Marjie Hyams was a different proposition, because although she'd recorded the odd solo with Woody Herman, and was featured for a few bars here and there on pieces like *North West Passage*, she had yet to make her own mark as a soloist, and so she was prepared to go along with what I wanted. Nobody had ever put together quite such a line-up before, with vibes and guitar featured alongside the piano, and by adopting the voicings we did, the band not only had an unusual line-up but a unique sound.

The sound itself was one thing, but I think the reason for its enormous success was to do with timing. In terms of personal timing, I was running low on money, running low on spirit, but instead of sitting around and worrying about that, I thought positively about what I could do to get out of it. I didn't want to live as an adult with rats running round the house the way they had in Battersea!

In terms of more general timing, I think there was a need for a more romantic approach to music, coming at the end of the first, very frantic, period of bebop. When I first arrived in New York for that three-month vacation, I just caught the tail end of the swing era. You could go to big hotels and hear bands like Tommy Dorsey's or Ray McKinley's. On the other hand, the bebop business had started and Dizzy and Bird were playing their unison lines very fast and very precisely, things they had endlessly rehearsed or worked on in all-night jam sessions. By 1949, the public was looking for something different from their frantic, fast-moving lines. In fact, during my time on 52nd Street, I'd got into that style myself the best way I could, but when it came to establishing a little niche of my own, something where agents would say, "I've got a man named George Shearing . . ." this quite different sound came into my head. I didn't do it in any calculated way, but I knew there was a necessity for a softer, more romantic approach.

Part of our success was also due to the personalities of the musicians themselves. Marjorie Hyams, for example, was a very fine musician. She was a thoroughly schooled classical pianist, well-versed in fugues and so on, but she'd taken up vibes in the early 1940s and, as I said, ended up playing with Woody Herman. We liked one another, and got along very well. She also wrote some originals for the Quintet including *November Seascape*.

I told her about some of my experiences, traveling on my own before the Quintet was formed. There'd been one place—in Philadelphia, I think—where I'd ordered room service to bring up some grapefruit juice, coffee, and toast to my room. The guy who brought it was very helpful. He set the tray down, then he took my hand, put it in the grapefruit juice and said, "There's your grapefruit juice." Then he put it on the melted butter on the toast and said, "There's your toast." Finally he dipped it in the coffee and said, "There's your coffee."

I'd never tried that recipe before, and I don't think I'd try it again! My hands had all three things on them by the time he'd finished. But to show just how conscientious he was, as the waiter left the room, he turned to me and called across, "Now, don't forget, Sir, the cold one is the grapefruit juice!"

When I told this to Marjie Hyams, I thought she was never going to stop laughing.

Chuck Wayne was an equally accomplished musician, and I'd heard him playing in his own trio with the pianist Gene DiNovi, who, incidentally, always credited Chuck with really developing him as a pianist. Chuck wrote some really interesting tunes, like his impressionistic piece, *In a Chinese Garden*. He was a great lover of Ravel, Debussy, and Delius, which is strange when you consider these composers didn't write much guitar music. But then I suspect his love of playing impressionistic material on the guitar involved a similar train of thought to what went on when I played accordion. I didn't think of myself as an accordion player—I imagined I was Jack Teagarden, and tried to phrase my solos as he might have done on the trombone. I'm sure Chuck used a similar technique to think of himself as some kind of impressionistic pianist, while actually playing the ideas on the guitar. You can let your imagination run wild and produce some pretty incredible effects.

The rhythm section, of course, had really jelled during our time in the quartet with Buddy DeFranco. Denzil had enough years of experience to know exactly when to use brushes, which he preferred to do, and how to propel the group along with the minimum of force. John played good time and good lines on the bass—although often I used to write parts out for him that became an additional part of the Quintet voicing. I realized that I couldn't have instruments that were hanging around trying to find something to do. So when I wrote bass parts, I voiced them so that John was playing notes that I couldn't do with my left hand, because it was playing the lowest part of the block chords.

A good example of this is our famous recording of *Autumn Leaves*, where what I had in mind was something similar to one of Bach's two-part inventions. If you strip away the Quintet harmonies and listen to just the bass line and the melody, they're pretty close to the kind of contrapuntal pieces that Bach wrote. But that's not all. I thought very carefully about the overall sound, and I also thought equally carefully about the actual chording I used, so that the inner voices of the chords have some movement in them to complement what movement there is in the theme itself. I was consequently always very scrupulous about what I played, and I took a lot of trouble to ensure that the guitar, piano, and vibes were dead in tune with each other. As a result, I used to rehearse quite a bit with just the three front line, to ensure that our note values were the same, that the force of sound that we used matched, and that we began to think together as much as possible.

This was very important, of course, when we went into a club and had to play full length sets, where we opened up the arrangements from the short form in which we'd recorded them for the 78's of the day and played much longer numbers. Virtually everyone would take a chorus from time to time, except on ballads, where we tended to stick closer to the record in order not to spin out a slow tune for too long. Later on, when I was drawn into the Latin business, we extended some of the pieces even more. I'd set up what classical people call an ostinato, and we'd repeat this vamp over and over while the drummer and percussionist were doing all kinds of stuff. We'd really let them go!

When the big break came during 1949 with the success of *September In The Rain*, and the Quintet really began to take off, it was Trixie who drove the group around and unloaded and loaded the instruments. We'd get into a town, find an apartment hotel, and then she'd go shopping, pick up some food, come back and cook dinner, after driving all day across country.

None of these things starts with a bang. To my mind, if something does, you have to be a little bit suspicious about it. If a thing

Denzil Best, 1945. (Frank Driggs Collection)

starts slowly and builds slowly, I think you're more assured of its likelihood of staying up there.

The Quintet was a fine example. It was formed in February of 1949, and it was available for the first few months at scale, which in those days was around $695 a week for five musicians. When we went on the road, I think it went up to $800 or $900. Transportation had to be paid, plus agents' fees. Trixie did most of the work of running the group herself.

One sign that we'd really arrived was in October 1949 when we made our debut at Carnegie Hall. I'd played there as support to Charlie Parker and Dizzy Gillespie the year before, just doing a solo piano spot, but at a time when I don't think anyone really knew I was in the country. This time, fronting the Quintet, was really different. It was a Horizons in Jazz concert, put on by Jimmy Diaz and Larry Robinson, and we shared top billing with Dizzy's big band. There were plenty of other great musicians on the program, including Harry Belafonte and Dave Lambert, and one sign of the influence we had already had in just a few months was that also on the bill was an *ad hoc* group featuring Terry Gibbs on vibes and Mundell Lowe on guitar, using the same instrumentation as the Quintet, with Al Haig as the featured pianist.

By the end of '49, things started to skyrocket. Trixie would be in the booking agent's office many hours a day saying, "Where are we going next week?"

"Chicago."

"And the week after that?"

He'd say, "What do you want? He's booked up two or three weeks ahead."

She'd come back with, "I want him booked up two or three months ahead. So we don't have to worry about it."

"Well, we never work that way."

"Just because you've worked that way for twenty-five years, there's no reason why you shouldn't alter and become a little revolutionary!"

I always agreed that there was no reason to go on doing things the way they had always been done, and I guess because Billy Shaw was starting up on his own, he took on board a lot of what we

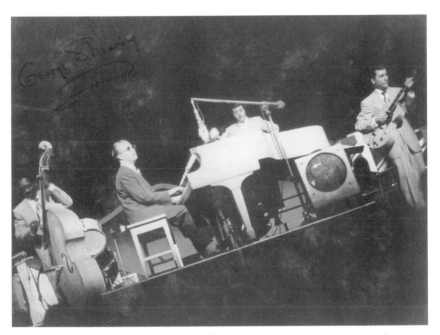

The original Quintet at the Paramount Theater, New York, 1949. (Frank Driggs Collection)

were telling him. Trixie managed the Quintet for about three years, until it became too much of an emotional strain—not only the hard work of driving, but co-ordinating the booking and everything. When we started, we had no road manager, no band boy, no booker, Trixie did the lot. We just had Billy Shaw in New York as our agent.

It got to the point when finally we could afford to get a band boy, but old habits die hard, and some time after he had joined, I suddenly realized that Trixie was continuing to load the instruments. I blew my top in a small town, somewhere out on the road, and I said, "Well, this is it. You're not to touch a thing."

So the time came to leave, and the band boy came to Trixie and said rather sheepishly, "Well, show us how to pack the instruments."

I wasn't having this, and I said to Trixie, "You sit right there! You're not going to do it!"

So we sat there waiting and finally Trixie said, "Oh, come on, George. Let's get going. Let me help him."

But I was still fuming, and I said, "No!"

But I have to admit that Trixie had a knack with instruments, fitting in all those odd cases. She could look at the station wagon and know there was only one way to get a double bass, drums, vibes, guitar, and a load of luggage into the luggage area, with room for the band members as well. At that time we just had the one station wagon and we traveled with all of us together on the road. Everything went into the one automobile, and the excess baggage went on top.

We just sat there for nearly two hours as the new band boy loaded and unloaded that station wagon but he just couldn't do it, so finally I gave in and let Trixie show him how.

Eventually, some time later, she had a breakdown in San Francisco, and suffered a miscarriage, so at that point I made John Levy, the bass player, my manager because the doctor advised Trixie to give up traveling and go home to look after Wendy. This was in the spring of 1951, and Al McKibbon came in on bass, to replace John. Actually Al had a much bigger sound, so it worked out well for all concerned.

8

EARLY TRAVELS

We stayed out on the road with our one station wagon and then as we made more money we bought two station wagons. For over two years we traveled that way, until that tour with Billy Eckstine, when I realized that I could afford to fly. Pretty soon, I decided to fly everywhere. So then we decided to buy a small van or truck for the instruments, and the rest of the group traveled in greater comfort with one automobile.

It was during these early years on the road in the United States that I began to work out many of my own preferences as regards constant traveling. For example, I never knew too much about showers with glass doors, as I recall, until I came to the West Coast. Mostly back East in the late 1940s, you would find curtains—and back in London, before that, we hadn't advanced all that far beyond the tin tub in front of the fire!

So I think my first experience with glass doors on showers was on the West Coast. I particularly liked having a nice big deep step to go down and plenty of room in the shower, where you can get a good deal of pressure out of the shower head. I found it reassuring to know I'd just got a room filled with finely running water, with no fear of the curtain hugging me around the legs, or the distance between the curtain and the bath being such that if the water was forceful enough it would go through, so I would find the floor soaking wet when I got out.

Over the years, I became somewhat fussy about things like this. Maybe this sounds a little materialistic if you compare it with people like Albert Schweitzer—who I'm sure would have considered such trivialities the last thing in the world to worry about, and was probably an extremely happy man—but I believe that by trying to seek these so-called trivialities when I can find them, I too have maintained my share of happiness. It depends on what one wants out of life. If you were to go away for a two-week vacation, just to get away from your present surroundings, you probably wouldn't care if you were in a basic chalet that didn't necessarily have all the conveniences in the world. But were you to be faced with spending eight or nine months of the year away from your home, I suspect that you would soon be looking for something a little more convenient.

For instance, I got to know the way the layout of certain hotel rooms worked. The seventeen group in, say, a particular Hilton, in other words the ones numbered 317, 417, and so on were one example. I could come into any of these rooms knowing that on the right is the bathroom and on the left is the closet. As I was coming in the front door, I didn't necessarily put both hands out because I knew where things would be. In the room proper, I'd immediately find the bed and the table beside the bed and know that the telephone on that table would be in a specific place, and that there'd be a bureau over there. I could go into one of those rooms and I wouldn't need anybody to assist me from the word go. I got to remember them.

After I'd been traveling the circuit for a while, in each city people would be wonderful with me. They'd remember the kind of room I liked, and very often I would go back to a hotel and get the same room that I got before, or at least, the same type of room.

Every so often I end up staying in a room that is really confusing, and I just can't figure it out. Many years later than those early days on the road, I was on holiday in the English Lake District with my second wife, Ellie, and we were put in the finest suite of a hotel on Lake Windermere. I'm sure this was done out of kindness and concern, but for me it was something of a disaster. Not only was the room very well carpeted, which made it difficult for me to tell where I was acoustically, but it was almost completely round. I think it's one of the only times I've needed to be led to the bathroom every time, and to paraphrase an old song, you pressed the first valve down, the room went round and round, and you came out . . . where?

Once Trixie became well again and got over her problems with being on the road, she went to Billy Shaw and asked him to give her a job in the office. I was away on tour at the time, but Billy told her he wouldn't take her on. She said, "Why?"

"You've got to be able to cuss and swear in this business!" She didn't agree with that, but anyway, Billy said, "If you want to see how the business is run, sit here." So she used to sit in his office all day and see how things were run and listen to him book his artists. It was a great experience for her, and she learned a lot about this business.

Billy was a great man, and because I was one of the very first musicians to sign up with him, his agency and my career in America grew up together, and, in due course, the agency became big. Billy and I had very similar temperaments, and we were both very impatient. So, often when we met in the office, there were fireworks. Finally, I said, "I'm going to keep out of the office. It's no good!"

Trixie was go-between between the two of us professionally, but socially we got on like a house on fire. He would come over to our house practically every weekend. It was tragic that he died as quite a young man.

He was coming over to us one Sunday, after going out to buy some movie-camera equipment. He said, "I'll be over Sunday and show you how to use it." On the Saturday his wife was setting off for the beach, and he was going to play golf, when he died of a heart attack, just like that. He was only about forty-five.

He made a great difference to my career—booked me into all the great clubs. He would sit down at the phone and somebody would call up and ask for Frank Sinatra. And he'd say, "Well, he's not available, but I have George Shearing here."

The guy would say, "Who's George Shearing? I never heard of him."

Billy would say, "Well, he is just about the greatest pianist in the world." And he'd tell him how great I had been in London and so on. And the other fellow would say, "But I don't need another pianist."

Billy would end up selling the Quintet. And it was fantastic. I've never seen a salesman for musicians as good as Billy. I was also represented for a time by Associated Booking, the Joe Glaser office, and in my opinion, Joe was the savior of musicians like Louis Armstrong and Ella Fitzgerald (before she moved on to Norman Granz). He was interested in really building up their careers, rather than just getting his percentage.

He came in to bat for me on several occasions, one of which was on one of our earliest visits to San Francisco with the Quintet to play for a man named Sid Woolfe, who ran several clubs in the Bay Area. Our contract read, ". . . to play at the Coronet or Martinique Club . . ." or something similar, and when we got there the San Francisco local of the Union told us they had disqualified the contract because it had more than one club name on it. Joe Glaser immediately got involved, and a message came through very smartly from the New York local, where I was and am still a member, "Uphold the contract or else!"

I don't know what "or else" meant, although I do know that Joe came up through the toughest kind of Chicago upbringing, and it did not do to tangle with him! I think the reason Sid Woolfe had tried to get out of the contract, and gone to the local of the AFM to help him, was because our appearance in San Francisco just happened to coincide with the most amazing array of other talent appearing in town. The town was absolutely inundated with star names for the same month we were there. Stan Kenton, Billy Eckstine, and Nat Cole were all in town at the same time, and I think Sid got cold feet. And still we lined them up round the block for a solid month, and all was well.

During that early period when I was being represented by Billy Shaw, I made some other long-lasting associations as well, particularly with George Wein in Boston. He opened a new club called Storyville in 1951, and he booked us in there to start off the whole thing. I'm sure we charged him more than he'd ever paid for any of his earlier promotions in and around Boston, but we sold out, and after that he used to book us to come back every year as a regular occurrence. In those days there were several clubs like that in cities around the country where we could eventually count on playing for a week or two at more or less the same period each year.

In Chicago, to start with, it was always the Blue Note on North Clark Street. We first played there when the Quintet had only just got started, and *September in the Rain* had not long been released. That gig was opposite Slim Gaillard, the multi-instrumentalist, singer, and humorist. He was two days late arriving and presented a doctor's letter to the manager Frank Holzfeind to explain his tardy appearance. Except, being Slim, there was a surreal punch line. The letter concluded by saying: "I have thoroughly examined Mr. Gaillard from head to toe, and I find absolutely nothing wrong with him." His act was equally surreal, with a lot of the songs he used to do with Slam Stewart as part of their double act "Slim and Slam," seasoned with funny remarks to the audience, some of them in his nonsense language of "vout." He'd even talk the same way backstage, saying to us as he went on: "I've gotta go out there now and play a little vouty, and get myself ready to perform on the macscrotimo later on in the show." It was all nonsense, but he delivered it in a very humorous way with fantastic timing. Later on, when we were both playing at Birdland, Slam Stewart would come in occasionally and fall right back into one of his bowed-bass routines that they used to do together.

We did well at the Blue Note, and after about three weeks, during which we were still playing opposite Slim, Frank Holzfeind took me into his office and said, "George, well done. Business has been good, and I want to give you a little something as a token of my appreciation. Don't tell your manager or your agent, just take this $200 and go and buy something nice for your wife."

And he handed me $200, which in 1949 was a sizable amount of money.

As it turned out, I did tell John Levy. In fact I gave him the money, and I said, "John, when we next come back here, or if at any time in the future we return and business is not so good, I want to give Frank his $200 back."

So John looked after it for me. It symbolizes the kind of trust that we set up with the club owners who took a risk on booking us when we were relatively unknown. When the London House opened up on North Michigan Avenue in 1951, I told George Marianthal, the owner, that I would only play there with the Blue

Note's blessing. In due course Frank agreed, and I ended up playing every spring at the Blue Note and every winter at the London
House. I was always very loyal to them both, and in return they
were extremely loyal to the Quintet.

After several months of traveling extensively across the country, there were some changes in the Quintet's personnel. The first
to go was Marjorie Hyams, who left after about a year and a half,
not long after we made our best-selling recording of *Roses Of Picardy* in July 1950. I think she just got tired of working for someone else and traveling so much, even though she was drawing a
good salary. So she came off the road, settled in Chicago, and
married a banker, Bill Ericsson. She carried on teaching and playing in the Chicago area well into the 1980s. Initially, Don Elliott
came in to replace her, and then Joe Roland. In 1953, Cal Tjader
took over the vibes chair. He was someone I'd heard out on
the West Coast, playing in Dave Brubeck's early trio. Cal was a
natural-born musician, and, as I've said many times before, a
rhythmic genius. He was a major part of the Quintet's move into
playing more Latin material, because he just loved those Latin
rhythms. By the time Cal joined, as I mentioned, Al McKibbon
had come in on bass.

With Cal on vibes and timbales, Al laying down as fine a Latin
bass line as anyone ever has, and with the addition of Armando
Peraza on percussion, our group of what I used to call "restless
natives" caused a lot of excitement. Al had been in Dizzy Gillespie's big band at the same time as the Cuban percussionist Chano
Pozo, so he knew the Latin situation very well. I didn't go out to
manufacture a change in the Quintet sound—I just took things
slowly, and assumed that the public would cotton on to what was
going on right away, which they did.

I'd heard Machito, I'd heard a young man who was then an
up-and-coming percussionist, Mongo Santamaria, with Tito
Puente, and of course, I'd heard Dizzy, so I had a clear idea of
what I wanted to do.

I think it was Cal Tjader who recommended Armando Peraza
to me, and he and Al immediately clicked. They got on really well,
so that when Armando played the timbales, Al would put the bass

down and play conga. With Cal playing percussion as well, and Bill Clark, who was our drummer at the time, joining in, it seemed to be all rhythm and no notes. I used to play that to the hilt in clubs, and we also recorded something called *Wrap Your Troubles in Drums* that gives an idea of how it all sounded.

I never had to write a bass part for Al on those Latin numbers. We might play something like *Old Devil Moon*, and Al would kid me saying, "George, where's *one?*" By which he meant where was the downbeat. He'd go straight into a figure that went something like "Bud-ee-bee-do-do, bud-ee-bee-do-do . . . one, two, three-and-four-and . . . two-and . . . and four-and . . . and two-and . . . and four-and . . ." He'd take it apart that way and match Armando's rhythms. People who don't really know Latin music would try and put the emphasis on the wrong *clave* beat, which is like putting the sock cymbal on one and three in Dixieland, instead of two and four, where you get the right sense of swing. Al always got the right emphasis in Latin numbers, launching from the "four-and" beat.

Also, when Cal joined, Chuck Wayne had decided to leave, so by 1953, the Belgian multi-instrumentalist Toots Thielemans was on guitar with the band.

From the outset, the original Quintet attracted some press attention because it was a racially integrated group. I can truly say there's not an ounce of racial prejudice in me—I can't tell the color of a person's skin, and I get on with people on the basis of who they are not what they are. But quite a lot was written on this topic in the early years of the group, and I remember one piece by the writer Al Fraser that said, "Although white, Shearing has just smashed down the barriers against Negroes in a Palm Beach Hotel. He will soon take the Quintet there, and its Negro members will share the same facilities as the whites."

This was when we were playing in a hotel in West Palm Beach, where, as was the case everywhere else we played, we went on the stand as a mixed group. I don't recall that suddenly the town completely opened to us, but at a time when it was not always possible in Florida, on this occasion everybody was able to stay in the same hotel. To be honest, that was seldom a matter that was a real concern of the Quintet in its early days, because—colored or not—the band members normally wanted to conserve a certain amount of expense. After all, they were working musicians, and as sidemen, they obviously lived under different standards than I was able to subsequently, and for the most part they wouldn't want to stay in the expensive hotels that we played in, on the salary they were getting at the time.

Yet it's easy to forget sometimes what a divisive society America was back then, even in the North. In 1951, I was going out to a Chicago hotel to hook up with Billy Eckstine and join the tour bus. I was staying in the Loop and the bus was leaving from the South Central Hotel on the South Side.

I took a taxi, and I said to the driver, "South Central Hotel."

Once we were on the way, he said, "Do you know that's a colored hotel?"

I said, "You don't say so. What color is it? I tried my darnedest to get reservations there yesterday but they were full up, so I was forced to take a reservation in the Loop until I could get in there."

When I got there I gave him a tip about three times as big as he would normally expect, and then walked straight across and got on the bus. He must have felt a complete idiot.

Another time on that tour, we were going along the freeway at about eighty miles an hour in Billy's car, and so Billy turned to me and said, " George, how fast are we going?"

I said, "Oh, we're doing about eighty."

He said, "Okay, George, you don't have to kid me about it any more. You can open your eyes. You don't have to kid anybody that you're blind any more for commercial reasons."

He had a great sense of humor—Billy was a nice guy, and I liked him very much.

That story about Billy's car reminds me of another incident with a blind musician named Joe Mooney, from New Jersey, who played accordion and organ. He began his career in a vocal duo called the Sunshine Boys with his brother Danny, who was also blind. By the time I first arrived in New York in 1946, Joe was leading his own quartet on 52nd Street at a club called Dixon's.

Some years later, Joe called me one night. He had come up to town because his father was dying and he had to leave for Philadelphia the next day. So I said, "Hey Joe, while you're in town, let's go around and do the town a bit—go to some clubs."

But he said, "Sorry, George, I can't. I've got to get up so early tomorrow morning to go to Philadelphia."

But I persisted, saying, "Joe, you come round with us tonight. We've just got this new Chrysler Imperial. I want to give you a ride in this new car we've just bought."

Suddenly Joe said, "What color is it?"

So I said, "Joe, what the hell difference does it make to you what color it is? Blue in Braille!"

Once the Quintet had been up and running for some time, we had to put the organization onto a firmer footing. Just before the formation of the group happened, maybe during the Buddy De-Franco period at the Clique or even before that, I'd got to know a guy by the name of Gene Williams, who had a band sponsored by another fellow called Ed Fuerst. They wanted some arrangements and I can't remember now whether it was Ed or Gene who approached me, but I did three or four arrangements for their band for which they paid me. They rehearsed them for a while and in due course the band played most of them, and that's how I got to meet Ed, at that time a successful insurance broker, who was later to play quite a part in my life.

I saw him again soon after that, when the Quintet had begun to travel and was playing out in Los Angeles at a club on 48th and Western, probably the Oasis. I met up with Ed out there, and we remained friends throughout the years. Eventually the Gene Williams band broke up. Maybe Ed finally decided that he'd sunk enough money into it, because he certainly lost a whole stack of money on that band.

The way Ed joined the organization of my group was around 1955, when I was having a little trouble with the band boy. Ed said to me, "You're going on tour with Count Basie and with a whole group of people. Why don't you let me take over the band boy's job?"

Now, here's Ed, an insurance company executive in New York with a beautiful apartment that he had designed himself for his own bachelor comfort. He had a very efficient housekeeper, who did all his laundry and cooked like an angel. He owned hundreds of records that were meticulously filed and catalogued. He was known among the jazz community as "Mr. First Nighter" because he never missed an opening night for any of us. In fact, many, many of the big names in jazz would congregate at Ed's apartment after their gigs for food, booze, and private times of playing and singing for one another. These times were very special.

Ed had never married. Yet, he wanted to go on the road as a band boy for me, put on Levis, drive the truck, and load and unload the instruments.

Sure he'd lost a lot of money with the Gene Williams band, but he didn't let himself get that low. Unless it was something that he really wanted to do, he needed it like he needed a hole in the head. So I said to him, "Eddie, you know, you and I have been friends for a number of years, and I'd hate to ruin a friendship because of a few stupid weeks or possibly even months of employment. After all, you come around and hear the band every so often, and at one o'clock you say, 'I think I'm getting tired. I'm going home to get some sleep.' We say goodnight and some time later I see you at a party or something, or we come to your house for a party. And everything's fine. But once you become employed by me, you know you can't do that. Maybe our job won't finish until four o'clock and then you'd have to see me home, or make sure that someone does. And I won't really be able to let you go home until the job's finished."

He replied, "Well, I guess I'm old enough to know that a job is a job."

"Okay, Eddie, as long as we have an understanding. But you're not really being paid just in order to hear Count Basie play."

"I don't really want it forever," he said, " but I just thought it would give you time to look for a band boy at your leisure, find the one you want and give me a few weeks away from New York. You know I like to get out once in a while."

On that understanding, I employed Ed and he got more or less the same salary as a normal band boy would get. I did pay him a little more. Perhaps $25 more than the average. And he went on the road, put the Levis on, and drove the truck and was having a real ball with it.

At that time—and as he had been for some years by the mid-50s—my former bassist, John Levy, was still on the road with us as my road manager and personal manager combined. In fact, to the best of my knowledge, John was the first black manager of a white act in the United States. As time went on, after Ed had joined as band boy, John was finding it more and more necessary every week to go into New York and take care of our business, plus he was trying to do a few things for a couple of other people on the side. He said he wanted to go back to New York and live there permanently, and he thought I needed another person anyway.

I said, "John, there are five musicians in the band. There's you and Ed to take care of them. I don't need a third person."

"Well," he said, "you know how often I have to go to New York to take care of your business. Ed's often the only one on the road. He can't pack up the instruments and take care of you at the end of the gig and everything."

I said, "John, we can't do it. From a monetary standpoint, I just don't see the sense in it."

Finally John and I came to an understanding whereby, instead of receiving a salary for doing the personal and road management jobs, plus a commission for doing the personal management job, he would work solely for commission on the personal management job. That way I could use Ed as a road manager and find another band boy. There was a guy that was applying for the job anyway.

Every few weeks, after that, Ed would say, "Well now, let me see. If you're going out to the Coast, I don't mind going out to the Coast in January. If you can stand me, I'd love to stay on." By now, John had come back to New York to open up the office, Ed had become the road manager, and the new band boy was doing the work that Ed had been doing. What eventually happened was that Ed went on being road manager for years afterwards, well into the 1970s, and helped me set up a number of things that made a difference to my home life. For example, he put an end to my W. C. Fields filing system. Before his intervention I would find things by knowing the number of pieces of paper in a file, and being sure that a certain address would be on this one because it had a tear on one side, or that that one had a line or so pressed down where I'd made a mistake so that it would have such and such address on it. If I spent enough time going through all my bits of paper, I would find what I was looking for.

Ed said, "Look, George, particularly if you're going to make notes of the addresses of disc jockeys who change every few months, I would be inclined to have their addresses on 3 by 5 inch cards."

Now that was against all my instincts of waste not, want not, and I said, "Gee, look at all this space, Eddie. Below where it says Jim Smith, so and so and so, there's three or four lines. Can't we fit in another name there?"

He said, "No. Better to waste the space and be consistent, and have one name on each card. Set them up in alphabetical order."

Then he helped me with the record file. Ever since then, I have had a beautiful filing system. I don't have any memory any more, but I have a good filing system! And the same with my record collection, for which Ed actually built some of the original shelving.

I've explained how Ed's job worked, but it's worth saying more about what John Levy's job entailed. A personal manager is a liaison officer between the artist and his or her agency. Most personal managers handle a few individuals, whereas the agency oftentimes will handle hundreds. It's the personal manager's job to create just a little extra service, for example, where he says, "Well, now let me see. George is in Chicago today and he's got four days blank and then he's in Milwaukee. What can we do with those four days? Not enough time for him to come back to New York and yet it's too long to just hang around in Chicago doing nothing." And he tries to find something suitable.

The agency has got other things to do other than just look at one person's bookings like that. John would see that the bookings coming in from the agency were properly scheduled and sensibly placed geographically. It's much like having an individual record promoter as well as having the company promote records for you.

In 1955, I left MGM and joined Capitol, but I was always aware that while Capitol was promoting my records, they were also promoting Frank Sinatra and Nat Cole—as much as those guys needed promoting—and then they had Peggy Lee and a zillion other people. On the other hand, although my individual record promoter might also handle a few extra people, he was being paid a salary directly by me to promote my discs, and therefore doing a little more of an individual-type job. This was the same thing as with John Levy and my live appearances.

John would scrutinize every contract, and see that everything was straight before it was signed. He'd have a certain degree of leeway to juggle things around, such as before we would travel out to San Francisco, we might have a job in Salt Lake City and that's an eight-hundred-mile jump. Rather than expect us to make that overnight, he'd push the opening date back a little bit—a couple of days—to give us a chance to get out there. Other times, the agency would offer a job, say, in Montana, in February. So John would say, "George doesn't want to go up there in all that ice and snow at that time of the year." It was his job to see that we weren't trying to get to inhospitable places in dreadful traveling conditions, but also to see that we weren't strung out somewhere with a couple of weeks with nothing to do.

In due course, John built up his management office in which I also had quite an interest. Over the years we handled people like Dakota Staton, Billy Taylor, Nancy Wilson, and Ramsey Lewis, as well as groups from overseas like Le Double Six of Paris.

In 1998, John was honored at a special event in the New York JVC Jazz Festival. The year before, when he was eighty-five years old, he wrote me a very moving letter of thanks, saying that I'd given him a chance when there weren't too many black bass players given that kind of opportunity, and that I'd extended that helping hand by making him the first black manager. "Now you're here for my eighty-fifth," he went on, "I love you. God bless you."

In 2000, his successor, Joan Shulman, decided to retire, and I called John to tell him about it. Well, he was eighty-eight at the time, but he immediately said, "George, I'll do anything I can to help."

That's typical of the man—he never puts himself first. He is one of the dearest friends I have, and he helped me a tremendous amount over the years. He was also very good at gently giving me good advice, which I always found invaluable. To give you a good example, one time quite early in the life of the Quintet, I went out and bought a rather fancy pair of shoes, which back in those days cost something like $50. I couldn't wait to get to work that night to show them off to the band.

When I got there, before I did anything, John saw what was going on and took me aside. "Look George," he said, "I don't know quite how things are in England, but over here I'm not sure it's all that wise to carry on like that. You're waving it in front of people's noses, who don't quite have the same opportunity as you." It wasn't a put-down—it was a help, and it put me on the right track as regards my modus operandi in what was still, after all, a new country for me.

9

LULLABY OF BIRDLAND

In 1952, Morris Levy, who owned Birdland, which had opened on the site of the Clique, came to me and said they were about to start a regular disc jockey show sponsored by the club. The club was at 1678 Broadway, at West 44th, a few blocks south of 52nd Street, and it's been built up so much in jazz legend by people with vivid imaginations that you might think it was a huge palatial place. In fact it was just a little jazz club, not very different from those on the Street itself, that held around 150 people, 175 at the most. Nevertheless, its fame had spread much wider than the immediate area, because it had had a wire in there for broadcasting almost since it opened back in 1949. Mostly, those radio shows had been eavesdropping on sets by whatever band was playing there, but now the local WJZ station in New York was going to take this new disc jockey program, sponsored by Birdland, and running from 11 p.m. for up to six hours every night, as well as featuring some of the bands playing there.

Morris wanted me to record a theme, to be played every hour on the hour, and he sent the music to me. It wasn't much good, and so I called Morris and said, "Look, I can't relate very well to this theme you've sent me, why don't I write one for you?"

He was immediately on the defensive. He said, "I'll bet you'd like to write one, because you have your own music publishing company, haven't you?"

He figured that if the show was a success and the tune was played every night, then the rights would add up to something worth having. But although I had set up my own publishing firm, that wasn't actually the reason I didn't want to record Morris's song. It just wasn't very good. So I said to him, "The reason I want to write a tune is so that I can feel comfortable about playing it."

"Well," he came back with, "we would feel comfortable about you recording a tune that we own."

So I suggested a compromise. I said, "Okay, I'll give you the publishing rights, but I'll keep the composer's rights."

Morris said, "Fine."

As it turned out, Trixie wasn't too happy with this decision. She was running my music publishing company—indeed there were eventually three companies, including one for ASCAP and one for BMI—and she really thought I ought to have kept all the rights for myself. But to start with, that was hardly a problem, because writing the tune wasn't quite as straightforward as I had expected. I sat down and wrote something, but when I played it to Trixie, she said, "This is terrible."

So for two days I thought the thing over. For some reason my mind went blank and although I wanted to write a song, I just couldn't think of anything. Finally I got to the point where I thought there was nothing for it but to send in the piece I'd written that Trixie reckoned was so awful.

That night, at our house in Old Tappan, New Jersey, where Trixie and I had moved not long before all this happened, I was sitting down to dinner, my favorite char-broiled steak. I'd just started to eat when I jumped up.

Trixie said, "What's wrong with it?" thinking there was something amiss with the food, because sometimes I would jump up with a yell if there was something on my food that was unexpected or which I didn't like.

That night there was nothing wrong with the food. I rushed over to the piano and said, "How's this?" I sat down and played right through *Lullaby of Birdland*. It just came to me, the whole thing, just like that. Within ten minutes I'd got the entire song worked out. Since then I've been back to the same butcher several times and asked him if if he could manage a repetition of that steak. Actually quite a lot of my compositions have come this way—very slow going for a week or so, and then the finished piece comes together very rapidly, but as I say to those who criticize this method of working, it's not that I dash something off in ten minutes, it's ten minutes plus umpteen years in the business.

It sounds rather flippant to say that, to justify why I can write something so quickly which will come out as a piece that people remember. I'm not pretentious enough to have thought from the outset, "I knew they were going to remember that song," but there's undoubtedly a catchiness in that opening phrase that people identify with me. "Oh, Shearing," they think—in other words, musically they know how to spell my name.

By contrast, I have to say that I observe a number of today's jazz musicians who are attempting to compose without much knowledge of jazz history. They don't know how it all started, and even some of those who do, don't really care. They take the attitude that, "This is what I want to do, and these are the few chords that I want to play to do it." My response is that if they took the trouble to listen to Teddy Wilson, Fats Waller, Art Tatum, and Coleman Hawkins, or to study wonderful orchestraters like Fletcher Henderson, Sy Oliver, and Bill Finegan, they'd have a much deeper grounding in music in general and jazz in particular.

That grounding has allowed me to record numerous different treatments of *Lullaby of Birdland* over the years. I've played it so many times that it is possible to get quite tired of doing so— although I never tire of being able to pay the rent from it! But by recording it in several ways, I've kept it fresh. I did it with a Latin feeling on an album with Ernestine Anderson, and I helped with a vocal treatment of it by the Blue Stars which was made many years ago. My good friend Dick Hyman made a wonderful arrangement of it for me to play on an American tour I did with the BBC Big Band. He left me a whole block of room to do a great range of things from some Brahms-type impressions to a bit of a Bach-like fugue, and ending up with a jazz shout chorus of the type I heard Mel Powell play in England with Glenn Miller's Army Air Force Band during the war. I've recorded it quite recently as well, with my "new" Quintet in 1994, and again when I took my current Quintet into the new Birdland in 2000.

Of course, since I wrote it, *Lullaby of Birdland* has been recorded hundreds of times by other musicians, including a French version, for which the title translates back into English rather quaintly as *Lullaby of the Land of the Birds*.

When I heard Erroll Garner's recording of the tune, it quickly became my very favorite recording. I wonder why I didn't write it that way—by which I mean I had a fairly brisk tempo in mind, whereas Erroll just took it very gently, he kind of lagged it along and scraped his way through it, so much so that you can almost hear the smile on his face as he's playing. In fact, my nickname for Erroll was always "the Scraper."

I first heard Erroll Garner on record in about 1945, and my thoughts about him have never really changed from that moment. I said to myself, "This is an astoundingly original style!"

From the outset, Erroll had a very personalized and highly unusual approach. In many ways, he was the most un-pianistic of all jazz pianists because he treated the instrument as if it were an orchestra, which made him one of a kind. If you're used to hearing records by Art Tatum, Teddy Wilson, or Hank Jones, all of whom treat the piano very legitimately as a piano, you won't hear very much of that in Erroll's playing. It's true that he did use a lot of single-note solos, but they were more than equaled by what I call his "shout" playing, the technique that he used after he'd finished such a solo. Rather than his fingers just cascading up and down the keys, he'd play these big, massive chords, which he used as what big band arrangers call a "shout," just like a huge ensemble of brass and saxophones. He would do that for four or eight bars followed by another four-bar single-note solo, all the time keeping a steady four to the bar with his left hand. It was almost as if he had Basie's guitarist Freddie Green, with his perfect time, kept prisoner inside his left hand. Regardless of how much his right hand lagged behind the beat, that left hand was always the time governor. There's never been another pianist quite like him, and I don't think there ever will be.

I first met Erroll in person after I'd moved to the United States, when he came back to New York from the West Coast, and I was playing opposite him at the Three Deuces on 52nd Street in 1948—a gig which lasted for quite some time. He was leading the Erroll Garner Trio, which was no less a line-up than Erroll on piano, Oscar Pettiford on bass, and J. C. Heard on drums. It was just ridiculous what they did, they were such a tight group.

Perhaps the best estimation of anyone's talent is, firstly, originality, which Erroll had in spades, and secondly, the musical and technical ability to put that originality into practice. His talent wasn't about being able to play everybody else off the stage by mastering their style and then some, but about being himself. It didn't matter to him what kind of piano he was playing—good, bad, indifferent, they were all the same to him—nor did it seem to affect him if the audience was talking. He would just play up a storm. Nobody else can play the way Erroll Garner did. I try to get close to it from time to time, and I received a nice compliment from Erroll's manager Martha Glaser, when she said that I'm probably the closest. That's good enough for me, because that's all I want to do—be as close as I can when I'm representing his style. I sometimes used to kid my audience by saying that Erroll and I were always being mistaken for each other, which is ludicrous, really, because he was much shorter than I am. But I loved Erroll.

After hearing how he tackled *Lullaby of Birdland*, I came to realize that the composer is not always right about his or her own music. Because when someone else comes up with another idea, they can enrich a piece by hearing something different in it. One of my very favorite composers of all time was Irving Berlin, and he wrote *Let's Face The Music and Dance* as quite an up-tempo number, but personally I much prefer taking it very slowly, and you'd barely think it was the same tune. I'm not saying one's right and one's wrong, after all if you have a group of people actually waiting to "face the music and dance," they want to hit the dance floor at what you might call the "businessman's bounce"—a sort of medium uptempo, which is how I believe Berlin wrote it. But the music and the lyrics are so lovely that they need nursing to draw all the music out of them, and that's why I prefer to play the song far more slowly.

Mind you, sometimes this can get a little out of hand. Miles Davis once made a very famous recording of my tune *Conception*. He was a master of playing the wrong bridge, or making up his own, which is what he did on that piece—although the most blatant example is in his version of Benny Carter's *When Lights Are*

Low, where Miles just transposed the opening eight bars up a fourth, instead of playing the beautiful bridge that Benny actually wrote.

The bridge, of course, is the eight measures in an ordinary popular song that connect the first section of a song with the final eight bars. Often the first sixteen bars are two runs through the same chord sequence and melody, which is repeated again at the end. Many, many songs are constructed this way, but a handful of very famous songs, such as *Back Home Again In Indiana*, are composed straight through and have no "bridge" section.

There was a bass player who was very late for a gig somewhere in the Midwest, and he finally stumbled into the bandroom minutes before he was due on stage. "Sorry, boss," he said to the bandleader, "I got hung up on the bridge in Indiana."

The bandleader fixed him with an icy stare and said, "There is no bridge in *Indiana*."

Coming back to the question of composition, it's long been a matter of debate among songwriters, whether the lyrics or the tune comes first. In a couple of my more recent compositions that hasn't been a question I've needed to ask, because I've written two sets of settings of Shakespearean lyrics, songs, and sonnets for choir. I did the first one in 1985 for the Dale Warland Singers in Minneapolis, Minnesota, and a second one in 1999, commissioned by a choir in St. Charles, Illinois. Although they were fourteen years apart, these two sets of choral settings both had a comparable mixture of poetry, and each runs for about ten minutes. I would like to write two further groups of settings, as together they would all make up a Shakespearean choral album.

In the last few years, I haven't written all that many originals for quintet, trio, or even my regular duo with bassist Neil Swainson, but I'm looking all the time for material that I can arrange for each size of group. For example, there are numbers that would suit the Quintet, but which we never got round to playing. Not long ago I came across a song called *This Is Mine*, which was ideal for the Quintet—after all I've done so much work with the line-up over the years that I know more or less immediately what would suit it, and how I would go about playing my part.

At the keyboard in New York, 1957. (Lebrecht Library)

I actually started composing during the war. The piece I mentioned some time earlier, *Delayed Action*, was actually one of the first that I wrote and went on to record. And then came a string of others, including *Bop's Your Uncle*. I wrote a number of pieces dedicated to the members of my family, at least a couple named after Wendy, and one for Trixie called *How's Trix?*

I mentioned the house that I had in New Jersey, into which we had moved by the time I wrote *Lullaby of Birdland*. Until I relocated to California in the 1960s, this was home—where I spent what time I had away from the road. For much of the 1950s I didn't really have a routine schedule, because my life was always so hectic. There was never all that much opportunity to plan, as things often came up at the last minute. Sometimes I'd decide to take some time off, and then a benefit or something would come up, which I couldn't afford not to do, so it was always impossible to plan my leisure time very precisely.

In the house, there was a large room with the record collection, which with the help of Ed Fuerst, I was able to catalog and file, keeping everything up to date. Even today at my home in New York, my discs are similarly ordered and cataloged so it is possible to find everything. In my music room at Old Tappan, there was a large Braille music collection, and that's where I would spend time studying and learning the scores when I began playing symphony concerts in 1952.

In fine weather I would spend a lot of time swimming, as there was a pool in the garden, beyond which were a further four acres of grounds round the house. When we first moved there, it was way out in the country and surrounded by woodland. The whole setting was very beautiful and quiet, but towards the end of my time there, people started building all around us. Of course we still had privacy with four acres, but it wasn't quite the same. Nevertheless, I could play all night as loud as I liked and there were no neighbors to bother or have complain.

It was also a good place to entertain when I was not traveling. Even during my vacations I'd like to get together with the fellow I dictated the arrangements to, or with some pianist friends. Also the house was close enough to Manhattan for me to go into the city from time to time, and make my way around the clubs to hear who was playing in New York. It was a similar kind of situation that Jack Kerouac described in his famous description of me in *On The Road* as "old god Shearing," where he talks about me at a Chicago club in 1957, listening "all ears opened like the ears of an elephant" and then sitting in. I was very complimented by that reference!

Every so often I'd try to take a complete vacation and lay off playing altogether for a short time, but usually by the time I was halfway through the holiday, I couldn't wait to get back to playing again. However, the antidote to being on the road was to lead a pretty quiet life when I was at home, and that's something I still try to do. When we moved into the New Jersey house, we made it clear to everybody that it was to be a place of rest and that it would be appreciated if they'd do us the courtesy of telephoning rather than bursting in. That meant that if I did want to study, to learn one of the big classical concertos for instance, I could do so for weeks on end without being disturbed by anyone.

I also like to read Braille books and papers, and as I said earlier, since playing bagatelle as a child, I've liked indoor games, so I'd play checkers or dominoes. I'd also spend quite a bit of time on the phone. The telephone is the greatest invention for the blind, because it keeps us in touch with everyone.

When we first found the house, we had spent about three weeks looking at real estate. We visited dozens of houses, until the agent took us to the one we eventually settled in. As we started to make our way up the driveway, Trixie said, "This is it."

The agent said, "You haven't seen the house, yet."

"Well, this is it," she replied.

She liked the grounds and the way it was beautifully laid out. There were five hundred fir trees, plenty of lawn and the house itself was colonial style, built in 1925. There had originally been an older house on the grounds, and we were only the third owners of the land. The original grant had been given by Queen Anne to one family and it belonged to them for well over a hundred and seventy years. The Watson family bought it from them, and sixty years later we bought it from the Watsons.

In the old days, silent movies had been made there all the time. The main local movie studios were at Fort Lee, and there was a lot right on the corner of the road where we lived, where a number of films were made. Mr. Watson had lived nearby in a small house on twenty-five acres with his father, until he met and married a silent-movie star, and built for her the house that we eventually moved into.

I eventually sold that house in 1961 to move West, and the man who bought it was an attorney. Years later, in 1976, he came to hear me when I was playing at the Café Carlyle in New York.

"I bet you don't remember me," he began, "but I eat my dinner every night at the table where you composed *Lullaby of Birdland*."

Well, not only did I remember him, his name was John Dorf, but I remembered he was an attorney, so I said, "I'm very glad you came by, because I think I've got a gig for you!" And I asked him to negotiate the purchase of the apartment in New York where I still live to this day with my wife Ellie.

But I digress. During my first marriage I moved my family to the West Coast. I spent some years at Toluca Lake, just outside Los Angeles. One thing that I liked about Los Angeles was that Clare Fischer, the arranger, used to organize something called the piano club. It was an informal group of pianists, and we would meet at someone's house and discuss what was going on in the world of jazz piano. It became a good meeting point for all types of pianists, and as well as Clare, I remember meeting other players such as Joe Sample at those get-togethers. It was felt by some of those who attended that Clare had originally organized it as something of a shopwindow for his own talents as a player and arranger, but in fact the diversity of those who showed up took the spotlight off any one individual and we could really home in on pianistic ideas. One pianist I knew well during this period was Jimmy Rowles, who also lived in the Los Angeles area. He had a very distinctive gravelly voice, and if we were discussing a pianist who had come to town whom Jimmy didn't like, he'd growl, "He's a real *visitor*!"

Although this was a time when I was able to meet other players quite often, Trixie was not that much of a social person, and so, for much of our life together, I didn't get too involved in many such gatherings that brought together other musicians and pianists. On one occasion after we'd moved West, I wrote a tune with Johnny Mercer, sitting on my patio at Toluca Lake in California, and we were playing and singing together. Trixie retired upstairs to her room with a migraine, but I think back on it now, and realize that had our roles been reversed, and it had been me who felt under the weather, there was no way I would have let that get in the way of seeing and hearing Johnny Mercer at work. The piece we wrote was a tune called *Too Good To Be True*, which unfortunately clashed with a more popular number which happened to have the same name. It's happened to me about four or five times that I've had that experience of working on a song and then finding out there's a completely different piece with a similar title.

In this case, nothing ever came of the song, but it was interesting to work together. Johnny knocked the words off in about fifteen minutes. He had an amazing ability with lyrics, which is one of the things I love in life. I have a great facility for remembering lyrics—I love the way they fit into tunes, and I think hard about how they should be read. There are situations where the tune might pause at a certain point, but to pause in the lyric at the same point doesn't make sense, and to give an example, I once discussed with Stephen Sondheim how I wanted to rephrase his lyric to *Send in the Clowns* so that it made better sense. I actually stopped him in the street and asked him about the line that goes: "losing my timing this late / in my career." That's the way many people have sung it, but to me it works much better if you put a big pause in after "timing", and then follow it with "this late in my career."

Johnny's lyrics tended not to have many problems of fit between the scansion of the words and the tune. Some of his rhymes like "Alabaster Palace / Aurora Borealis" from *Midnight Sun* are just so inventive and magical, and they draw in a wide vocabulary in an incredibly inventive way, just as Ira Gershwin and Cole Porter had done before him, and Sondheim has continued to do.

The piece we wrote together was a number I intended to record on one of my Capitol albums, and although it wasn't by any stretch of the imagination one of Johnny's best lyrics, it fitted my tune really well. And so *Too Good To Be True* was recorded.

While I'm on the subject of lyrics, a man by the name of George David Weiss put the lyrics to *Lullaby of Birdland*, but the name that appears on the printed copy is B. Y. Forster, because in those days it was against the rules for an ASCAP writer, which he was, to write with a BMI composer, which is what I am. The only way you could get around it was by using this kind of nom de plume. Weiss wrote a number of other tunes, like *Mr. Wonderful*, under his own name, but despite the name on the copy, it was he who added that particular lyric to my tune. Since Weiss was ASCAP and I was BMI, I guess you could say that it was a half-ASCAP tune.

In the fullness of time, I gave my music-publishing businesses to my daughter, Wendy. Originally this aspect of my affairs was entirely managed by Trixie, but when she died, the publishing rights passed to Wendy, who now has all three of the companies I set up. The first of them, Shearing Music, was an ASCAP firm, although I was never allowed to belong to ASCAP because I joined BMI soon after arriving in the United States. Our main business, Bayes Music, which took its title from Trixie's maiden name, was a BMI firm, and it handled most of my writing. The rest of my work was in Engam Music. This name came from joining the first syllables of "England" and "America." This is a simple way of arriving at effective titles that I have used a few times—the record label I established in the early 1970s was "Sheba," the first sylla-bles of "Shearing" and "Bayes," and that company is also now with Wendy.

I know now what I didn't know then, which is that setting up this kind of business on your own is tough when you haven't got a bunch of people working for you all the time, promoting and managing the discs when you are out on the road. Sheba was, for quite a lot of its existence, a rather well-kept secret, and nowadays, who remembers it? Probably only a few collectors who happen to have some of the discs I recorded at the time, but otherwise it's largely forgotten, and most of the music has never been reissued. It's proof that for most musicians, personally owned record com-panies do nothing to help achieve a peaceful and trouble free life!

≡ 10 ≡

ON THE ROAD

There is one great advantage of our ability to be able to judge people immediately by their character rather than be distracted by the color of their skin, or perhaps their shifty eyes, or their beauty or whatever. For instance, quite early in the life of the Quintet, we were playing what was then the only integrated hotel in Atlanta, Georgia—the Waluhaje, on West Lake Avenue. A woman came over to me and said, "Mr. Shearing, my name is so and so, and I enjoy your music very much, and I'm white."

"Do you mean outside or inside?"

"Well," she said, "you know the way we are down here."

"No," I replied. "That's why I asked you. Frankly, you're speaking in those terms to the wrong guy. Because if you had been accustomed to spending fifteen or sixteen hours in an air-raid shelter in London, it might have changed your views about things. You had to go down to the shelter whenever the raids were getting very heavy. Now it might be that years and years ago you had a falling-out with somebody, and maybe decided not to talk to him. But as soon as the siren went, if you happened to be standing at the side of that person, or anybody else at all, you'd forget your differences and say 'Let's go down to the shelter.' When you have been involved with things like that, you don't have time to think about whether he or she is black or white."

Blind people are very fortunate in that respect. Sometimes I wonder whether even those people who are ostensibly not racially prejudiced just might have a few little reservations about it. For example, in those days if they were in a restaurant in a mixed party, they could see people staring at them. We're protected from all that. Not that I would care. I feel that I'm one of these people who probably wouldn't care even if I could see them.

There was another incident on the road—another racial situation. All the Quintet went into a little roadside restaurant, the kind of joint we called a "greasy spoon." It was in the South, and after we placed our order, we were doing a considerable amount of waiting for everyone in the band to be served.

So finally Trixie asked, "Could we have two more coffees?"

And the waitress said, "I'm sorry. We don't serve colored people."

Straightaway, I said, "You don't? Then I think you should have informed us of that before we placed our order." So I turned to the band and said, "Okay, gentlemen, let's go."

She said, "Aren't you going to eat your toast and pay for it?"

"No. The time may come when I might need any one of these people to see me around. When I call upon them to do it, I know they'll be there for me, because they're friends of mine."

And I added, "In these circumstances, I think it's their turn to call upon me. Good-bye."

When we got outside, John Levy patted me on the shoulder. He said, "Are you crazy? They'll have the police after us!"

I said, "Well, John, in that case, you're my guide dog!"

Members of the Quintet sometimes turned things around and played tricks on me that they could only get away with because of my blindness. The bassist who was with the group in the early 1950s—Al McKibbon—was a specialist in practical jokes and pranks. We were playing in a club in New York, and George Wein, who was the owner of Storyville in Boston at that time, came into town.

Al said to me, "Hey, George Wein is here. Why don't you do your impression of Tatum for him."

So when it came to my solo feature, I gave an impression of Art Tatum, as much as anybody can give an impression of that musical god. When I got through, McKibbon said, "He's here, you know."

"Who? Wein?"

He said, "No, Tatum!"

When I heard that I couldn't wait to get off the bandstand to apologize to him. So I went right over to Tatum when I came off and shook his hand, saying, "I'm sorry, sir."

He said, "All right, man. You're swinging, Dad." He wanted to make me feel good, and eventually I got over it.

I'd first met Tatum in my early days on 52nd Street, when I first came over. He had already had such a strong influence on me, from records, that I felt he was the complete solo pianist. That impression strengthened when I heard him in the flesh, and I never really liked hearing anyone else play with Tatum. He was so consummate as a soloist that to add guitar and bass or other instruments would be a bit like adding a third voice to a Bach two-part invention. Gilding the lily, so to speak.

Having heard Fats Waller in England, there was a little bit in common between the two of them as both of them played stride, and anyone playing in the stride style couldn't avoid incorporating something of Fats, as well as the other great Harlem players like James P. Johnson and Willie "The Lion" Smith, but Tatum had his own musical vocabulary. His runs and figures were unique, but they were the essence of jazz.

When you meet somebody whom you idolize all your life, you tend to go up to them and say things like, "I'm delighted to meet you sir, I've been a fan for so long. I've got all your recordings, and I've listened to everything."

That's exactly what happened with me and Tatum. I must have been his most boring fan, as I went up to him and he let me talk—gush all over him verbally—and after about three or four minutes he finally said, "Glad to meet you, son, are you going to buy me a beer?"

Hearing Tatum in the flesh and on record at the time was truly impressive. In later life, it is possible to discern a number of pianistic tricks that he used fairly often and listening to the old records again now, there are times when it would be nice to hear a half chorus without one. The sound that he made on the piano was good enough without them, and it was his whole sound that was one of the greatest things about him. When you come across one of his little tricks—a particular run or ornament—for the tenth time in his arrangement of a particular song, you think, "Well, it's still marvelous," but not "Isn't that wonderful."

McKibbon would occasionally play other tricks like that one with Tatum. For instance, he'd set off to take me somewhere and he'd gradually speed up until he was going what seemed to me like ten miles an hour. He'd start running—just to keep me moving, and all the guys would stand around and laugh at the speed we were going. Our bongo drum player from the same period, Armando Peraza, did the same kind of thing.

Armando is one of the nicest people I ever met in this business. He ended up staying with me nine years, during the life of the first Quintet, which was longer than anybody else apart from John Levy. Armando's a very loyal, very hard-working guy. He came originally from Havana, and I think he's better than any of his contemporaries as a Cuban percussionist. This speaks for itself, really, because he's worked with everyone from Perez Prado to Machito in the Latin world, and with Dave Brubeck, Cal Tjader, and Stan Kenton in the jazz world.

He plays in a very authentic style, although occasionally he'd come on the stand and play with all kinds of troubles—his hands all cracking open with calluses. Sometimes he'd tell me, "My hand is very painful here."

I'd say, "Do you want me to cut it short, so you can go off?"

But he'd always reply, "No, I have to play. Have to play and keep them hard. That's the only way."

As I said, he is the nicest person in this business, and he was quite a showman too. I was told by the other members of the Quintet how he used to do a thing with a glass of water that was just marvelous. He would balance a glass of water on his head, play bongo drums, and he would never spill a drop. And he would go through the motions—plenty of gyrations. He was great.

McKibbon and Armando both played tricks on me, but from time to time I was able to play some pretty comprehensive practical jokes myself. One I remember particularly well took place at the Fairmont Hotel in San Francisco. There was a bunch of us at a table—in fact it sounds like a name-dropping session, but it's true—Billy Eckstine, Nat Cole, June Christy, Jimmy Lyons from KNBC, plus Trixie and me. The conversation got round to the subject of blindness, and Nat Cole suddenly asked, "George, how do you tell the difference between different denominations of dollar bills? Doesn't all paper money feel the same?"

Well, as it happened, Trixie and I had got our reply to this kind of question set up a long time before. So we went straight into our routine. The idea was that if I'm handed a one-dollar bill she was to do nothing. If it's a five, she taps me once, but I pretend to smell the money. They hand me a ten, she taps me twice, and again I smell the bill. Twenty would be three taps, a fifty is four, and a hundred—I don't know, we never got there.

So I say, "Nat, the way I handle money is that I can smell the difference in the notes."

Now, of course, everyone at the table immediately wants to put me to the test. So they hand me a ten. Invisibly, Trixie taps me twice. I smell it and say, "It's a ten."

Then they hand me a twenty, and it's three invisible taps, and I smell it and say, "It's a twenty."

Then it's a five. One tap, a quick smell, and I say, "Five!"

Now Trixie spots that the next bill is going to be a one, but to cover her traces, she says, "I don't like the way you people are looking at me. You give me the impression you think I'm giving him a tip-off. I'll move away, so that you can be sure that George really is smelling the difference."

So sure enough, just as she moves to sit somewhere else, the next bill is a one. I smell it and say, confidently, "It's a one!"

Nat can't believe it. He says, "How DO you do that?"

So I gently explain to him, "Nat, for every different monetary denomination, they use a different grade of ink. And each ink has its own particular smell. The problems only really start to arise when the smell wears off and you've got to start feeling the difference in paper grade using your nose!"

Finally Nat just walked away, shrugged his shoulders, and believed me. I didn't tell him the truth about that gag for another five years! By that time he had gone round the world telling people that I could smell money!

During the years of the first Quintet, we had some unusual visitors dropping in to hear the band. One of them was the singer, Tony Martin, who had become a big star in film musicals during the 1930s. He was best known for a tune called *Tenement Symphony*, which he originally sang in the Marx Brothers film *The Big Store*. The night Tony came in to see us at the Round Table in New York I said that we were honored to have him in the room. I went on to tell the audience that the first time I had heard Tony Martin he was singing *Tenement Symphony* and I thought it was the best thing that ever happened.

I finished up by saying, "To show my appreciation of Tony Martin's performance of that song, I would like to play *Tenement Symphony* and dedicate it to him." I played an introduction and chorus leading to the big bridge passage and built it up. I was just going to build it up some more to the second chorus and be very majestic about it, but as I reached the start of the melody, Tony, completely uninvited, was at the microphone singing. This is the kind of thing that producers dream up to put in movies, but it happened in real life. And he sang it beautifully. When he finished, I got up from the piano and shook hands with him and we embraced each other.

He came in a couple of times after that.

It's one thing when a great singer grabs the moment—and the microphone—and produces something magical, but there were other less exciting moments. One thing I got to dislike, and still object to, was when I would be at the microphone speaking to a club audience and they'd go on talking among themselves. It got to the point where we were refusing to play some clubs because of this. I was more prepared to understand it if I knew that the management was with me, and the problem of an inattentive audience was a problem shared. But in some cases you'd speak to the management about it and they'd say, "Well, what are you going to do? We're selling liquor." From remarks like that, I'd realize that there was no sympathy to my point of view.

Another thing that used to bug me was going into a club where all kinds of money has been spent on the décor of the room, but on stage there was nothing more than a couple of cheap microphones and a mediocre piano. I have always felt that if you're going to do something, do it the whole way, and above all do it to support entertainment that you are paying thousands of dollars for. Protect your investment by giving it the tools to work with.

If I've got the backing of the management, and an audience is making too much noise, rather than scold, I try to do it nicely. I will say things like, "The final decision is with you. But it strikes me that if you've taken the trouble to come into the club and pay all kinds of minimum cover charge, then you would want to hear what you're paying it for. If you don't, that's fine. If a few of you don't and a number of you do, it's unfortunate that the few are going to interfere with the wishes of the many."

Occasionally, there's nothing for it but to take action. We were playing the Hawk—that's the Blackhawk in San Francisco—when a troublesome man came in. Now the Hawk was one of the nicest rooms as far as the listening audience is concerned, but this fellow started to make a little noise at his table. So I made a bit of a quip about the noise in the room.

But he wasn't having that and shouted, "Be quiet! Blow your horn, man! Blow your horn. What do you mean, be quiet? We pay money to come in here!"

So I said, "Waiter, would you either see that this gentlemen is removed from the ringside or do something about it? Because I don't think he should interfere with the listening of everybody else." So they made him leave.

I don't want to come on like a prima donna, but if a club owner pays me a certain amount of dollars to come into a room and play, he's not doing it for the good of his health. He's doing it because I can bring people into that room, and I bring them in because they want to listen. If they're prevented from listening, then I think the number of times they're going to go into that room to hear me is limited. They just won't continue to go there, and of course the same applies to the audiences that come along for anyone else who plays there as well.

Sometimes, when a club closed down or stopped hiring the same standard of attraction, I would feel that I had to go somewhere else in that same town and bring my loyal audience in again. I suppose this is justifying my salary, but I have often felt over the years that I have to protect those people more than the club owner.

That's not to say there aren't some club owners for whom I would go out of my way to help. At the height of our success, when the Quintet was able to charge much higher fees than it had done to start with, some commentators wondered how a small club like the Blackhawk could continue to afford us. But the reason we played there very often over the years is because we decided to give them a break.

It was always a pleasure to play the room. The Blackhawk management knew its music, and the house band was led by the fine bassist Vernon Alley. I also found that we could do good business there, and play other types of events in the same city. For example, some time around 1960, I played a sold-out concert with André Previn at the Masonic Auditorium in San Francisco, and then a few days later we went into the Blackhawk. You might think there's a conflict between playing in a major hall with top-price tickets, and then appearing at a nightclub in the same city where we could be heard for the price of a drink.

But there never seemed to be any conflict, and to some extent I felt that if I had brought a bunch of musicians all the way out to San Francisco from the East, it was incumbent on me to do whatever I could for them, because between there and Chicago there wasn't an awful lot to do. On the way we might play occasional colleges, here and there, but for a band like ours, there was not a lot to do work-wise, and it was a costly proposition to bring guys out West.

Thinking about what a pleasant room the Blackhawk was to play, it had its counterparts in one or two other places. There was the London House in Chicago, where, as I mentioned in an earlier chapter, we used to play a couple of times a year until it finally closed and turned into a Burger King in the 1970s. The only drawback with that club was that it was primarily a restaurant. So people were not always there simply for the music. The pay was as safe as a house, we lodged at the Executive House almost next door, and I enjoyed the atmosphere a lot. But the background noise was always very busy, and from time to time, when someone would say to me, "We came to hear you at the London House,"

I'd have to correct them and say, "You came to *see* me at the London House!"

Another club that springs to mind was one in Detroit named Baker's Keyboard Lounge, which was on Livernois Street at Eight Mile Road. It was always an absolute pleasure to play for Clarence Baker, who ran the place for over forty years until he retired in 1985. In many respects, it was about the nicest room in the country. It was always well decorated, and often refurbished, but he always had a seven-foot piano in topflight condition and a really good sound system.

It was a very small room and there was no alternative pianist or group. Often in those circumstances, the management would get nervous. After you'd been off for twenty-five minutes they'd say, "What do you think? Isn't it time you came back on?"

But not Clarence. I recall a real case in point. One night there, we came off at twenty after twelve. The club closed at two, so when we came off for that break, I said to the guys, "I'll tell you what we'll do. We'll come back at ten minutes to one and play until ten after and then play a short final set from one thirty till two."

Clarence said, "Oh no. What'll you do that for?"

So I figured that at that time of night perhaps the break was too long for him, but he said, "No, you shouldn't do that."

"Why not?"

He said, "What you suggest is really too short to come back. Why don't you stay off until five after one, and go back for the last fifty-five minutes?"

So there we are. We had a thirty-five minute break, and I said, "Fine Clarence. We'll go and get some food."

That was always the way I preferred to deal with club owners. If I knew the guy well enough, I would always rather have a gentleman's agreement with him as far as the schedule is concerned than have a watertight contract.

One room I enjoyed visiting was Bradley's in New York, which opened some time in the 1970s. I never actually worked there, although I did sit in occasionally right up to the time it closed in the 1990s. Usually in Manhattan I played at the Café Carlyle or the Blue Note, but if I could, I'd take the opportunity to go down to Bradley's and hear whoever was playing there. Often it was Tommy Flanagan, who was somebody I admired and got along with very well on a musical level. Strangely, though, one thing I'd wanted to do with him never happened, which was to make a duo album at two pianos as I'd done with Marian McPartland and Hank Jones. I asked him one night if he'd be up for it, and he said, "Yes, as long as everything is above board and straight."

This saddened me, because I thought I knew Tommy well enough that he, of all people, would realize that everything would be honest and upright. Thinking about it in retrospect, I got the record company to approach both Marian and Hank, and perhaps things would have worked out differently if I'd got them to approach Tommy instead of doing it myself. I was sad the record never happened because I loved Tommy and what he did at the piano, but after he said that, a slight coolness developed. I guess that's a family trait with me. My mother and her sister disagreed over something, and never spoke to each other for thirty years afterwards, so I guess we Shearings do not forget. If I've had a difference with someone and they come up to me and say, "George, I don't know whatever made me do or say that, I've thought about it and I don't know how I can ever repair the situation," that's enough for me, and I'll do my best to put it behind me. After Tommy said that to me, I never discussed the idea of playing two pianos with him again, so we never got to make the disc, although we continued to be friends, and I would still go to hear him from time to time at Bradley's or wherever he was playing in town.

Keeping the Quintet going involved a number of changes of personnel, and as the repertoire grew, and our stylistic range broadened to include Latin material, our choices involved finding people who could really play well across a very broad swathe of material. Occasionally, the very best musicians weren't the right ones for the good of the Quintet as a whole.

We found one musician who was one of the most exciting we ever had, and that was Philly Joe Jones on drums. He broke us up. He was marvelous. I was so happy with him, apart from the fact that he had a personality problem. He had a drug habit. It meant that he was so unsure of himself that if anybody said anything to him, he would take it the wrong way and get into a fight. We nursed him along until another musician joined the group who was equally as great and was also difficult. He had been on drugs and was trying to get straight. So we had the brilliant idea of suggesting one of them keep an eye on the other, with the idea that it would stabilize Joe, owing to the fact that we'd given him this responsibility. This really worked for a while, but finally he snapped.

We were out on the road, when the manager of the club where we were playing in Minneapolis came to me and said, "George, one of your musicians is using some bad language to one of the women customers."

Philly Joe came up and said, "You talking 'bout me? You're a goddam liar!"

So I said, "C'mon, let's go talk about it."

Joe needed to be taken aside, so we went outside for a walk, and he more or less exploded at me, "Prejudiced sonofabitch!"

"Look," I said. "Let's take this thing at its worst. Let's say the argument with the customer, or the way the manager has treated you, did turn out to be the worst case of racial prejudice you've ever seen in your life. You're not working for this man. You're working for me. I've had a mixed group for years now. You know there's not an ounce of racial prejudice in me, and you're working for me for fifty-two weeks in the year. You happen to be at this club for one week. As it happens, I don't think the problem is down to racial prejudice. If you think so, that's your prerogative, but it's not your prerogative to tangle with him. When we come back to this town we may be in this club, we may be in another club. If I choose to play this club next time, in spite of the fact that the manager may be racially prejudiced, I want to prove to him and to the citizens of this town that a mixed group can get along together. This is the only way we're ever going to break it down. We're not going to break it down by causing fights in public."

He was a little loaded at the time, because, in an effort to keep straight, sometimes drink would take the place of drugs. He said, "You're right."

We went back to the dressing room and I said, "Give this man some black coffee."

Joe started off to get his coffee, and as he went the rest of the guys were talking about it. He disappeared out into the kitchen, saw the manager out there, and started a fist fight with him.

As it happened, the man with whom he was fighting—and this was the only physical incident I had in the whole life of the Quintet—happened to have a good deal of jujitsu under his belt. So he got Joe's arm in back of him, and got him down. But then he figured, "Well, now the man has to play, and he's the drummer, so I don't want to damage his arms."

As a result, he let him go, and immediately, Philly Joe went and got a bottle, smashed it, and went after the manager with the jagged edge. Again the manager disarmed him, and although he could have, he agreed not to press charges.

Nevertheless, this was a federal criminal offense and I couldn't permit Philly Joe to stay with the band. I went to him and said, "I'm sorry. We both tried, but one of us didn't quite make it." And so I let him go.

It's a shame because he was a talented and intelligent man, and indeed, he never said one word of criticism of me after I let him go. But it does show that even the most brilliant musicians don't always fit. Although it seemed longer, I think he was only with us for about ten days or so, but during that time I really came to appreciate his musicianship. He was a very talented pianist, with almost as much skill as he had on drums, and he had previously been leading his own fifteen-piece band. If he had stayed straight and been a little bit of a businessman as well, that man could have gone to the moon with his career. It was very frustrating to see that talent go to waste. When Joe left, Roy Haynes took his place and there were no more problems. Roy stayed for a while. He is a lovely man and I loved his playing, but after a time he went back to his old job with Sarah Vaughan.

In 1955, the Quintet moved from MGM to the Capitol label. It's probably the case that we'd gone just about as far as we could with MGM. They'd been responsible for the making of the Quintet, and they'd pushed that concept along from one album to the next. But when a record company, in just the same way as an agent or a manager, feels that they've done everything they can do for you, then you have to have a think about moving on to somebody else who might have another idea, or a different way of doing things. I can't remember now whether we approached Capitol or they approached us—whether the chicken or the egg came first— but it was the start of a dream period for us, because Capitol came up with great ideas from the start, and they poured in money to make them happen.

So we began a long association, which produced a whole series of albums and a variety of musical carpets on which the sound of the Quintet rested. There were settings with brass, strings, brass-and-woodwinds, vocal groups, Latin sounds, in fact a whole range of different elements with which the Quintet was able to work quite amicably. I was very happy with my producers there, all of whom really knew what they wanted. One of them, David Cavanaugh, came up with the idea of all the albums relating to a kind of tapestry. Capitol tied this up with a very clever sales pitch, so that the covers and titles projected an image of what at the time was seen as glamour and sophistication, and most of the sleeves featured photographs of voluptuous-looking women. I used to kid audiences that because I was fortunate enough to read Braille, I'd chosen them myself, and it often took quite a time for the penny to drop.

The album titles included *Blue Chiffon*, with songs such as *Love-wise* and *Nocturne*. Then there was *Satin Brass*, which featured the Quintet backed by a brass choir. Another was *White Satin*, and then, with a bit of a pun on "Latin" and "satin," there was *Satin Affair*, which mixed Latin rhythms with string settings. I think the first string disc was *Velvet Carpet*, but we also did things like *The Shearing Spell*, which mainly just featured the Quintet. There was another one called *Latin Lace*, on which the liner notes said, "add a little spice into your pad with these twelve hot little numbers!"

This was part of the whole sales strategy. People would come up and get the titles a bit muddled.

"Oh, Mr. Shearing, I've got your album *Blue Velvet*!"

"Don't you mean *Blue Chiffon*?"

"And then there's *Green Satin*!"

"I think that might be *White Satin* . . ."

But of course, it achieved exactly what the folks at Capitol had intended, and the colors, the tapestry idea, got people talking, and more importantly, remembering, the discs.

It was during this time that we made our first collaborations between the Quintet and a full orchestra, in some sessions we did in 1958 with Billy May. The two of us, Billy and I, used to put Dave Cavanaugh on unmercifully. We'd know that he'd have all the guys booked for a seven o'clock session in the evening, and one of us would call and say, "Look, Dave, we're just not going to be ready."

We'd give him an hour or so to stew, and then we'd ring back and say, "It's okay. We've put our heads together, and we're going to be ready!" Of course, we'd really been ready all along, with all the arrangements worked out and the Quintet parts rehearsed, but we took the opportunity to get Dave's nervous juices flowing. He was an arranger himself, so he knew exactly what was involved.

As an arranger, Billy's background was very much in the big bands, and much of what he wrote stressed the brass and saxophones, but in the late 50s and early 60s we did many other things together, with strings and woodwinds, brass, choirs, all kinds of combinations. He had marvelous ears, and at one of our earliest record dates in 1958, I remember playing him my final chorus on *Cuckoo In The Clock*. It had some quite tricky chords in it, and I asked him, "Do you need the inner voicings?"

"No," he said, "I've got it." He had completely got the whole thing down after hearing it once, and before long he'd arranged it for full orchestra. That kind of technique is not uncommon among arrangers. Robert Farnon has similar gifts, and I remember back in the old days before I left England, Laddy Busby was famous among London musicians for being able to write out two parts simultaneously, a tenor sax part with his left hand and an alto sax part with his right. This was particularly impressive, because it involves transposing into two different keys at the same time.

I loved playing with a big band. As well as those records with Billy, I was lucky enough to have the opportunity to sit in with the Basie orchestra from time to time, when we were out on the road together. Actually, I was tempted to listen more than to play, because of the nature of the band, which was always one of my favorite groups—so much so that it was always very tempting to play in a style like Basie's, because it fitted the band so well.

To be working in the record business at that time was to lead a charmed life. We were able to do the most ambitious projects, and for the most part we never had to worry where the money was coming from. One of the most ambitious things Billy May and I did was an album called *Concerto For My Love*, which was made up entirely of love songs, like *Love Letters*, *Love Child*, and *Portrait of My Love*. There were ten or eleven other instruments on it, plus a fifteen-voice choir, so that overall it was a big, big production, but nobody ever seemed to give a thought to the finances. Nowadays we come to do an album and the first question is often "What's the theme?" The second is "What's the budget?"

Just imagine going to a record company today and saying, "I want to do an album with twenty strings, ten woodwinds and five brass, plus twelve voices." Unless they're rolling in money or in love with you, they'll say, "What? Are you out of your mind?"

It's not anybody's fault, but the whole business has changed irrevocably, and in today's climate it's so easy to obtain CDs or even make your own, that a lot of thought and tight financial planning not only goes into the production of an album but its whole development, the video, the press kit, the marketing. That having been said, back in the late 50s, Capitol was very shrewd in terms of the market at the time, because every album gave the public something that was recognizably familiar, but which always included something a little bit different or new.

That's not to say that from time to time I didn't have to use all my powers of persuasion to take Capitol along with my ideas. I guess this began the moment I first suggested leaving behind the *Velvet Carpet* kind of disc where the Quintet was very much in evidence. The company was very apprehensive the first time I proposed a Latin album.

"George, you've been doing all these quiet mood albums for so long, people have got to know you for that."

I suppose in retrospect that was a healthier attitude than today, where the questions are more likely to be: "Who are you going to record with who has as big a name? How will you present it? Who will the guest be? Elton John?"

This demonstrates the kind of shopwindow mentality that goes on in the industry today. Back in those days, Capitol simply wanted to protect the predictable salability of their merchandise by being consistent.

Anyway, I said to them: "Trust me!"

We made our first Latin album, and it sold over 80,000 copies, which at that time was a very healthy quantity for an LP. It was because Capitol was prepared to back us to do these discs that had a link to the familiar kind of album I had been making, but each recording pushed a little further into new territory. We stayed with the company for about fourteen years.

A lot of people thought that as each new disc appeared with the big bands or strings that "Shearing's going cocktail!" or "Shearing's gone over to 'polite' jazz!" Not at all. I believed that with each disc I was introducing another element into which jazz could creep—and believe me it was necessary to creep in some of those settings where the traditional noisiness of jazz has no place or point. If you're playing an album of ballads with orchestral backing, you can introduce all kinds of levels of subtlety of improvisation. In the case of the blues, it was possible to get politely funky, but in those settings it wasn't appropriate to go really "down home."

Capitol also gave me the opportunity to record a fair number of solo piano pieces, and I was able to explore a similar range of subtlety there. For example, there's a version of *I Cover The Waterfront* where I allude to Debussy. I like the idea of bringing in what I know of classical impressionism into my jazz playing, and that piece is a perfect example of using the musical language of Debussy and Ravel to create a specific effect. You wouldn't try to put French impressionism into *St. Louis Blues*, but a song like *I Cover The Waterfront* has a much more apposite mixture of subject matter and musical structure. If you go down to the seashore and hear the sound of the waves rolling in, and the wind, it seems to me that's just the set-up for impressionistic music, and it's something I can do as a solo pianist that would be impossible with the full group.

Looking back at the repertoire I recorded during those fourteen years with Capitol, it was pretty wide ranging. Some of it was dictated by material that originated with my various publishing companies, but that was a fairly minor consideration. Mainly, I wanted to record what interested me, and that included pieces by other pianists whose work I liked. One I'd single out was Ray Bryant, several of whose pieces we did with the Quintet, including *A Bebop Irishman* and *Bel Air*, both of which had excellent bebop lines that were a little out of the ordinary.

During that period, apart from the orchestral sessions, whether you heard the Quintet on record or in live performance it basically sounded much the same, except that we might be inspired by an enthusiastic crowd, which makes a lot of difference to the playing. Instead of seeing how correct you can get something in the studio, and going over it time and time again until it's perfect, you lose that restraint and feed off the warmth and feeling of the crowd. We did the same kind of mix of ballads and up-tempo pieces in person that we included on our discs—some jazz, some not so much jazz—and our audiences were generally large and enthusiastic.

That didn't always please the critics. In fact the die-hard jazz critics all said I'd commercialized and that they would limit the number of stars they gave to any one of my albums. But success in the eyes of the critics isn't everything. I well remember bumping into Dave Brubeck somewhere on the circuit in the late 1950s and saying, "David, I understand you just lost a critics' poll. You might be able to afford a band boy now!"

And he said, "I just got one."

Which all goes to show that critical opinions do not always equate with popular success. Of course, we need critics, as any artist does, to spread the word and offer evaluations, but if we happen to do something of which they do not approve, life does go on!

One activity that met with a great deal of critical success and popular acclaim was the work we did with singers. My favorite singer of the 1950s and early 1960s was Nat King Cole—just as Mel Tormé was later to become my all-time favorite. Both men were such consummate musicians, and of course Nat had been one of the great jazz pianists before singing took over his career.

When Nat and I were putting our album *Nat Cole Sings / George Shearing Plays* together in 1961, he said, "Let's do *Pick Yourself Up*." Back in the forties, this had been a number that I used to play at breakneck speed, and I thought surely he's not going to do it like that? So I asked, "Do you really want to do it, Nat?"

"Oh, yeah," he says. And at this marvelous, relaxed tempo he snapped his fingers and went into, "Uh—Pick yourself up . . . . . . dust yourself . . ."

"Ah! Very well, Nat!"

Because with just those few hints he'd given me the whole atmosphere right there for how he envisaged this particular track. Frankly, I think that *Pick Yourself Up* was just as brilliant in its own way as *Let There Be Love*, although that seemed to be the number from the album that everyone went crazy about, particularly in England. *Pick Yourself Up* was my personal favorite in that medium, catchy, tempo, not least because of the way Nat's ideas dovetailed with mine. For instance, at the end of the first chorus of vocal, Nat left plenty of room for the Quintet to play a variation of the melody, just for a few bars, which I voiced so that it really fit the sound of the group, and this kind of melodic variation was a feature of the album as a whole. We did some great ballads on the recording as well, like *Lost April* and *Serenata*, and I loved getting together with Ralph Carmichael to put the string orchestrations in place for them.

About eighteen months before that, in May 1959, we'd made one of our most popular albums with another singer, Peggy Lee. The disc was called—forgive the pun—*Beauty and the Beat*, but it didn't involve anything like the same amount of preparation as the

Nat Cole album, because it was recorded at a disc jockey convention in Miami. The fun thing about it, of course, was that the whole industry was there, all the main record companies, and a lot of the people who were generally involved with the record business. So this gave us a built-in audience response, in fact it was an incredible audience and the whole atmosphere of the album was charged up because of that. I'd have to say, however, that whereas Peggy Lee was a great singer, she was never a great musician in the same sense as Nat or Mel. While Peggy and I were rehearsing *Some Other Spring* for this album, I suggested that rather than do it as a ballad, to take the tempo up a bit, with a real Billie Holiday, mid-tempo swing to it.

Peggy quipped back, "Oh, come on, George, are you trying to tell me how to sing?"

I went to Dave Cavanaugh, who was producing, and told him that if I didn't have an apology from Peggy by the next morning, I was off the album. Well, the next morning Dave and Peggy came to my room, she apologized and the session went on.

Other singers we recorded with in that same period included Dakota Staton and Nancy Wilson. I have very firm opinions about what I do—how I play almost orchestrally behind a singer—and I brought that approach to all these albums. I'd met Nancy in 1960, shortly before we made *The Swinging's Mutual* album together, and she was also managed by John Levy, so I knew quite a lot about her and her career. Taking that idea of playing orchestrally behind a singer a stage further, my favorite of the records I did with Nancy was one for which I wrote all the arrangements. We recorded it in the summer of 1962 under the title *Hello Young Lovers*, and Milt Raskin transcribed my ideas for the orchestra. These days, some record companies don't seem to like fade-outs, but I managed a particularly effective fade on the title track of that album—it almost sounds like the lovers walking off into the sunset. In fact on that disc I only actually played on one piece, *Miss Otis Regrets*, and I used the harpsichord on that. Sadly, at the time of writing, it has yet to be reissued on CD.

My biggest regret from that period is that I never got to record with Frank Sinatra, the more so as we came really close to making an album together.

The Quintet had played opposite him for two weeks in Carnegie Hall, and not long afterwards we did something similar in Boston. On both those occasions, he had his own accompanying group with him all the time, and I was with the Quintet, so we did not actually appear together on stage. But hearing him from the wings, I dreamed of playing a ballad for him. Even today, when I listen to his voice on a number like Jobim's *How Insensitive* on his *bossa nova* album, or on any one of his own numerous classic-ballad performances, it still sends shivers down my spine. I really wanted to have the chance to record with him, because I felt I could bring a certain sympathy to his ballads and draw out the tenderness in him. He had a unique talent for finding an emotional angle in a lyric. He never overdramatized it, but with his precisely placed low notes he gave the impression of gently making love to a song.

Once, when I was playing at the Café Carlyle, Frank came in to hear me. He was sitting quite close to the bandstand, and I knew he was there, but for some reason I didn't have the nerve to ask him to come up and sing with us. I think in retrospect it was because although I had met Frank socially, and played opposite him, I hadn't really worked *with* him. I knew what keys he sang in, and what register best suited his voice, but I wasn't sure that he knew that I knew. Also, I was in the habit of playing quite advanced chord changes, and maybe he would not have responded affirmatively to some of my harmonic ideas. As a result, I was worried that he might refuse the invitation to join me on stage, so we never did get to do a ballad together in a club setting.

It must have been some time after that, quite a period after we'd played opposite one another at Carnegie Hall, that I had dinner with Frank. During the course of the evening, I confessed to him, "I have one unfulfilled desire, and that is to play a ballad for you."

"Ballad?" he replied, "Let's do a whole album."

Lists of tunes were exchanged then and there, but we were both so busy we never did get round to it. It was something I think we both regretted. However we did both take part in a special charity fundraiser at Radio City in 1982, a concert for the Memorial Sloan-Kettering Cancer Center in New York, at which Luciano Pavarotti also appeared. It was an extraordinary event that raised two million dollars in a single night. The evening was one of the most memorable of my life. I have a permanent reminder in the form of a citation, in a beautiful leather box, given by the Rockefeller Foundation and read out on the night by Frank.

Over the years, I got to be really tired of the media attacking Frank. What those attacks failed to notice was the dignity with which he went about things, and the fact that once he was involved, the big corporations threw in their backing at a level that was way beyond sponsorship. Most of the charity events that Frank became involved in were planned years ahead, and had this kind of heavyweight backing. And at the same time, Frank quietly did many things behind the scenes that showed he retained the common touch. When the singer Sylvia Sims was ill and had to undergo a serious operation, Frank footed the bill for the whole thing without even thinking about it. He often went back to his hometown of Hoboken, New Jersey, and helped somebody out there. And for my own part, I have a letter from Frank following that charity concert, saying, "Thank you very much for your help, and if you ever need mine, just let me know." That was the Frank Sinatra I knew.

As an overall performer, I think Frank was the best there was for many long years. Towards the end, there was a feeling that that utterly distinctive voice was starting to depart from us, but even then, he could do something extraordinary. I remember that towards the end of his life, we were in Las Vegas, and I had gone along to be a spectator, and just listen to Frank.

There was no announcement, the orchestra played two chords, and the next thing I heard was, "I never knew the charm of Spring . . ."

Wham! He came out on stage, singing, and the presentation sent a chill down your spine, with the mixture of simplicity and the onslaught of his attack.

At one time, my second wife Ellie was working as a back-up singer on commercials and studio sessions, and she was hired to sing on Frank's *Trilogy* album along with fifteen other singers.

Frank sent us a copy with a note that said, "Many, many thanks, Ol' Blue Eyes."

So I sent him back a short note that said, "Many thanks, Ol' No Eyes."

I didn't get the chance to speak to him for a couple of years after that, although the story of my reply had crept into print in an Australian paper. When we finally met, I asked if he'd been offended with my response. But he just said, "How can I be angry with you, George? I love you, you silly man!"

That's my Frank Sinatra.

One session I was very happy to be involved in from the early 60s was with the Montgomery brothers, Buddy on vibes, Monk on bass, and, of course, the marvelous Wes on guitar. They were instinctive musicians, and none of them was really a reader. On *Darn That Dream*, Wes sang out a slightly different version of the theme, and so we played it his way. He and Buddy played the theme an octave apart, and I added my Quintet harmonies in between, so we actually made a Shearing Quintet out of the Montgomery brothers and me.

The session happened during the Capitol days, and it happened because Capitol wanted to do a recording with Cannonball Adderley, who was signed to Riverside. In return, Riverside agreed, but on condition they got George Shearing to record with the Montgomery brothers for their Jazzland subsidiary. It was a very healthy exchange, and the kind of thing that was possible during those years when the record business was in its heyday. I met Orrin Keepnews from Riverside during the time we recorded that session, and he was a very dedicated, enthusiastic man. No producer can make a silk purse out of a sow's ear, but the exceptional producer is the one who hears something original and then has the courage to go through with something the public doesn't initially understand until they've been able to hear it properly for themselves. Orrin did that with Wes, just as he'd also done it with Monk.

Going back to the changes in personnel in my own line-ups during those years, one of my favorite groups was with Vernel Fournier on drums and Israel Crosby on bass. In June 1962, we had gone into Basin Street East in New York as a trio, and two nights of our season there were recorded, making up a couple of albums. Israel died right after that trio session. For a few years before we worked together, the two of them had been very much associated with Ahmad Jamal. After Israel's death, Vernel went on working with me in the Quintet for a couple of years.

While Vernel and Israel had been with Ahmad Jamal, the Belgian multi-instrumentalist Toots Thielemans was in my Quintet—in fact he was in the group for about six years up until 1959. He originally joined as a guitar player, but once I found out how great his harmonica playing was, I'd always introduce him to play a solo. I always tried to make a point of ensuring that all the members of the Quintet were featured as soloists when we played, even if the sets were so short that I had to focus on two musicians in one set and two more in the next. Usually the last one to be featured would be the drummer, because traditionally, drums finish the show. It was that way with Denzil Best in the original Quintet, and it's that way today, with Dennis Mackrel, who usually closes our sets with a long solo.

Coming back to Toots, I think that if he hadn't been a musician, he'd have become a mathematician. He is also amazingly quick thinking, as a musician and as a man. We were staying at the Hollywood Hawaiian one time, and out of the corner of his eye he caught sight of a little girl falling into the swimming pool. He had stripped off his shirt, dived in, and fished her out, before any of us had any idea he was gone. He's an incredible on-the-spot-Charlie when it comes to speed of thought and action.

In 2002, I took part in a celebration of his eightieth birthday at the Blue Note in New York. From time to time the club goes in for big celebrations where they expand an anniversary into a season of concerts, and every night they feature different musicians associated with the player whose birthday it is. I was happy to appear, to help celebrate my long association with Toots.

He was with me for five or six years, and he latched on to the Latin thing very effectively, scraping out rhythms on the *guiro*. Sometimes I'd drop out, and the entire group would be playing drums or rhythm instruments. I'd leave them to it, because it was pure rhythm, really exciting. This might go on for five minutes or more.

Around the time I introduced the Latin material to the Quintet, we used to go and hear Tito Puente, who was becoming known as "King of the Mambo" during the 1950s. If I have one criticism of Tito's work at that stage, it's that his band was very polished and squeaky clean. It sounded lovely, but it was the opposite end of the spectrum from Mongo Santamaria's band, which sounded as if it had come right out of the bush. I'm not trying to put either of them down—not making the kind of comparison that saxophonists once used to make between Charlie Parker and older hands like Freddie Gardner—but trying to point out where there are layers of inhibitions.

Tito would have wonderful, crafted arrangements, so he had a really well-set band, as opposed to Mongo, who had skeleton charts and a lot of improvisation on that skeleton. It seemed to me at that time that one of them was about the minimum of jazz versus the maximum of jazz, and conversely, the maximum of inhibition versus the minimum of inhibition. Ironically that didn't apply to Tito's own playing, and fronting a band he was always a wonderfully dynamic performer himself.

That having been said, in due course I became good friends with Tito. He appeared on my eightieth birthday concert at Carnegie Hall, and I appeared as a guest on one of his albums, playing *Lullaby of Birdland.*

It probably goes back to that early gig at the Clique with Buddy DeFranco, where we were opposite Machito, but whenever there's Latin music going on I seem to know instinctively what to play, and to be totally in synch with Latin rhythms. For example, I never comp, in jazz terms, when I'm playing Latin material, I attempt to play genuine Latin piano, just as I heard Machito's pianist doing back in the 1940s. I knew immediately then that what he was playing was right for the surrounding elements, and having been exposed to that, I was able to grab onto it and use it in my own playing.

Ultimately, it all boils down to inhibition. If you're afraid of things not sounding as tidy as you'd like them to, then you'll remain in an area where you can be sure you're not gumming up the works. On the other hand, if you're really sure of the path you're taking, then you'll continue on it with confidence, knowing that those not already on it will come round to it and follow your lead.

One popular misconception is that there is a connection between Afro-Cuban and Brazilian music. To my mind, there's very little direct connection between them, apart from the fact that in the United States there is a marked tendency to play *bossa nova* too loudly. I once sat in with Luiz Eça in a little club in Brazil, and he wasted me with the complexity of his rhythms after about three choruses. We're just not subtle about *bossa* in America, you get this "bang, bang" ground bass and everyone pounds it out like mad.

There are exceptions, and Clare Fischer is a miracle at Brazilian music. He was into it very early, when he recorded an album of *bossa nova* with my old colleague Cal Tjader. Anything Clare directs is never too loud, which is why I had him orchestrate a whole *bossa nova* album for me. He's a very subtle arranger, and he's the kind of musician who very rarely enters a musical conversation on any subject in which he can't partake on an equal level with the acknowledged experts in the field. He's a wonderful musician.

Around the end of the Capitol period, I became associated with Baldwin pianos. Actually I had originally intended to come to an arrangement with Steinway, but they told me that their prime requisite was that I have a Steinway piano in my home. Well, by that time I had a Bösendorfer at the house, and I certainly wasn't going to get rid of that to replace it with an American Steinway. I might have considered getting rid of it for a Hamburg Steinway, but not for one of the American instruments. So, I went to Baldwin, who really didn't care what kind of a piano I had at home, as long as I played a Baldwin on stage.

I always tried to get an SD-10, their big nine-foot model. And I was usually successful, because the company would bring one over for me if they didn't have one at the club or concert hall where I was appearing. I think their best workmanship went into this model, and I always used to say it's like the difference between properly brewed and instant coffee. There's no doubt that the SD-10 was extremely tastefully brewed, with a mellow tone and a good sustaining power. It comes into its own on those classical pieces where you want a very slow decay on the notes, like the slow movements of Mozart concerti.

During this period, the Quintet had plenty of experiences out on the road. Sometimes the elements conspired to prevent us getting to where we were supposed to be. One night in the early 1960s, we were heading for the gymnasium at the University of California in Santa Barbara, but it rained all day, and by the evening a real storm had blown up. We battled through, but around eight o'clock, the time we were due on stage, we were still on the road, some miles away in Ventura. One of the guys in the band called ahead to say we expected to be about an hour late.

We finally got there just before nine, and we had to set up in front of a huge crowd of over one thousand students. Just carrying the instruments inside the gym, everyone got soaked, and there were no curtains, so we had to put everything together dripping wet in full view of the patient crowd. We set up fairly fast and began playing about a quarter after nine or so with our theme, *Lullaby of Birdland*.

The audience loved it, but I felt I had to apologize in some way for keeping them waiting. "That's not our style," I said. "And there is no excuse for it. The rain slowed us down a little, but really, it was entirely my fault. You see, tonight it was my turn to drive."

11

CLASSICAL CONCERTS

The first time I played a classical concert was in Rochester, New York, during 1952. Trixie had to calm me down with aspirin and hot milk before I went on. When I started doing them, I was always a nervous wreck before I played every symphony concert.

In jazz, you perform arrangements made by yourself, or someone in the band, or a proficient arranger, but in most cases these arrangements use technical devices that are thoroughly tried and tested by the performer. Classical music places very different technical demands on a pianist, which, as a jazz musician, one may or may not possess to an adequate degree. If you're not in possession of them, they have to be acquired, and it is a time-consuming job to acquire a degree of technical facility that you may not already have under your fingers. I had been playing classical transcriptions almost all my adult life, starting with Braille editions of Liszt, for example, when I was still at Linden Lodge, but there's a big difference between playing and practicing classical music on the domestic level to performing full-length pieces in public.

Back in the 1950s, when I first tackled it, it took me a couple of weeks of intensive work to learn the first movement of the Schumann Piano Concerto. It involved a level of technique which, at that time, I had never displayed publicly with any degree of consistency. That's to say, not nearly the consistency that I was able to achieve in jazz, because jazz is something I did every day.

Jazz consists of the type of arrangement I described plus improvisation, and even at the highest level of jazz, one tends to improvise within the limited scope of one's own technique. This is common sense, I think, so that you minimize the chances of getting technically too far out of your depth. But in classical music a good deal more discipline is required—every note really counts and the accuracy of playing is of prime importance. I'm not saying that you can get away with mistakes in jazz, but within the field of improvisation you're not half as worried as you are in the classical arena.

For one thing you can have a memory lapse very easily in classical music. One single movement of a concerto can take approximately twenty minutes to play, all of which has to be memorized. In jazz, since a lot of it is improvisation anyway, there's no one to say that you're playing it incorrectly. Whereas, in a classical piece written by a composer, everybody plays the notes written on the score. There's no improvisation allowed. When I began, I often felt that the classical critics were lying in wait for me, who was known as a jazz performer, to give a bad performance of a classical work. I once asked quite a well-known critic whether, if he heard a performance of a classical piece given by a proficient jazz musician, he would hear it with a completely unbiased opinion, and have the same kind of reaction that he would with a classical performer. And he said he didn't think he could.

So I accepted the view that most critics of classical music just could not hear and really accept a classical performance given by a jazz musician on level terms. This is why, throughout the 1950s and 1960s, I always maintained the redeeming factor of playing jazz in the second half of the program. But at the same time I decided that I would aim to perform classical music in public, as much as I was given the opportunity. I found that the more I did it, the more I got used to doing it, and the less nervous I became. I also got more practiced at preparation.

I remember giving a performance in Sacramento in the mid-1960s, for which I spent three or four days beforehand with a friend of mine in San Francisco, a professor at San Francisco State, Dr. Wendell Otey. Our preparation regime was a mixture of working on the Mozart Piano Concerto No. 20 in D-minor, K. 466, and tandem cycling through Golden Gate Park.

The way that man disciplined me during those few days really set me up for the performance. Obviously I had already learned the score, and given a good deal of time to it, but the way he disciplined me made sure I got all the romanticism out of it and played it as a work from the classical period, which really made all the difference in the world.

There was one incident while I was playing that same Mozart concerto at a concert in Buffalo, New York, quite recently. When I came offstage, my second wife Ellie, who was standing in the wings, asked me, "George, did you have a memory lapse?"

I said, "Only about thirty bars—how could you tell?"

"I noticed you were leaning towards port," she replied.

"I never touch the stuff . . ."

"Come on," she said, "You know what I mean."

And of course, she was right, I had been leaning in towards the orchestra on my left so that I could hear what chords they were playing and was able to improvise something in the style of Mozart until I got back in synch with the original composition. Probably only the conductor, Ellie, a few members of the orchestra, and I were really aware of what happened, although there are almost always a few really knowledgeable members of the audience at classical concerts, and I suspect some of them may have noticed. This kind of lapse is an absolutely terrible feeling, but it happens to the greatest. The famous story goes that in Carnegie Hall, Rachmaninoff and Heifetz were giving a recital when Heifetz had just such a memory lapse. So he sidled over to Rachmaninoff during their piano and violin sonata and hissed, "Where are we?"

And back came the answer, "In Carnegie Hall!"

Although I do have to work hard on preparing classical pieces, there are some big differences between the jazz world and the classical world that my friends in the classical domain can never quite get used to. One thing that really gets up the nose of the classical performer is the way that most jazzers can just fall out of bed, wander on stage, and come up with a program—just by improvising. A good example of this happened on one of the very few occasions when Ellie and I performed together. She is a mezzo-soprano, and while we were living in San Francisco in the mid-1970s, we did a benefit concert for St. Paulus Lutheran Church, which was our church at the time. She and her accompanist Russell Stepan were going to do the first half of the program. Ellie would open the concert with Rachmaninoff followed by a group of Lieder and some French art songs. Russell would close the first half with piano pieces by Brahms, Bach, and Rimsky-Korsakov. I would then do the second half of the program.

Well, in the couple of weeks or so leading up to the concert we went away on a short cruise, and all the time we were on the boat, Ellie was memorizing German and French lyrics, humming to herself, pulling out the printed music and so on—in other words doing the full classical-preparation bit. After a day or two she started asking, "What are you going to be doing?"

I answered, "I don't know. I haven't really thought about it."

So she said, "Well, you'd better start thinking because the concert's less than a couple of weeks away."

When we got back to our apartment, Russell started coming by every day to run through their part of the program, and again Ellie would ask, "George, have you decided what you're going to play, yet?"

"I still don't know—but don't worry, I'm getting it together."

"George, it's in three days!"

Then the day before the concert, and we were making our way to the hall for a sound check, when she asked me again. And I said, "Just about got it . . ."

Finally, we were in the car on the way to the concert, and she said, "George, you're on in approximately two hours, what are you going to play?"

I never did tell her.

Ellie opened the program with Rachmaninoff's *Vocalise*. When my turn came, I began with the same Rachmaninoff *Vocalise* that Ellie had sung in the first half, but my version rather quickly turned into *Love Is A Many Splendoured Thing*. One of the pieces Russell had played was the Brahms E-major *Intermezzo*, and so I continued with the selfsame Brahms intermezzo, but after a few bars it turned into *Taking A Chance On Love*. I eventually announced it as "Taking a Chance on Brahms." As Russell and Ellie sat in the front row, the nickel gradually dropped—*they* had planned my program! But this kind of last-minute invention just doesn't happen very often in the classical world, and many classical musicians find it annoying, possibly because they find it rather hard to do!

Nowadays I don't play classical music very much for fun. In fact I don't always go near the piano at home unless I'm working on something, and that's the same with both jazz and classical music. If I have a concert coming up, then I go to work on the music—usually a bit too late—but that's when I'll play classical music in the house. That's not to say I don't listen to it, or take an active interest in what's going on. Both in Manhattan and at Tanglewood during the summers, I get to a lot of concerts, and with a constant stream of visitors, there's always the chance to talk about matters classical.

One of the reasons I loved to do mixed classical and jazz programs was because I believed very strongly that both the classical and jazz worlds could benefit by this kind of concert. When I began doing them in the early 1950s, I think there was a real sense that concerts of this stature helped to "elevate" jazz in terms of its critical and audience reception. And as far as the classical side was concerned, it was often the opportunity to hear a symphony orchestra appearing for fun. In very practical terms, if two sides of the audience are well represented, two sides of the box office can be drawn.

Back when I started doing these mixed programs, I think only André Previn and Benny Goodman had done anything similar. Now, half a century later, the barriers that I felt were there in the 1950s have broken down a lot, making it possible for a whole range of performers such as Wynton Marsalis or Fred Hersch to play in both areas of the music at a very high level. I remember how much I used to wish that there were more jazz attractions who could do this, because I believed it was a very important phase, much more so than somebody writing an extended work for jazz combination and symphony orchestra. Such innovators were also very important, of course, but I was convinced that someone who could play Mozart or Rachmaninoff or Gershwin in the first half of the program and jazz in the second would help what was then the social position of jazz tremendously. Taking such action myself, and encouraging others, certainly helped to disprove the erroneous theories that many people held at the time that jazz could only be played by a bunch of degenerates in some cellar—and that such musicians should have no real education.

Over the years, I have played classical pieces with upwards of a dozen orchestras all round the United States. One of the most prestigious, with whom I did a tour of the California coast and several individual concerts, was the Boston Pops under Arthur Fiedler. He was a very humorous individual, and at the start of the tour he knew I was nervous about playing classical concerti with the orchestra. Just before we went on, he sidled up to me and said, "You know, George, I think it's time I changed my socks. I took them off last night, threw them at the ceiling, and they stayed there!" Then without more ado, he propelled me onto the platform and we went into a Mozart concerto.

That helped me relax, by having a laugh as we went on, and it was typical of Arthur to size up the situation and react accordingly. But there were some musical occasions where he was not quite so sympathetic. For example, the Quintet joined the orchestra to play an arrangement of *Scheherazade*, which is in five-four, with a very natural feeling of rhythm that goes "ONE-two-three-FOUR-five," in other words with the emphasis on the first and fourth beats of the bar. But Fiedler conducted it rigidly as "ONE-two-THREE-four five." This gave it a rather lop-sided, hurried feeling, so I said to him, "Maestro, I know you were in this business before I was born, but do you think I could have the accents on one and four?"

He said, "George, the horns come in on three, so I am emphasizing the three."

"I don't think the horn entry will make a lot of difference," I said. But it was a lost cause, so as I made my way back to the piano stool, I said to the Quintet, quietly, "Listen to me and *do not* watch him—if you do, you will come unstuck!" They followed me, in what was as natural a feeling of five as Paul Desmond and Dave Brubeck playing *Take Five*, which also stresses the first and fourth beats.

Such occasional disagreements aside, Arthur was good fun and good company, although his eating habits were somewhat inflexible. I remember once Ellie and I took him to Trader Vic's in San Francisco, a place that no longer survives today, but which, at the time, was the best Polynesian restaurant in town.

Arthur ordered matzoh-ball soup.

Ellie told me that there were immediate looks of consternation on the faces of the waiters. But they took the order, unusual as it was in a Polynesian restaurant.

Now right around the corner was David's Deli, which was famous for its matzoh-ball soup, and I don't know to this day if Trader Vic's sent a runner, but within a very short time the soup arrived. After a spoonful or two, Arthur asked the waiter, "When were these matzohs born?"

"This afternoon, sir."

"Is the mother doing all right?"

After this rather unusual meal, he came back to our apartment for a drink. It was the time when the Cuisinart food processor had just come on the market, and Ellie had one. Arthur followed her into the kitchen to see how it worked. He helped himself to Ellie's stock of carrots, and before long he had sliced, diced, and slivered bag upon bag of carrots, totally captivated with all the things the machine could do. But then that's hardly a surprise because Arthur was fascinated by all things mechanical, and in particular fire engines. I believe he was made an honorary member of the fire brigade in Boston as a result of his interest.

Coming back to the subject of music, I mentioned the Mozart Piano Concerto No. 20, K. 466, but I've also performed several other Mozart concertos, particularly No. 19 in F, K. 459, and No. 23 in A, K. 488. A particular favorite of mine is the Double Piano Concerto in E-flat, K. 365, which I first performed in the 1970s with Clara Siegel, who was a wonderful pianist and piano coach, based in Chicago. Normally I learn the Braille score, but in the case of the Double Concerto, I don't think one had been published at the time I wanted to play it, so Clara actually sent me a tape, and I learned the piece by ear from that. It's not really a method of learning that I'd recommend, because you have to have a very discerning ear, and you miss out on the subtleties that are generally marked on the Braille score—the phrasing and fingering.

I've learned a variety of other pieces, ranging from the Gershwin Concerto in F to Bach's D-minor Concerto, and pieces by Poulenc and Delius as well.

Traditionally, a classical soloist both in Europe and America never uses the score when playing publicly, but memorizes the entire part. The music of J. S. Bach makes the point as to why this is a particularly suitable practice for a blind musician. In my study at home, I have the scores for Bach's "Well-tempered Clavier." The sighted edition, which I have for visiting friends to use, is just two fairly small volumes, but my Braille edition is the size of six suburban phone directories. Volume one becomes three huge Braille scores, and so does volume two, so you can imagine how large the scores could be for some of the lengthy classical pieces I have played in concert.

One piece that was quite a challenge to learn was the *Concerto for Guitar and Jazz Piano* by the French composer Claude Bolling. The piece is included on my album *Across The Clock*, made in 1980 with Angel Romero, Ray Brown, and Shelly Manne. Nobody had ever produced a Braille edition of it, and although Claude Bolling had recorded the piece himself a year or two before I tackled it, instead of learning the music from his record I used the printed score, which Ellie played to me bar-by-bar until I had learned it entirely.

As I mentioned, J. S. Bach is still one of my favorite composers. As you go through life you realize that old Bach really knew what he was up to. He would make a two- or three-voice invention sound like a full piece—it might not cover the whole range of the instrument, it might not give the same impression of depth as a thirty-two-foot organ stop, but it would have its own beauty and simplicity. I think you have to grow old enough to appreciate that.

I also mentioned my collaboration with Gary Burton on *Out of the Woods*, which brought elements of Bach's baroque style to the Quintet. The way Gary came to join the group is quite a story. I've always been very reluctant to fire musicians. If a guy comes late several times, or uses bad language or other unprofessional behavior, I'll let him go, but for the most part I will not do anything to instigate the departure of a member of the band.

Gary Burton. (Mike Doyle/Symil Library)

When Gary applied for an audition, I told him I'd give him a chance, but I was naturally reluctant to replace my existing vibes player. He actually said, "You can't afford not to hear me."

He was right! He was really something, and I immediately thought when I heard him, "He's just got to be in the band." I'm very slow to fire anybody from a band, but in the event, I made space for him, he joined the group, and we became fairly close. Although we never hung out together, he learned enough Braille to write me little notes, and that was something I always appreciated. To be honest, I'm always overjoyed when a sighted person learns Braille, because it creates a whole level of personal communication that is otherwise denied, and it demonstrates a whole extra level of commitment when someone who doesn't have to learn it goes to the trouble to do so.

As I said, I had a fight with Capitol over doing an entire album of Gary's compositions. In those days recordings were plentiful, and they didn't worry too much about how they would sell something, because almost everything we recorded sold reasonably well. On some of our discs, they had put up the money to back the Quintet with a twenty-piece band or with twelve voices, and as I look back on it now, the time really does seem to have been what I described in the last chapter as a golden age of recording. However, despite the fact he had already done a couple of albums for RCA, Gary came into the band as a twenty-one-year-old unknown, and this was particularly true in terms of Capitol's view of him. So when, at my instigation, he wrote an entire album for the Quintet and four woodwinds, Capitol got cold feet. I had to battle hard to get them to proceed with it, because I knew what an exceptional musician he was.

It was a good group at the time, with Shelly Manne joining the rest of us for the studio sessions. Shelly never went on the road with us because he was in such demand as a session drummer, but he came in on all our Los Angeles recordings at the end of 1963 and beginning of 1964.

Gary had laid everything out very carefully, and he made a tape for me of exactly how he wanted me to play my parts. I had to work hard on the arrangements in order to learn everything because his concept was highly original and not all that easy or straightforward. I'd been used to working with top-flight arrangers like Abe Most, who was actually one of the woodwind players on the album, but Gary's work was just as good and it was such a joy to have him in the band. Also, although you might not realize it from his later work in which he has exclusively specialized on vibes or marimba, he was also a marvelous pianist. We played things like *Dialogue for Two Pianos*, a number that was partly written and partly improvised, and he certainly played a lot of piano!

I also played harpsichord on *Out of the Woods*. Overall, I think the harpsichord is quite limiting except to create a baroque sound. There are several sounds you can get from it, what with the different stops and manuals, but I prefer piano. Even though the harpsichord was around in Bach's day, I still prefer to hear his music played on the piano. My favorite interpreter of Bach is András Schiff.

During the same period as the recordings of Gary's compositions, I also recorded Quintet versions of music by Chopin and Grieg, one of which was an arrangement by Milt Raskin of *Solveig's Song* from Grieg's incidental music to *Peer Gynt*. That was on an album called *Old Gold and Ivory*, which Capitol marketed at the time by saying it "brings a modern burnish to timeless favorites." The favorites in question also included the theme from *Scheherazade* by Rimsky-Korsakov, *Variations on a Theme of Paganini*, and the *Ritual Fire Dance* by de Falla. In addition I included *In An English Country Garden* by the man I used to announce as "the Lone Grainger"—Percy Grainger. All these pieces were suitable for the Quintet to play in the other half of those concerts where I performed a classical concerto with an orchestra.

Quite apart from performing classical music, I've also had some very close friendships with various musicians in the classical community. The King's Singers in England recorded and gave concerts with me, and several of them became my good friends. Another was the French-horn player Barry Tuckwell, whom I got to know in the 1980s. We first met when he attended one of my concerts at the Barbican in London with my bassist Neil Swainson. Barry came backstage during the interval, we got into conversation, and I told him that I liked his Jerome Kern recording, on which he played *Long Ago and Far Away*. I noticed he was carrying his horn, having come from an earlier rehearsal.

"Why don't you come up and play it with us?" I asked him.

"I don't remember the tune," he replied.

"I'm sure you could, with a little help," I suggested.

Neil taught it to him in the intermission, or at least reminded him of it. And then we went onstage and played it.

"That's it," I said. "I think we're going to record together."

To my mind there's nothing more beautiful than a French horn nursing the interval of a seventh, and when I was working out the repertoire, the first song I thought of was *I've Got You Under My Skin*. Immediately I thought of a Schubert-like theme that I could use as a countermelody as he played Kern's tune, and it wound up with him doing the Schubertian theme while I played the tune. In the arrangement, I made sure he had plenty of sevenths to play!

When he came over to our apartment in New York for rehearsal, he didn't bring his horn. I gave him the parts that day, which was a Sunday, and he pencilled in notes to himself. He isn't a jazz musician, so although on the recording you can hear what sound like improvised choruses, I'd actually worked all of those out for him to play. Improvisation is not necessarily the long suit of the classical musician, but I was able to demonstrate to Barry how to play what I'd written so that it would sound spontaneous, as if it were being improvised. In any event, there was a lot of material for him to take in. We began recording on Monday, and his first wrong note was on Tuesday afternoon. What a professional! He was the height of perfection on what must rank as the most unreliable instrument in the brass family. It was great working with Barry, and he had the same certainty about everything he did that I found with Mel Tormé, when we played together. In French-horn terms, of course, Barry is in the same league as the great Dennis Brain, whom I heard in his prime, before his early death in the 1950s, or Dennis's father Aubrey, who was another very distinguished player.

Some classical musicians can handle improvisation. I remember one of the most exceptional was a blind organist by the name of Ed Jenkins at the Perkins Institute in Boston, to whom I gave a theme I'd worked out. I can remember that theme so clearly it's as if I'd just written it today, but I also recall that when I first wrote it I knew it would be good for a fugue. Sure enough, Ed improvised a prelude and fugue out of it. It was so convincing you'd think it had come from the old man Bach himself.

Another marvellous improviser whose name springs to mind is the Dr. Gerre Hancock, the Organist and Master of Choristers at St. Thomas Fifth Avenue in New York City. On one occasion when he came to my house for dinner, we sat at two pianos and improvised duets on various show tunes he knew. But Gerre is unequaled when he improvises at the organ during a church service. If he knows I'm in the congregation, he'll go out on a limb for three or four minutes between the verses of a hymn, which is a very long time in terms of a church service, and sometimes even I wonder how he is going to get back to the main theme. When he's successfully navigated his way back after a long excursion, Ellie will whisper, "So there!" into my ear, so I get the point that not all classical players are unable to improvise!

≡ 12 ≡

ELLIE

A life of constant touring does very little to preserve a marriage unless your wife is able to be with you most of the time. After Trixie's illness, she seldom accompanied me on the road, and instead she devoted her energies to running the office, to our publishing companies, and seeing that Wendy was properly brought up. Meanwhile, traveling remained an important part of my career, taking the Quintet's music to new audiences all over the United States and beyond.

Slowly but surely we drifted apart, and, in due course, inevitably, there was a divorce in the family.

Although I have often been asked what happened between me and Trixie, I really have nothing to say on the subject. I'd go along with the sentiments expressed in music by the great blues singer, Jimmy Witherspoon, along the lines of:

> *Last night we had eggs and bacon*
> *Today—ain't nothin' shakin'*
> *Ain't nobody's business what I do.*
>
> *If we spend all day havin' a fight,*
> *When we wake up nex' mornin', everything's all right*
> *Tain't nobody's business what we do.*

Suffice it to say that when you're lonely and traveling a lot, and you meet somebody very carefree and vivacious, that can be very dangerous to the established order of things.

In 1971, Trixie and I were living in Toluca Lake near Los Angeles. Our daughter, Wendy, and our housekeeper, Kitty Burns, were also living there. On Christmas Day, we were having a large luncheon party, and among the guests were Leonard Feather and his wife, Jane, Gene Webster, the producer of the radio series I had at the time, and Russell Stepan, a fine pianist. Russell had asked if he could bring a friend and I had told him that he certainly could.

Russell's friend turned out to be Ellie Geffert, a Lutheran minister's daughter who was born and raised in Harvey, Illinois, a suburb of Chicago. Russell and Ellie had studied piano with the same teacher, Ruth Alexander, at the American Conservatory in Chicago. Having known each other since the age of eight, they were old friends, and in many ways more like a brother and sister.

At lunch, I was at the head of the table with Russell on my left and Ellie on my right. Leonard was seated to the right of Ellie and so on down the table. Trixie, Wendy, and Kitty were at the other end. During dinner, it seemed that our end of the table was having more fun. I found out that Ellie was doing session work as a singer at the studios. She was one of thirty singers who had already done the soundtracks for *Finian's Rainbow*, *Star*, *Hello Dolly*, and *On a Clear Day*. To keep the wolf from the door, as she put it, she was also a substitute teacher in the Hollywood schools, teaching music and remedial reading.

After lunch, I wanted Ellie to hear a particular recording of Renata Tebaldi. Although Ellie worked as a session singer, her whole background was in the classical field. She had been the alto soloist with the Norman Luboff Choir and had sung under Erich Leinsdorf, Leonard Bernstein, Zubin Mehta and Lorin Maazel as a member of the New York Choral Artists. All of this work had been done with the New York Philharmonic.

Ellie watched as I crossed to my collection of LPs that ran floor-to-ceiling and wall-to-wall of the living room, which had a big roaring Christmas fire. I ran my fingers down the sides of about three albums and pulled out the one I wanted her to hear.

"Extraordinary", she thought.

What she didn't know is that I had Brailled the side of each album with the title and artist. I knew I had impressed her! However, I was still a married man and Ellie was dating others.

We didn't see each other for two years after that first meeting, at a time when I was passing through San Francisco, coming off a tour and on my way to a divorce. By then, Trixie and I had been married for 32 years but the traveling and long periods of time apart had taken its toll. Ellie happened to be visiting Russell and his partner, Ron Staeheli, who was a bassoonist with the Oakland Symphony. I called Russ and suggested that I take them all out to lunch at Sears, a San Francisco institution in the form of a small restaurant just up from the St. Francis Hotel on Powell Street. I understand that when Ellie was told about the invitation to dine at Sears, she quipped, "Where are we going to eat? In the Mail Order Department?" I was starting to get to know her sense of humor!

After a lunch of fresh raspberries, even though it was early spring, and wonderful dollar-size Swedish pancakes covered with real maple syrup, we returned to Russ and Ron's apartment. We sang and played for each other until about 5:00 when the doorbell rang. It was Tressa Lewis, a wonderful jazz singer who was to be my date for dinner. Tressa joined in the music-making and when I felt that it was time to take our leave, I asked if anyone knew of a restaurant where the two of us could get a nice dinner. At that point, Ellie's ecclesiastical background came to the fore and she came out with the name of *her* favorite place, Chez Michel. Later, she told me that that suggestion may have been very Christian of her but it was also very dumb. Here, another lady and George Shearing were having a wonderful dinner at her favorite restaurant!

The next morning, I called Ellie and asked her if she'd like to pick me up at the Bohemian Club, where I was staying. We'd have a drink at the St. Francis, a quick walk in Union Square and then I'd be on my way to Los Angeles. She accepted. By that time, I knew that I wanted to see her again but I didn't want to appear too eager.

We had our drink and our walk and then I thought the moment had come. So I asked if I could call her the next time I was in Los Angeles. I also told her that I didn't drink for the first forty-six years of my life and that, sometimes, just sometimes, if I was having a late drink in a lady's apartment, that I'd been known to fall asleep on the couch. I hurriedly added, "And you wouldn't like that, would you?"

To which she answered, "Why don't you try me?"

As they say, the rest is history!

The first time Ellie invited me to her apartment, it was after I had sent her three New York strip steaks from Kansas City, where I had played a concert. As a teacher, she had never seen steaks that thick—about 2 inches. When she called to thank me, I suggested that we share them and that, perhaps, *steak au poivre* might be nice.

"Absolutely," she retorted, "what a wonderful suggestion!"

Little did I know that when she put the phone down, she thought, "What the hell is *steak au poivre*?"

Being from the Midwest, her mother fried everything until it was well done. She didn't know that meat was any other color than gray!

One of Ellie's traits is that when your back is against the wall, you do some research. So from her extensive collection of cookbooks, she found the recipe in Vincent Price's *A Treasury of Great Recipes*.

Saved!

But I was arriving on Friday and this was already Wednesday night! Undaunted, Ellie called her dear friend, Florence Gabrielsen.

Florence was a spry 84-year-old former home economics teacher who always kept a bottle of champagne chilling in her fridge. The call came through from Ellie and Florence was on her way . . . champagne and all. When she arrived, the bottle was uncorked, a couple glasses of the bubbly downed and the cooks were at the ready. Florence read the recipe and Ellie cooked. They, of course, split the third steak I had conveniently supplied.

Friday evening arrived as did I—with a 1959 Chateau Lafitte Rothschild. When Ellie saw the bottle, she exclaimed that the cork alone was probably worth $5! She told me that the recipe for the steak was an old family recipe, one that had been in her family for years. I have since found out that minister's daughters can fib better than anyone else! But, I must admit that it was definitely an "MM" or, as Ellie put it, a "memorable meal".

By then I had obtained a divorce and we started dating seriously. In 1975, we finally decided to get an apartment together in San Francisco. We set up housekeeping in the top two floors of a wonderful Victorian townhouse on Presidio Avenue between Washington and Jackson. While we were living there, we were invited to a party in Toluca Lake at the house of my old neighbors, Bob and Dolores Hope.

Ellie and Bob were talking and she mentioned where we were living. Now, Bob knew that we weren't married and said in his most shocked tones, "Ellie, do you mean to tell me that you're living in sin?"

"No!" she replied, without missing a beat, "in San Francisco!"

I learned that Ellie could handle herself in any situation. After the Bob Hope incident, my longtime friends in San Francisco, Bill and Dickey Quayle, finally gave me the push to think seriously about marrying this minister's daughter from Harvey, Illinois. Bill was a fellow member of the Bohemian Club and they invited us to join them for the Spring Picnic at the Grove, where the summer encampment convenes every July. It's a beautiful setting in acres and acres of redwood trees along the Russian River, north of San Francisco.

Traditionally, the wives are in charge of the potluck meal. Despite not being a wife yet, Ellie still volunteered to prepare the starter or *hors d'oevres*, a liver paté, the recipe for which had come straight out of the pages of *Gourmet* magazine. Ellie is no slouch in the kitchen and, being another Leo, was not afraid to show off her culinary artistry.

The table was set, the wine was poured, knives and forks were at the ready. Ellie proudly presented her paté to a round of applause. Bill Quayle offered to slice and serve it for her. Knife in hand, Bill attempted to make the first slice. Being a true Bohemian gentleman, he tried again . . . and again . . . and again. But to no avail. The paté was as hard as a brick!

Bill, always helpful in a crisis, then suggested that, perhaps, the beloved paté could be used as a doorstop!

A few days later, I was visiting the Quayles on my own. They owned a beautiful home on Broadway, overlooking the yacht club and the Golden Gate Bridge. Their living room was on the top floor and, to reach it, one could either take the elevator or climb the outside stairs. Bill and Dickey loved dogs, and at that time, they owned Clydesdale, a blonde labrador retriever with paws as big as the hooves of the famous draft horses—hence the name.

Now, Clydesdale had a problem. He was notorious for the degree of flatulence that he seemed to harbor at all times and which was to be avoided at all costs. Somehow, Clydesdale knew I was blind. And, being a helpful sort of creature, would lead me up those stairs farting silently, but wagging his tail to be certain that I knew where he was!

It was this particular visit to the Quayles that gave me the push to propose to Ellie. As soon as I walked through the door, both Bill and Dickey said, "If you let that one go, you're crazy!"

It was then that I remembered that Ellie had told me that she had four Lutheran ministers in her family—her father, brother, uncle and grandfather. And, I remembered her joking that because of all these clergy, all the services were free to the family . . . weddings, funerals, baptisms and confirmations. I liked the arrangement.

So, early in 1983, on a flight from Salt Lake City to New York, where we had moved in 1978, I suddenly asked if we could get to Salzburg, Austria via Chicago. Ellie had attended the Music Festival there a couple of times and always thought that I would enjoy it. She thought how wonderful it was that I should finally show some interest in attending. But why go via Chicago when we already were living in New York? She took out the map in the flight magazine and put my finger on New York and then moved it to the left where I could "see" where Chicago was.

Why go west to go back east, as it were?

Well, I kept insisting on going via Chicago until she got so frustrated that she blurted out, "But, George, why do you insist on going from Chicago when it's so far out of the way?"

Smiling, I answered, "So your brother can marry us free!"

Ellie and I were married on 28 July 1984 in Trinity Lutheran Church in Harvey, Illinois where her father had served as senior pastor for 52 years and where Ellie had been a Sunday School teacher and organist in her younger years. Her brother, Melvin Geffert, officiated and Dr. Oscar Remick gave the homily.

Her oldest and dearest friend, Audree O'Connell, was her matron-of-honor and Ed Fuerst served as my best man. About 30 people attended, just family and close friends. Afterward, the delicious wedding luncheon was served at Les Nomades, a private eating club in Chicago.

Then it was off to New York and on to Salzburg and the start of a still-exciting life together.

I once asked Ellie about what she regarded as the most "memorable meetings" of my friends in the business. The first she recalled, from before we left San Francisco, was Joe Williams, the singer.

I think the first time I heard Joe must have been when he was singing in Chicago with Jay Burkhardt's band in the late 1940s. Then in the mid-50s, of course, he joined Basie, and from time to time the Quintet toured with the Basie band, so I got to know several of them very well: Marshal Royal, Freddie Green, and—of course—Joe. Eventually, in 1971, I asked him to record with me for my own Sheba label. I loved the purity of his voice and his feeling for the blues. One way or another over the years I worked quite a lot with Joe to the extent that we built up a great rapport, which was demonstrated the very first time he met Ellie. She'd heard of Joe, but she'd never actually met him until the day he came to call.

To reach our apartment one had to climb a long flight of stairs on the outside, followed by another set of stairs on the inside. Joe came up these stairs towards the door that led into our foyer. As he reached the top, it happened that I was sitting at the piano in the living room, and when I heard him hit the final step, I played a chord. Without a pause, still with his raincoat on, Joe turned towards Ellie and sang *Come Sunday* to her, slowly, and beautifully. She was completely speechless, with this marvelous voice singing directly to her, all on the basis of that one opening chord.

When he finished, I said, "Ellie! I'd like you to meet Joe Williams!" But he'd already made his introduction in the most perfect way possible.

Shortly after that, Joe and I did a long concert tour together for Columbia Artists. It involved a lot of traveling around the United States, and the road manager decided that it would be more efficient and easier for us to travel by bus to the next venue after each concert. We would check in to a hotel in the morning, giving us the chance to sleep until it came close to the time of that evening's show. It wasn't the most comfortable way of getting about, although we did avoid a lot of traffic, and we got from place to place about as quickly as possible. However, Joe made those journeys particularly memorable, because just before we set off he used to order a huge quantity of popcorn, and as the bus roared through the night to wherever we were going, he and I would sit and share a bucket of popcorn and talk until the small hours about times gone by, the people we'd met and the music we'd heard. We often worked together again in the years that followed.

Another musician who was also on that long tour with us was Joe Pass, who had played guitar in the Quintet during the 1960s. I admired and always will admire Joe's playing. But even more I admired the way that he pulled himself out of what you might call the "junk-heap." He had been a mainliner, hopelessly dependent on drugs, and he had really hit rock bottom. When I first heard about him in the early 1960s, he was in rehab at Synanon in Southern California, under the care of a remarkable man by the name of Chuck Dederich. One of the newspapers once said that Chuck "had the battered face of a professional wrestler, the soul of a philosopher and the command presence of a combat general." He was certainly a powerful personality, although in later years, he attracted a lot of criticism when Synanon turned from a self-help collective into a kind of cult. However, when Joe was there, under Chuck's guidance it was a very positive experience, helping addicts to use their talents and skills to survive in a drug-free environment. Joe later told me that when he arrived there, he literally crawled in through the door with all that he had left in the world—thirty-seven cents and his guitar.

With Joe Williams. (Author's collection)

Joe's skills as a guitarist were what he used to survive, and in due course he attracted quite a bit of attention for some discs he made while he was still at Synanon. At that time, I was living in Toluca Lake and I needed a new guitarist, so I went and asked Chuck about him, and he said, "George, Joe's getting on all right, and he's behaving pretty well at present. Give me a year, and I think he'll be ready."

So I gave him a year, after which I went back to see Joe, and he joined the Quintet. He was always impeccable, and stayed with the band for three years from 1965–68. He was free of his habit when he joined us and never once slipped back for the rest of his life. But this wasn't an end to our drug-related problems, and I recall that on one occasion Joe took me aside and strongly advised me to part company with Bob Whitlock, who played bass in the Quintet for some of the time that Joe was with us.

Matters had come to a head shortly before that discussion, when Bob called me one night to ask if he could come over and see me. I agreed, but almost as soon as he arrived at the house, he broke down in tears, sobbing, "I'm on drugs, man!"

I said, "So, you're on drugs. What are you going to do about it?"

He stopped crying and began to think about what he was going to do. Later I discovered that he had been forging my name at the pharmacy to get drugs, but at the time I was unaware of that, and I kept him on. It was at that point Joe Pass came to me and said, "Man, you know what this guy's doing?"

"Yes," I said, "but I don't know if he's got your strength. We'll find out."

"Let him go," said Joe. "Because by paying him, you are supporting his habit, and he has got to know what it's like, as I found out, when you are down to your last penny. You must let him go and let him get down into the gutter, for his own good."

As it turned out, I didn't fire Bob and he was still recording with our group as late as 1968. Eventually he left, and worked around the Los Angeles area. I later heard that he dropped out of the music scene for a while in the mid-70s to check into a rehabilitation center. In due course, he went back to his old academic career at U.C.L.A., where he worked for some years, before setting up his own computer company.

Ellie and I have always enjoyed puns as well as the kind of practical joke that goes back to my first experiences of pranks from my time at Linden Lodge and in the various bands I played in during the war. One of the first dreadful puns I really laid on Ellie was when we went to England together for the first time. We were staying at the Berkeley Hotel, and one morning she looked out of the window and it was a beautiful sunny day. Not long before, I'd introduced her to Walter Crombie, an old friend whose family had a jewelry store in Bond Street in London, and somehow the bright sunlight put her in mind of all the sparkling jewels. So she said, "It's a beautiful day outside—I think I'll call Walter and order my tiara!"

"Well," I said, "if you're going to do that, you'd better hurry up and do it, because he's going to sell a number of those today."

"Really?"

"Yes. He'll sell more of those today than on any of the other three hundred and sixty-four days of the year."

"Really?"

She said, "Why's that?"

"Ellie, don't you know? There's a tiara boom today!"

One pun I laid on Eddie Monteiro, the accordionist who worked with the singer Nancy Marano, comes from a later visit to England when Ellie and I were spending the summers in our little cottage in the Cotswolds. I was talking to Eddie on the phone, and I told him how the cows in the field by the cottage used to come right up to the windows. "So one day," I told him, "I asked them which Duke Ellington composition they liked best, and they 'Mooed Indigo'!"

"George!" said Ellie. "That's a four groan conclusion!"

One factor in my life from some time before I met Ellie was that this was the one period when I had a guide dog. His name was Leland, Lee for short, a beautiful golden retriever.

I had Lee for about ten years, and as a matter of fact I traveled with him quite a bit. Soon after he arrived, Trixie came with me on one of my longer trips, when we went to Japan, but Lee was

With Lee, late 1960s. (Author's collection)

with me too. He seemed to have a second sense about when the plane was taking off or landing. He'd put his head on my left knee as if to say, "Well, Buddy, we're on the way, now!" or "We're about to come in to land!"

He was a marvelous companion with a great temperament. By the time I got him, it seemed as if I'd always had dogs as pets. For a long time, Trixie and I had had two boxers called Major and Minor, and I used to joke to her that all we needed in addition was a miniature poodle, so we could call him Diminished.

I'd never had a guide dog before Lee, and I've never had one since. You could say that when I married Ellie I married my guide, but we've never again had a dog.

I got Lee in 1962 from Guide Dogs for the Blind in San Rafael, California. I trained with him for one month but, before I got him, Lee had been in training much longer. When he was eight weeks old, Lee was given over to a Puppy Raiser to live with the family until he was about fourteen to eighteen months old. While living with the family, Lee had been observed daily as to how he reacted to family situations, such as a baby, children, and other everyday experiences. The Puppy Raiser adhered to the strict diet for the dog provided by Guide Dogs and made sure that he was immaculately groomed.

About the time that Lee was eighteen months old, he went back to the Guide Dog campus. The resident veterinarian gave him a thorough examination to make sure that he was in fine physical shape. Of course, the dogs are all neutered for obvious reasons. And then, Lee began his formal training with a professional trainer. This lasted another four to five months. Now, he was ready to meet his new master.

I arrived on campus and was warmly greeted by the staff. I was shown my room which I shared with another student and then taken around the rest of the facility. For the next three days I worked with "Juno" who was actually a human trainer. He played the part of the dog receiving my commands and giving instruction when I failed to convey my commands clearly.

Then it was "Dog Day," the day I actually was introduced to Lee and the bonding began. The trainer described Lee to me and told me about his personality. I wish I could have told Lee about mine! But he learned quickly enough.

Then the real work began. We began walking with the dogs just around the campus. I can remember one very serious reprimand that Lee got one day when we walked in the dining room for lunch. We were headed for a table when a trainer said, "Mr. Shearing, step aside. Lee, NO!"

I heard him clout Lee and felt the dog go sprawling across the floor. He then explained that it had taken years to get a law passed that would enable us to bring guide dogs into any restaurant. Lee had put his head on one of the tables where the food was. The trainer said that if the dog did that in public, the law that they had worked so hard to be enforced would be rescinded. I understood. Lee never put his head on a table again.

Our next step was to take a Guide Dog bus into San Rafael and learn about crossing streets and finding our way from Point A to Point B. There was always a trainer with us but not necessarily next to us. They would oftentimes be a step or two behind but at the ready to help if we got into trouble.

When we graduated to working in downtown San Francisco, my heart was in my throat! Now, we had to learn about stairs and escalators, revolving doors and public transportation. I remember having to negotiate the crowded and cluttered streets of Chinatown and I will never forget the day I could feel the wind in my face as Lee and I walked across the Golden Gate Bridge together.

What an exhilarating experience!

For the first time in my life I felt the independence that sighted people must feel but take for granted. It was wonderful.

You might ask, "What happens to the Puppy Trainers when, on Graduation Day, they hand over these now-grown-up dogs who had lived with them and their families all those months?"

There might be some tears, of course, but not for long, because Guide Dogs soon delivers another squirmy, cuddly little 8-week old puppy. This way sadness is replaced quickly with another happiness.

I had Lee for ten years. During this time, my good friend Bob Newhart told a true story about Lee and me on national television.

To this day, he still tells it on his personal appearances and just last year he told it while I was in the audience for an appearance he made in Prescott, Arizona. I simply cannot resist sharing it with you.

I was on a flight from Los Angeles to New York. In those days, there was always a fuel stop somewhere in the Midwest. We landed in Chicago and, during the time of refueling, the passengers usually left the plane to stretch their legs. Remember, this was in the days when one walked down stairs that were rolled up to the exit. I remained inside the plane with Lee tucked under my seat, chatting with the passenger next to me. After a time, the pilot came back and asked if I'd like him to take Lee for a walk. I agreed, thanked him and gave him the dog. About fifteen minutes later, my seat partner commented that about 40 or 50 people seemed to be milling around the bottom of the stairs, reluctant to get back on the plane because they saw the pilot with a guide dog!

When I was performing, Lee would oftentimes come on stage with me. He would lie under the piano until it was time to take a bow at the end of the show. Then, he'd come over next to me and take his bow as I took mine. I also wrote *Lee's Blues* for him, a song which had the lyric, "You ain't nothin' but a guide dog . . ."

But, working with puppies can also be embarrassing! Some years ago, PBS wanted to make a documentary film in which I would tour the Guide Dog facility in San Rafael and talk about my experience there. The film was called *Out of the Shadows, Into the Sun*. One scene was shot in the "puppy play yard," a large, grassy rectangle where the little puppies could run and play. Around the enclosure were some ten people, Ellie included, each holding an eight-week-old golden retriever under each arm. The cameras were all set up and whirring away. I was kneeling alone in the center of the play yard. At a given signal, all the puppies were let loose. I clapped my hands and they all came scrambling up to me. I picked one up, caressed it, petted it and, holding it very close to my face said, "Oh, you cute little doggie. One day, are you going to be my guide dog?"

Unfortunately, I was talking up the tail-end of the dog!

For some reason, that part of the scene was cut from the documentary but we got hold of the 27-second film clip. About two weeks later, I appeared on the *Today* show. We told the producer about the clip and he asked if he could use it on the show. So, nationwide, I appeared talking up the wrong end of a dog! The audience roared and the switchboard lit up like a Christmas tree with watchers screaming with laughter.

I was very fond of Lee, but eventually he passed on. Looking back on it now, I tend to feel that in some respects, having a guide dog is a bit like carrying a white cane—it's an advertisement of blindness. Maybe that's because I've lived for so long in Manhattan. Certainly in Toluca Lake in the 1960s and early 70s, having Lee was a boon, because with him I was able to walk independently around the neighborhood because he knew his way around the streets in all directions. We had a regular walk round a long block, which began by going from my house on Navajo up Toluca Lake Avenue, making a right on Foreman, and heading up to Riverside Drive, which is where most of the local stores were, like the drugstore and cleaners. With Lee, I could run all my own errands to those stores, which gave me plenty of independence.

The guide dog world led to some interesting meetings. I attended many gatherings with folks who raised funds to assist in the training of dogs (and their owners). I also got to know Betty Ford, the wife of President Gerald Ford. Ellie and I were having a private tour of the White House. Betty Ford got word that we were there while she was in the helicopter flying back from attending a ballet performance in New York. She sent a message asking if we would please wait until she arrived. We did and Betty met us in the Map Room. Soon joining us was Liberty, the Fords' golden retriever, who proceeded to lick my face from chin to forehead in one go. We later heard that one of Liberty's puppies had been sent to guide dog school and was now working with a blind man in Canada.

Talking about presidents, I was going to perform at the Cheltenham Jazz Festival one summer. Of course, the local Cotswold paper wanted my bio and picture for publicity. Ellie dutifully took the story and picture to their local office and told them to just print the bio as written without changing a word. They agreed. However, the editor decided to show his or her knowledge of American presidents. When the story ran, in the part where it told about the three presidents for whom I had played at the White House, instead of printing it as Ellie had written it: "Mr. Shearing has played for three presidents, Ford, Carter and Reagan," it read "Mr. Shearing has played for three presidents, Jimmy Carter, Ronald Reagan and Henry Ford."

I was often asked by Guide Dogs to attend cocktail parties that were fundraisers for them. Of course, Lee was the real star and showed off his ability to take me diagonally from one corner of the room to the other, guiding me around chairs and tables laden with glasses and plates. On one occasion, Lee as ever performed this task admirably. However, later on in the party, one of the guests came up to me and asked, "Did you know that, half way across the room, Lee turned his head slightly to the left and, without missing a step, took a big slurp out of someone's martini?"

I hope it didn't have too much vermouth!

Jimmy Carter was the most relaxed of the three presidents for whom I played. He would chat to Ellie with his arm on the back of her chair, very informal and pleasant, and he was quite a jazz enthusiast. I got to know Ronald Reagan a little better, because we were both members of the same club in San Francisco, the one I mentioned before where I'd introduced Ellie's accompanist, called the Bohemian Club. Now that sounds like somewhere that caters for a bunch of badly dressed artistic slobs—but in fact it is exactly the opposite, and it's frequented by very successful businesspeople, not to mention musicians and politicians. I met Reagan there when he was still more famous as an actor, but his life changed when he became first the Governor of California and later President. I played for him at the White House, and when he came across to thank me, I said, "I'll see you at the Grove next summer."

He turned to his guests and said, "George just told me he hoped to see me at the Grove. That's the Bohemian Grove in San Francisco, and it's a club where I was allowed to go before I got this job! But now, what with security men and so forth,

I've become a group, not an individual, so much as I like it, I can't go back there until I've stopped being a group!"

He was quite right, as apparently the Club prevents serving Presidents from going there because of the invasion of privacy caused by such an influx of people, not to mention the threat to security that is caused.

The name of the Bohemian Club has come up once or twice so far in this chapter, and I ought to say a little more about it. As I've mentioned, it is the opposite of the image its name suggests. Its membership consists of distinguished individuals from the arts, science, business, finance, and government. I was introduced to it by a friend from the financial world, Bud Keaton, who was my sponsor when I was put up for membership. It's an all-male club, although women are welcomed as guests at various functions at the city club such as art shows, concerts, and dinners, as well as at the family picnic each spring at its summer home, the Grove, on the Russian River. When Trixie and I separated, I went to the Club's main home in San Francisco to live. It's a very pleasant residence, a landmark building on Taylor, between Post and Sutter, and Lee and I spent some time there, when we were not on the road with the Quintet. It was less easy to take Lee to the Grove, because the other members, who went there to relax away from the city, tended to spoil him, by giving him hunks of bread or biscuits, which is not the way to treat a guide dog. I used to plead with them not to do this, but some of them thought they were being kind, and carried on slipping him treats in secret—which was the quickest way to destroy his health and well-being.

That apart, the Grove was the most pleasant place to stay, not least because among the members were several very good amateur musicians. Bud Keaton himself was a clarinet player, and there were several other highly competent woodwind players, so it was not unusual to wake up in the morning to the sound of Haydn or Mozart chamber music being played by an *ad hoc* collection of players. This would entertain all of us, and at various times, when the Grove Encampment was well attended, this could mean several hundred people, during the summer encampment.

I said earlier that after Lee, I didn't have another guide dog, but that Ellie has become my guide, and that has been true since the moment we started to be together. To show her how much I appreciated her guidance, I bought her a little dog bone on a chain, all made out of solid gold. But quite early on in our relationship, she almost had to turn it in.

We were going to meet my attorney in a particular restaurant on Melrose in Hollywood, and it was at a time when Ellie used to drive me about in her little Volkswagen. We duly arrived, went in together and sat down at a table, where we ordered a nice bottle of wine. My attorney is one of those people who is always spot on time, but to start with, we thought nothing of it when he was a little late. But then half an hour passed. Then forty-five minutes. We had had a couple of glasses of wine each, when it finally dawned on Ellie that the restaurant we were supposed to be in was three blocks further down. So she called and discovered that the attorney had been patiently waiting at the other place. When she confessed to the maitre d', he said it was such a good story that the wine would be on him.

The next night, she took me back to the restaurant we'd gone to by mistake, and throughout the evening they kept asking us, "You are supposed to be here tonight, aren't you?"

When we eventually moved to Manhattan, the apartment Ellie and I came to in 1978 was a marvelous find, and I expect to end my days there. This is because it's the perfect place for a one-pair-of-eyes family. Although we spent our summers for fifteen years in England, or more recently in the Berkshire Hills in rural Massachusetts, close to Tanglewood, when we leave New York for the summer we have to leave together. It's not as if one of us can just pop back to the apartment. Where we go, we go as a couple. But during those times of the year when we're based in the apartment in New York, it gives me a considerable amount of independence. I can go out from there to drop a letter in the mail, or I can leave packages with the doorman to give to the mailman, and everything you need can be delivered to the door, whether it's six gallons of bottled water or greengroceries, or a bunch of flowers. Overall,

With Ellie. (Author's collection/Richard Avedon)

it's a very convenient place for a blind man and a sighted woman to be living.

I think I've worked more consistently since I've been there, too. The Café Carlyle is not too many blocks away, and even the Village is not much more than twenty minutes drive. There's a real focus to life, and in particular to musical life, in Manhattan, and with that extra degree of independence, it means that, for example, I can go out with a friend, or visit a radio studio on my own, and then come back and let myself into the apartment, if Ellie's out. Or the doorman calls up to the apartment for her to let me in if she's there. With a 24-hour-a-day doorman, things can be delivered any time, and it's another bonus for me that when something arrives for me, I can have them bring it up and meet me at the elevator, which is all part of being as independent as possible.

≡ 13 ≡

TWO BODIES—ONE MUSICAL MIND

In 1977 I began to feel that I was coming to the end of a phase with the Quintet. How many times was it possible to play *September in the Rain*? After all, by then I'd been playing it almost every night for over twenty-five years, and I began to feel a bit like a typecast Shakespearean actor. You know the kind I mean—the leading man who only ever performs a very small number of different plays because he's so popular in the roles he has made famous. Imagine playing Hamlet every night for ten years!

To start with, he might have said, with even intonation, "To be or not to be, that is the question."

Five years later, he had developed to the point where he was saying, "To be or not to be, *that* is the question."

And a little later on it had become, "To be or not to *be* . . ."

There are many classical musicians who find themselves similarly trapped by their repertoire, and the changes they make are often this kind of small adjustment of nuance or detail. But a jazz player ought not to be trapped in this kind of way.

As I said earlier, I tried to ring the changes by varying the treatment of all my most popular numbers, but ultimately with the Quintet arrangement of *September in the Rain*, more often than not I ended up playing it more or less the same way every night, because that's the way that audiences can sing along with you.

What brought it home to me that I had become caught in this trap was when I was in a shop close to my home, and the girl behind the counter asked, "Are you George Shearing?"

I said, "Yes, I am."

And she turned away towards the other girl in the store, who obviously didn't know her music so well, and said, "You know! George Shearing . . ." and then she sang a few bars of the song.

I thought to myself, if she sings it like that, and knows my phrasing so well, that's all that everyone who's ever heard it really wants to hear. And I recognized that I was on automatic pilot most of the time, playing in a way that was almost the exact opposite of all my instincts as a jazzer and an improviser.

As it happened, I came to this realization at a time when there was a real economic crunch going on in the music business, particularly for those of us who believed in and were identified with a certain form of music. With the explosion of the pop and rock industry that had taken place during the 60s and early 70s. I had remained relatively insulated from falling sales or dwindling audiences, but now there was no doubt that it made economic sense to go down to just bass and piano.

In many of the articles and reviews that were written at the time, you might have got the impression that the Quintet just suddenly stopped one day. In fact, it was a much slower process than that. I made the announcement that I was going to discontinue the group in the fall of 1977, but the way bookings work so far in advance, I was already obliged to take the Quintet on a Community Concerts tour early the following January, and there were to be other reunions during the course of that year. I remember telling Whitney Balliett that on our final tour we did fifty-six concerts in sixty-three days, and I think that finally did me in, as far as the Quintet was concerned.

From some time before we disbanded, it is true that all my attention, and most of the attention of the journalists who wrote about me, was focused on my duo with bassist Victor Gaskin, and we put ourselves on the map, so to speak, with a nine-week season at the Carlyle Hotel in New York, once the New Year tour with the Quintet was over at the start of 1978. A little later that year we were featured on a jazz cruise to the West Indies, alongside Dizzy Gillespie's quintet and the Thad Jones-Mel Lewis band.

Playing as a duo with Victor allowed me to play a different role from anything I'd done for a long time. I became less a leader and more of a pianist again, and I felt I was once more getting to grips with real creative possibilities. I could explore the piano as a much more complete instrument, instead of playing those block

On the road with the Quintet: Larry Blackshere (vibes); Rusty Jones (drums); Andy Simpkins (bass); and Earl Klugh (guitar). (Author's collection/Columbia Artists)

At the Capital Jazz Festival, London, in the late 1970s. (Mike Doyle/Symil Library)

chords in harmony with the vibes and guitar. The more people you have on the stage, the more structured your work gets, and the more structured it is, the more it tends to be played the same way all the time. It was only after I'd changed to mainly working in the duo format that I realized how little enthusiasm I'd had for the Quintet in latter years, because it only allowed me a very limited range of possibilities to keep that enthusiasm riding high. Now, the economy of sound of the duo, and the freedom from what I had begun to feel were musical fetters, rekindled my enthusiasm to a remarkable degree, and I felt I had a new source of creative energy.

I've shared that with all my bassists over the years, but particularly Victor Gaskin, Don Thompson, and for over a decade now, Neil Swainson. There was an added dimension to my work with Don, because he was a very fine pianist, and from time to time he'd put the bass down, and we'd play something at two pianos, or he'd take a solo at the keyboard. I could almost have had a whole band with Don on his own, because he also played excellent vibes, and quite passable drums! He's a very talented man, a good writer and arranger, who's led several of his own groups in his native Canada including a very original nine-piece band, plus working for a long time with Rob McConnell's Boss Brass. Like a lot of the most talented musicians, he's very modest about his abilities, and doesn't really flaunt what he has—in other words, although he is a consummate musician, he doesn't spend all day telling you about it. He was a good duo partner from 1982 until 1987, with all the qualities that I look for, which are basically those of a Ray Brown. Because Ray was one of the first bassists I played with when I came to the United States, sitting in with him, Ella, and Hank Jones, he set a standard that I have always seen as the benchmark.

Forty years after first meeting Ray, we recorded an album together in 1987, with Marvin "Smitty" Smith on drums, called *Breakin' Out*. They both played really well, but Ray—however good he sounded, and however concentrated he was on making music—always had his mind on practical matters as well. At one point in the session, he motioned to Ellie, who was in the control

The duo with Don Thompson. (Author's collection)

A tandem ride with Neil Swainson. (Author's Collection)

booth, and stuck his hand in his mouth, meaning, "I think he's forgotten about lunch!" He was right. I would have gone on all day, not least because it's always been my instinct to get everything possible done while you are all in the right frame of mind, really focused, and able to get the most out of the situation. Talking of getting a lot out of a situation, on that session I was very impressed with Marvin "Smitty" Smith, because he was willing and able to change his normal way of playing to match up exactly to mine. That's a test of musicianship, which he passed with flying colors.

As well as launching my first duo with Victor Gaskin in 1978, there was another creative highlight on the horizon, the start of my partnership with Mel Tormé.

I first met Mel when I went along to hear him at a club during the time I was living in San Francisco. But we didn't work together until some years later, in 1976, when George Wein presented Mel with Gerry Mulligan and me, plus an all-star band at Carnegie Hall. With the success of that meeting in mind, it wasn't long after breaking up the Quintet that I started working regularly with Mel. I'm not sure that when George first had the idea of putting us together, he realized just how long our association was going to last. We made a lot of recordings and concerts together over the years that followed.

Mel and I worked as a duo, as well as with Donny Osborne, his drummer, and my bass player, either Don or Neil, so this meant we were on the road together for quite a while as a quartet. Nonetheless, we thought so similarly in terms of music that we clicked together whatever the setting, from a duo right up to a big band. By the time of the Carnegie Hall concert, I'd been a great fan of Mel's for several years, and I used to go and hear him every time he was around in New York if I wasn't working. So when the opportunity came up to work with him regularly, I couldn't wait to take it.

Both Mel and I felt that we were one musical mind contained in two separate bodies. He is the only person I've ever worked with where I always knew we could go on stage and do a show at the very highest level, without any rehearsal at all. It really was a case of having one musical mind. For example, our favorite composer was Frederick Delius, whose work we both loved, and I'd often throw in a little quote or an allusion, and Mel would take it all in his stride, often just letting me know with a phrase or a sequence of notes that he'd noticed and was returning the favor. One number we used to do was *It Might As Well Be Spring*, and I think the moment we both discovered that we knew our way round Delius's music was when I worked in a little quotation from *Brigg Fair*. Mel came right back at me with the next phrase.

This Delius thing went on and on, and each of us often sent over tapes of pieces or performances we thought the other would like, but the most memorable example of it came about on the occasion of Ellie's fiftieth birthday.

She and I had been out on the road, and we came back to visit her favorite restaurant, which was called the Box Tree. I didn't want her to know that I'd hired the whole place for the night, so when we got home from the tour, I said to her, "Look, I'm very tired from all this traveling. I know it's not much of a fiftieth birthday present, but is it all right if I take you to the Box Tree?"

"That's wonderful," she said.

During the couple of days between getting home and her actual birthday, I'd disappear out of the door with my secretary from time to time. Ellie was a bit puzzled about what I was up to, but she little suspected that I was rehearsing a six-piece choir in a special happy-birthday fanfare that I'd written for her.

On the day itself, I had the neighbors come in, and David and Sara Hadden, who had been invited to the party. Sara said she couldn't stay long, as she was being taken to the theater.

Ellie asked her what she was going to see, and she told her, *Children of a Lesser God*. "You'll love it," said Ellie, "It's a wonderful play. John Rubinstein was terrific!" She left, but as the door closed behind her, Ellie suddenly said, "Something's going on. That play closed three months ago!"

I somehow kept a straight face, and then I said, "It's nearly six, we'd better get ready for the limousine to pick us up."

"What limousine?"

"I can't have any fifty-year-old woman hailing a cab on the street."

When we rang the bell of the restaurant, the first inkling Ellie had that something was going on was when she saw Marvin Fisher, the composer of *When Sunny Gets Blue*, dressed in a suit and tie. Marvin always spent the entire weekend on Long Island and this was Sunday. As she rounded the corner, she saw friends from California, New York, people she had worked with in theater, and her oldest and dearest friend, Audree O'Connell, whom I had flown out from the West Coast. When Ellie asked her what she was doing there, Audree announced, "I'd fly across the country to watch you turn 50!"

Dinner was served and Ellie and I were seated with Audree and Mel Tormé, who was singing in town. As yet, no one had wished Ellie a "Happy Birthday." I had instructed them all to keep mum because I had something else up my sleeve. Between the main course and dessert, Ellie noticed some people coming in and thought they were part of the second seating. Then she recognized one of them as a member of the New York Choral Artists, the professional group she sang with. In fact, they were all members of that choir.

What Ellie hadn't realized was that I had rehearsed this choir in a special *Birthday Fanfare* I had written and arranged for them to sing in her honor. It was sung gloriously and they followed that with half an hour of English madrigals. But the musical magic didn't end there—Mel got up and sang an *a capella* version of Delius' *Brigg Fair*. It was utterly beautiful and it ended an utterly beautiful evening.

Before getting back to the subject of Mel, there was a follow-up to that story of Ellie's birthday. A few years later, when it was my birthday, I was playing at the Barbican in London with The King's Singers, with whom Neil and I had recently done a recording. We did a few things from the album, and before we went on, they happened to mention that as it was my birthday, they'd be singing something for me. There are six King's Singers, and the piece I'd written for Ellie was in six parts, and you can imagine my huge surprise when they sang this same piece for me claiming *they* had written it. Of course, Ellie had purloined the score, and with the collusion of their manager had got them to work it into our concert. Now it's become quite a contest between us to see who can upstage the other on our respective birthdays which are just nine days apart.

Mel couldn't have been more different from the type of singer—and I've worked with many of them over the years—who expects you to play exactly the same on the show as in the rehearsal. For that kind of performer, if you don't stick to exactly what was worked out, they're thrown. They just don't have ears that are compatible with a spontaneous jazz accompaniment, so that once an arrangement had been sorted out, there it would stay, set in stone. To some extent I had taken the same kind of rigid approach with the Quintet, particularly on the numbers where the guitar and vibes were doubling the melody I was playing on the piano. On the other hand, with Mel, I could change notes all over the place, and he'd be right there on the second eighth note, his ear was so keen.

To be honest, rehearsal was never necessary with Mel, we were so in tune with one another, and our music kept fresh and exciting because I rarely, if ever, played an accompaniment for him the same way twice. Obviously we often had something of a musical plan for what we were going to do, but it amounted to little more than the kind of skeletal arrangements I used to have with the semi-pro London bands with whom I started out. With them you'd say, "Okay, fellows, intro, two and out!" by which you'd mean a four-bar introduction for the piano, a couple of arranged choruses, maybe with a singer on the second, before you all got together for the final "out" chorus. That's a plan, but it by no means suggests that you have to play every note the same in every chorus. There are numerous people for whom, when I've played or recorded with them, I became a mere accompanist, which is something I've never wanted to do. If I can work with somebody who has ears like Mel Tormé then I'm free to do as I wish with the harmonies.

There was only one occasion I can recall when Mel wasn't able to solve a musical problem with that fantastic musical ear of his. He had just competed a new orchestration for the Boston Pops, with whom we were performing together. During the rehearsal,

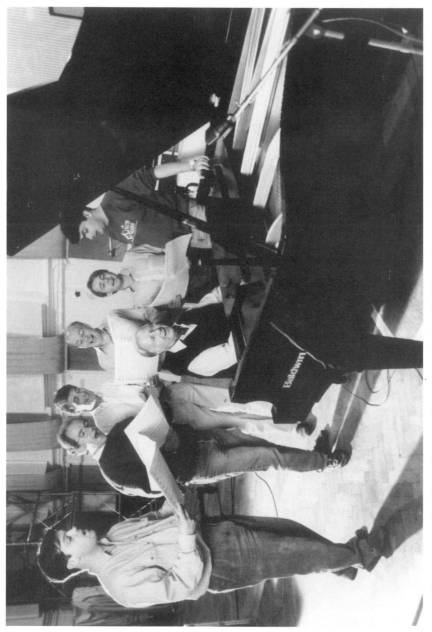

Recording with the The King's Singers. (Author's collection/EMI/Peter Vernon)

there was a wrong note somewhere in the arrangement, but he just couldn't work out where it was.

I said, "Mel, would you mind if I took over?"

"Yeah," he replied, "I wish you would."

Now Mel had tried to hear the problem through the sound of the whole orchestra. The only thing I did differently was to listen to the troublesome measure from each of the sections of the orchestra in turn.

First I called, "Strings!"

On my downbeat, they played it through and there was no sour note. Then, "Brass!" Same thing. Finally, "Woodwind!"

"Aha! Second clarinet, you're playing a B flat and it should be B natural."

The orchestra gave me a round of applause. But it was really common sense, and by isolating the sound, I was able to diagnose what had gone wrong.

Overall, I guess Mel and I had the same kind of rapport that Sarah Vaughan had with Jimmy Jones, way back when I first arrived on 52nd Street, or that Hank Jones had with Ella. Of course, Ella dealt with a repertoire that included fewer ballads and more straight-ahead jazz songs. That meant that the kind of numbers Mel and I specialized in would not come under Hank's fingers as often as they did for me, although of course Hank was such a consummate pianist he knew exactly how to deal with them when they did.

Mel and I could sit down and I'd say, "Do you know such and such a song?"

He was a monster when it came to remembering lyrics, and he really knew a lot of tunes. Almost always he'd come up with the song I'd called. Over the years, I've memorized a lot of lyrics too, because I love to sing, although I don't do it if there's anyone around who can *really* sing! Usually, I'd know exactly where to pitch the song to suit his voice, and we'd begin. Only very rarely would I have to move half a tone higher or lower, but generally we'd be in exactly the right range from the word go. And then— which is the incredible bit—we could immediately have done it professionally in front of an audience.

Mel was an extraordinary man. He was a great lyricist in his own right. He was a writer, a television show host, and at one point he even managed Judy Garland—can you imagine those two personalities together? I loved him dearly, he was a beautiful man, and of course we shared a sense of humor. We would laugh for hours at the same jokes.

We did an album together which includes a live version of a *New York, New York* medley, which started with the well-known intro: *doop, doop, dooby-doop, doop, doop, dooby-doop*. But instead of beginning the *New York, New York* theme, I'd go off into something different, like *Me and My Gal*. He'd pick it up, and then I'd be back at *doop, doop, dooby-doop*. Each time a different song.

He said, "Okay, George, I think they've got it now . . ."

But I kept on, until he came over to the piano and lifted my hands off the keys.

Come to think about it, we've made a lot of money kidding each other on stage. We had a thing going about what Christmas presents we'd given each other, which in reality was nothing. Mel would tell the audience that he had sent me a gold cheese grater, which was strange because I don't like cheese. He added that he received a lovely note of thanks, saying it was the most violent novel I ever read!

Another time, knowing that he liked to dabble in the markets, I said to him, "I've just found a stock that you might be interested in: American Thermometer. I bought it at 66½, took it home, shoved it up my ass, and it went immediately to 98.6." That joke ran a long time between us.

We worked together in all kinds of settings, from just a duo right up to full orchestras or big bands, like the BBC Big Band, which toured in the United States with us. I loved playing with that big band as much as any over the years, and I was particularly pleased that for that tour there were arrangements of many of my pieces in the band book. I had done some of the arrangements myself, and others had been done by old friends such as Dick Hyman.

Celebrating the 35th Newport Jazz Festival with Mel Tormé. (Author's collection/JVC/Michael Rose)

On the road with Mel Tormé and the BBC Big Band. (Author's Collection/Peter Lambourne)

Perhaps the most bizarre appearance we made was on the NBC *Today* show on television in the late 70s, where I sang and Mel played the piano. The host Tom Brokaw came over to me and said, "Is this the first time you've ever sung?"

"Yes," I said, "standing up!"

Our first recording together for Concord, released as *An Evening with George Shearing and Mel Tormé*, was made in the Peacock Court of the Hotel Mark Hopkins in San Francisco. It was a benefit for Guide Dogs for the Blind. We were aiming at an intimate sound, but the room itself has a very live acoustic. So how did we go about it? Speaking for myself, when I arrive at a room like that, I come in, try the piano and hear how it sounds in the space. If it reverberates you cope with it, and you can foresee problems before they come up so that you change what you are doing accordingly. I do it more the older I get, assessing the elements around me ahead of time, so I know how to deal with them. It's not good enough, for example, that the piano was tuned the week before—I want it tuned on the day of performance by someone who has some kind of ear. This kind of attention to detail and thinking means we will always perform to the highest level, whatever the acoustic problems of the space in which we are playing.

During the years that Mel and I recorded for Concord, we used to appear annually at the Paul Masson Winery at Saratoga in California, which became almost as regular as the kinds of bookings the old Quintet had in the 50s at the London House in Chicago. I got Mel in there and I helped to get Stephane Grappelli onto the roster, too. Eventually, both of them ended up recording several albums of their concerts there. It was an open-air auditorium right in the middle of the winery itself. I don't mind playing outdoors if the climate's right, but I don't like my hands to be cold when I play. The Paul Masson venue had a very benign climate, and I used to enjoy staying at the Chateau there, way up in the mountains in the California wine region, being waited on by the staff! It was a perfect setting for Mel and me to perform.

I have exactly the same kind of rapport with my current bassist, Neil Swainson, as I had with Mel. Sometimes I just have to nod my head slightly in Neil's direction, and he knows there's a

Reunited with Stephane Grappelli at Paul Masson winery, early 1980s. (Author's Collection)

substitute chord on its way. Immediately he figures out exactly where I'm going so that he's right there with me.

During the time I was recording for Concord, I also recorded with the guitarist Jim Hall. He's a real individual when it comes to the guitar. When we played as a duo we tended to stay out of each other's way very well, only coming together when a musical embrace seemed to be in order! In those same years I also recorded with Ernestine Anderson and with Carmen McRae. With Ernestine, although it began with just piano and voice, things were not very straightforward. To start with, we just wailed through everything, and as she was on a separate track, she had the opportunity to go back afterwards and re-do anything she wasn't happy with.

Carmen, on the other hand, was so well-prepared, the whole album took us only three hours and fifteen minutes to record. I had always loved her voice, going right back to the days of her early recordings, when she had such a beautiful sound, and of course she was very involved in singing bebop was well as the standard songs. So that was a very satisfying album to make, adding yet another successful collaboration to those I have had since I broke up the Quintet in 1978.

Earlier, talking of birthdays, I mentioned how organizing something for our respective celebrations became something of a cutting contest between Ellie and me. One marvelous thing Ellie arranged for me, which it would be hard to better, was on the occasion of my sixty-fifth birthday in 1984, when she secretly contacted just about everyone who had known me during my career and got them each to write a personal greeting. She had them transcribed into two books of Braille by a woman called Diann Smith, who did a really fantastic job in preparing all these dozens of letters for me to read.

On the evening of my birthday, I'd been playing at Paul Masson, and afterwards we came back to our room late at night. As I sat on the bed I realized I was sitting on something. I was just going to chastise Ellie for leaving things lying around, when I realized it was a book of Braille. As soon as I read the first lines, there was no stopping me—I was up half the night, reading all these letters from my friends and colleagues starting with Steve Allen and running right through the alphabet. Typical of what I found, from early on in the collection, was this generous note from Dave Brubeck:

> Every time I play my piano I see your face before me. There is a photo of you on my office wall, and I often wonder, when I look up, if George would like what I'm playing today!

A lot of the other notes made me look back on my life in a way I had never done up until that point. Leonard Feather, for example, welcomed me to Medicare by saying:

> After all these years there are so many shared events to look back on—in London, New York and out here in L.A., and who knows where else—going back more years than either of us would care to remember. The Rhythm Club in London, the Three Deuces, the Apex Studio, where we made the Discovery session (would you believe that was January 31st, 1949), the MGM studios, and on and on . . . What is most wonderful about this passage of all this time is that instead of becoming older and tireder, you keep getting better and better. The only sad part is you still have no sense of humor.

One surprise memory of those early London days came from a good friend in the musical world, with whom Ellie and I had spent many evenings over the years playing bridge—John Lewis of the Modern Jazz Quartet. John reminded me that our contact went back much earlier than my arrival in the United States, when he said, "I well remember our first encounter in 1943, when I first heard you playing with Stephane Grappelli in London at Hatchett's."

You might wonder how a blind man can sit down at a card table with sighted players, but we use a pack of cards that combines the ordinary symbols of the sighted deck with Braille. I started playing bridge when I was very young, and Ellie had also played from well before I knew her, so we always took the opportunity to play when we could. Although I have a very well-developed memory, from learning music and remembering lyrics, I find bridge is a bit of a battle between the power of my memory and my lack of concentration. I don't always concentrate as hard as I should, but even so, I prefer bridge to other, simpler, games, and as well as John Lewis, we've had many musical bridge partners over the years, including the swing bandleader Les Brown and his wife Claire. I took to Les the first time I met him, when someone invited me over to his house, and his first words to me were, "Sit your ass down here . . ." I often used to go along to hear his band when he was playing in and around Los Angeles, between television gigs, because I enjoyed his marvelous simple, straightforward orchestrations, and the way the band would swing. It was a very underrated band, given its consistency over the years. Whenever he spotted me, he often included a little pastiche of the Quintet, inevitably followed up by an announcement saying, "Sorry, George!"

Members of the original Quintet were included in my birthday book, too, and Marjie Hyams wrote, "When we met you were just a boy, George, but as you used to say, 'Time Marjies on' (and on and on)." And there was a really touching letter from my good friend and former bassist John Levy, which really sums up what our long, long association was all about. He wrote:

> The relationship which we have shared over these many years is one so deep and true that words such as 'thank you', 'appreciation' and even 'love' ring hollow and cannot do justice to my feelings. Your encouragement and support, the way you stood behind me especially during those early years, was largely responsible for the success of my career and my acceptance into this industry. But even more important was your faith in me as a person. And let's not forget all the great music we shared. To have been your bassist and then to have been your personal manager, allowing me to play a small role in furthering your great success has been an honor for me. But above all I am most proud to call you Friend.

Amid the many messages from my other musical colleagues was a note from Marian McPartland that concerned one thing we had in common, having both come to the United States from Britain. She began: "It seems like just yesterday that we were at the Statler Hilton Hotel in Cleveland and you were trying to get a decent cup of tea from room service!" And she went on to recall how we had come to know each other:

> I also remember the Silhouette Club in Chicago around 1949. Jimmy and I were enthralled by the Quintet. I think that's the first time we met, and I became one of your many friends. In fact if all your friends were laid end to end (and maybe some of them have been!), the chain would reach from here to London and back again.

Over the years I have appeared on Marian's *Piano Jazz* show a number of times, and it was always an enjoyable experience playing on the program. She has used the opportunities that broadcasting has given her very well, to introduce a variety of music and musicians to a large radio audience.

Other musicians who contributed pieces to my birthday collection were inspired to verse, including Tommy Flanagan, who wrote,

> *Said a famous pianist named Shearing*
> *I'll play on though the coda is nearing*
> *Here on earth or on high*
> *As ever—for aye—*
> *Out of sight, but not out of hearing!*

Considering how much music I have made since 1984, it's a surprise how many of those who wrote to me then seemed to expect me to be about to retire. I'd not long since finished a tour playing opposite Bob Crosby and the Bob Cats, which we'd all enjoyed a great deal, but Bob wrote:

> Welcome to the 'Social Security' club. Now you can start collecting the fruits of your labors. No agents' commissions! No more road trips! Relax and enjoy. Imagine yourself in a large comfortable chair, your stereo and the wonderful memories

of your association with so many great artists and the joy and happiness you have brought to millions.

I might not have been quite as ready to retire as Bob suggested there, but there's no denying I loved the organized Dixieland that Bob's band used to play. To me it was always much more rewarding than the free-for-all that often passes for traditional jazz, where nobody thinks about staying out of anybody else's way. Of course I knew all the famous compositions his band had recorded, particularly the pieces by Bob Haggart like *South Rampart Street Parade*, *My Inspiration*, and *What's New?*—a piece originally titled *I'm Free*, but which acquired its new title along with its lyrics.

Four years after this birthday tribute of mine, I had a chance to record a Dixieland session of my own for Concord *George Shearing in Dixieland*. I've always remained a great fan of the style, and I took the opportunity to orchestrate all the repertoire for the recording, working out the charts myself. I actually left relatively little room for free jamming, as I was using a four-piece front line of trumpet, trombone, clarinet, and tenor, and I wanted to keep a clear separation in the roles of the different instruments.

As well as liking Bob Crosby's band, I'd always been a fan of Vic Schoen and the things he recorded with the Andrews Sisters, with pianists like Billy Kyle and Frank Froeba in the line-up, and that was the kind of sound I was after. I asked Warren Vaché to play trumpet for me, and we also had Kenny Davern on clarinet, Ken Peplowski on tenor, and George Masso on trombone. Concord gave me a considerable amount of freedom, which I enjoyed, because in one or two other companies I can think of, there are producers who try to suggest things to artists, and tell them what to do, if they're not powerful enough to name their own ticket. For most recording projects, I don't think there's anybody who knows better than the artist about what to do, and I've always prided myself on doing things that are enjoyable to do musically and which will sell.

The Dixieland album was certainly very enjoyable, and in making it I went quite a long way out on a limb from the kind of music I'm normally known for. But I've got very diverse tastes, as both a listener and player. Indeed, if I thought I could play it well enough, I'd record a classical album, too. I've performed classics in public, of course, but I've never felt ready to record even the Mozart concerti that I've played a lot over the years.

In his typically English way, the broadcaster and one-time King's Singer, Brian Kay, took a rather different attitude from Bob Crosby to the milestone I had reached in 1984. His note said: "There's a malicious rumor going round that you are sixty-five years old, and we simply cannot believe it. We thought you were *much* older!" And Henry Mancini took a similar tack: "Don't feel too bad about reaching that milestone. I've got wine in my cellar older than you are!"

There was a reminder of an earlier neighborly connection in Bob Hope's note from Toluca Lake, that said he missed me, but not my guide dog, as his hedge was just starting to grow back!

Then there was the note from Stephen Sondheim, whose show *Sunday in the Park With George* had recently opened, and who said, "I hope you've noticed that I admire you so that I've named my latest show after you." And finally, Frank Sinatra wrote,

> Wish I could be with you tonight to lift a cup, however I'm singing for my supper in Monte Carlo and couldn't possibly get back in time to congratulate you with a big hug. You are a wonderful, decent, sensitive and great man, and I expect you to be around so that we can both celebrate the year 2000.

14

TODAY

Through the years I've been with several record labels. First there was Decca in England, then my first American recording was on Savoy and the launch of the Quintet on Discovery. I joined MGM in February 1949 and stayed with them until I began my long association with Capitol in the fall of 1955. That ran until the end of the 1960s and after recording in the early 70s for my own label, Sheba, I went first to MPS, and then to Concord, where I had another long-running business relationship, including all my work with Mel Tormé.

At the beginning of the 1990s, I made another move to Telarc. Things began for them with a couple of live albums from the Blue Note in New York, where I appeared during February 1992 with Neil Swainson on bass and Grady Tate on drums. I never had to say one word to Grady or Neil about the musical conception of the album; we just played. We covered all kinds of material from bebop pieces by Charlie Parker and Bud Powell to Brazilian tunes by Antonio Carlos Jobim. Plus there were some originals, too, by me and Neil, including his waltz *Horizon*.

Later that same year, I made an album in London with Robert Farnon for Telarc, called *How Beautiful is Night*. Bob wrote the arrangements and conducted a full orchestra. I've been a fan of Bob's since the days of World War Two. In the world of composing and arranging, he's known as the guv'nor and deserves all the many accolades he's received over the years. Our first recording together, *On Target*, dates from my MPS period, in 1979. That was an interesting recording, because I originally made the trio cuts in Villingen-Schwenningen in the Black Forest. Hans Georg Brunner-Schwer, the producer, decided it was going to be a Bob Farnon album and that we would lay in the orchestral tracks at a later date in England. So Bob received the cuts from MPS and worked on the orchestrations. I had the MPS engineer record an "A" on the piano for the orchestra to tune to, and they only did so in Wembley, two years later!

Hans Georg, the owner and chief engineer of MPS, is one of the nicest people in the world, with a marvelous family and a great studio in his house, although you did occasionally get the impression that he loved everything he did so much that he was reluctant to see it leave his shelves. Nevertheless, the studio he had set up was fantastic, and overall it was one of my best experiences in terms of recording of my whole career. When you went to the Black Forest to work there, you flew first class, stayed in the finest hotel in the area, and were well paid. This was followed up by regular accounting, so the company was good to work for, except as I say it sometimes took a long time to get things out. It certainly can't have been cheap to bring in Bob and a big orchestra to complete the disc we made together. Overall, recording with Hans Georg was a joy and a privilege, never just another job.

When I was reunited with Bob for the Telarc recording, *How Beautiful Is Night*, we did the whole thing live with all the musicians—my Quintet and his orchestra—together in the studio. Prior to the sessions, Bob came over to our cottage in the Cotswolds during the summer before we recorded, and spent the whole day with us. He had no manuscript paper with him, just a notepad and a pencil. He'd jot down a note or two here and there, and more often than not he'd write down a word, rather than a musical idea.

Later, his son told Ellie that what Bob did next was to go home to the Channel Islands, where he would sit down in his favorite chair. Once he's there, he thinks and thinks, and then he thinks a while longer. Then he pulls out some manuscript paper and starts writing. There's no piano involved. And the sounds that come out from the orchestra are not to be believed.

I can't think of anybody better at writing a beautifully orchestrated ballad than Robert Farnon. But he has his jazz moments too. He has been a good friend of many jazz musicians over the years, including a lot of the guys who played at Minton's, as well as leading the Canadian Band of the Allied Expeditionary Force during the war. He stayed on in London to write for Ted Heath,

Ambrose, and Geraldo, and to make his own discs for English Decca. In the days when I had my own radio show on WNEW in New York I played several of Bob's jazzier London recordings from the 1940s, including *You're The Cream In My Coffee*, which I announced as *You're The Crime in My Café*.

On four of the tracks we recorded together in 1992, I featured a group playing in the style of the old Quintet, with the English musicians Frank Ricotti on vibes and Allan Ganley on drums alongside guitarist Louis Stewart, an Irishman who had played in my trio in the 70s, and Neil Swainson on bass.

Two years after that, after endless requests to do so, I put together a Quintet again for a complete album called *That Shearing Sound*, which we made at a New York studio in February 1994.

Why did I decide to resurrect the Quintet?

I guess I felt the time was finally right, after being asked time and time again when I was going to make another Quintet record or if the band would ever tour again. I thought to myself, that maybe, just maybe, I could bring back the romantic sound of the Quintet with its quiet, self-contained feeling. Maybe there was something similar about the musical climate in the mid-90s to the time I first started the group as an antidote to the frantic energy of bebop—at any rate, I felt that we'd once again been through a rather frantic phase and it was time for something more placid and more melodic. There are periods in our lives when we seem to be more receptive to peaceful or to frantic things, and this was definitely a peaceful time.

When I started writing the arrangements for the album, I was like a kid with a new toy. I'd wake up every morning with a new idea for the project, and couldn't wait to work it out for the group. The sound wasn't new. It was back to the ingredients of the original Shearing sound, but I'd been away from it long enough that I was no longer on autopilot.

The main decision I made was that although the sound was the same, I wanted all new musicians who had never played in the Quintet. I didn't want the problem of selecting former Quintet members.

Neil Swainson, of course, was the automatic choice on bass, and Dennis Mackrel was the perfect drummer. On vibes was Steve Nelson, a Rutgers graduate who had played around New York with several bands and recorded with Kenny Barron and Bobby Watson, and who's subsequently been a member of Dave Holland's various groups. On guitar was Louis Stewart.

After that, we continued to record as a Quintet, but I also recorded a trio album with Louis and Neil, and a solo piano album.

Back in the 1940s, when I was starting out, Billy Shaw used to book me through promoters who wanted another of his more famous acts. Often a condition for getting Dizzy Gillespie was that a promoter took George Shearing first. By the 1990s, with many years in the business, I'm glad to say the tables were turned, and I was able to do my bit to help three younger pianists whom I admired immensely and still do. They are Fred Hersch, Bill Charlap, and Benny Green, musicians whom I discovered on record, but having done so, made efforts to hear in person. All three of them share with me some of the same aspects of our musical thinking.

In 1998 Pat Philips and Ettoré Strata produced an eightieth birthday concert for me at Carnegie Hall. There were more friends on stage as well, because they asked many musicians including Tito Puente and Nancy Wilson to be part of the show. To prepare the guys in the band, I sent out the music well in advance for the tunes that the Quintet was going to play with Nancy, which I'd selected from our album *The Swinging's Mutual*. The numbers included *The Nearness of You*, *Green Dolphin Street*, and *All Night Long*. When we actually got together to do the show she was magical, although it was well over thirty years since we'd originally recorded these songs.

Later, Nancy told Ellie in the wings that it was "just like the album!" Ellie told her how I'd sent the guys tapes of the songs, so we could get them exactly right. I still think Nancy is marvelous, and it was great to work with her again in that setting.

Also on the bill were John Pizzarelli and his trio, Dave Brubeck—who played two-piano pieces with me—and, as I mentioned, Tito, who brought down the house playing percussion with the Quintet for some exciting Afro-Cuban music. It was very informal, Ellie was on stage with us, and as people came on, she welcomed them and then they went on to sing or play. Needless to say, the hall was sold out, and it was a very memorable event for me. What I remember most was the love and fellowship I felt around me, coming from both the performers and the sold-out house. It was like having a gigantic hug. People from my past came up and talked of our days together, like George Wein, who reminisced about Storyville. John Levy, who was in the audience, wrote a lovely note, saying, "It was an overwhelmingly moving night for me. One which I will never, ever, forget."

In October 2000, after returning from our summer vacation in the Cotswolds in England, I took the Quintet back to Birdland. At least, that's what we called the resulting album, but in reality that's something of a misnomer, because it was more about going back to the Birdland concept. Today, with the new club on West 44th Street, the place is entirely different from the original club on Broadway, and the only similarity is in the name. There was a lapse of over thirty years between the last time I played the original Birdland and the first time I played the new club that took its name.

The new place works well as a room to play, and I seemed to sense what the audience wanted. But I missed old Pee Wee Marquette, the midget who used to announce the bands at the old club in his tiny high-pitched voice. Everyone who played at the original Birdland really used to put Pee Wee on unmercifully. I could hear him talking away somewhere below my elbow, and I always wished someone would bring him up level with my left ear. From time to time Slim Gaillard used to get a chair and put it on stage. Because Pee Wee was so small Slim thought he ought to stand on it to reach the microphone. As he was talking, Slim would raise the microphone as high as it would go—and Slim was a tall, tall man. Then he'd say to the crowd, "I just want to get the microphone ready for Pee Wee."

Despite all that, Pee Wee didn't seem to mind having gags made about him. He remained one of life's comic eccentrics with a highly unusual choice of words.

When we were back at Birdland with the new Quintet in 2000, I wanted to try hard to maintain something familiar about the group's sound—to recapture its special qualities for those who did not hear or were not particularly knowledgeable about the original band. So we played numbers such as *Lullaby of Birdland*, or *Autumn in New York*, and I kept the basis of the locked-hands style, using the familiar vibes and guitar voicings, but mixed with a slightly more contemporary feel. After all, we've all heard a good deal of music since those first recordings came out in 1949, and several of today's Quintet, including Neil Swainson, Reg Schwager and Dennis Mackrel, weren't even born when I made those original recordings!

A year or so later, we had a rather different experience, collaborating in the studio with guitarist John Pizzarelli on the album, *The Rare Delight of You*. He and I had listened to each other's work before we got together, so it was easy for us to do the arrangements for the album. I'd known the Pizzarelli family for a long time. They're all very musically minded, and I enjoyed playing with John, my old friend Bucky's son, as he is not only a gifted guitarist but also a fine singer. Bucky himself is an old friend and a marvelous guitarist in his own right. Recording with John had an added bonus: he really knows his wines, and he promised to come over and give Ellie a lesson in pasta making, the way his Mom does it!

Much of the time now, I appear in a trio with Neil on bass and Reg on guitar. We've been doing it for so long that we've fallen into a well-established pattern for our concerts. I have always thought of what I do—even the most straight-ahead jazz imaginable—as show business. So I put on a properly thought-through program, towards the end of which Neil and Reg play a duet to give the old man a "breather." Then I come back to play a solo, maybe sing another, and talk to the audience. I'll let you in on a secret. If I like the piano and the way it responds, I'll play something in a very impressionistic way. If I feel that the piano is not friendly, I'll play something honky-tonk by Scott Joplin or Meade Lux Lewis. Then we finish together with something very spectacular, before playing out with something like Cole Porter's *Every*

Time We Say Goodbye. Or, if we are in a more humorous mood we do a composition of Erroll Garner's called *Loot To Boot.* But there will always be a little humor in what we do. Most of our concerts also have at least a reference to J. S. Bach, so the classical influence is often in evidence.

One number we often play is *Come Sunday,* where I put in a little rocking gospelly section for the audience to clap or snap their fingers along with us. I usually end up saying to the audience, "Now just watch me—because it's fairly easy for you to watch me, but I have a hell of a time trying to watch you!" We start out loud, and I get them to place their claps quite carefully—not on beats one and three, but on two and four. Then we get quieter and quieter, and they snap their fingers more and more softly, until Neil and I drop out altogether, and there's nothing but the finger snapping left. This kind of audience participation is fun for them and, more often than not, it leads into a standing ovation. Then I feel that my purpose has been better served, in terms of connecting with the audience, than just getting up there and playing a set.

It can be hazardous, when, after my solo feature, I announce Neil's return to the stage, and then go into a rapid bebop tune on which we play some pretty dramatic fast choruses until we trade fours or eights. On one particular occasion, when I was back in the UK at the festival in Bath, the tune I selected was Bud Powell's *Wail.* I talked a bit at the microphone, and then, having announced Neil's return, I sat down and began. I hadn't reckoned with the fact that the Forum Theater is like a labyrinth backstage, and it took some while for Neil to find his way from the greenroom back to the platform. For about a couple of choruses, I played on, wondering what had happened to him. There's a BBC recording of that concert, and you can hear the roar from the audience as we were eventually reunited a considerable number of measures into the number!

Around the same time, I was invited to play at the Cork Jazz Festival in Ireland. On the flight over on Aer Lingus, I noticed that, for the only time in my long experience of flying, the safety cards in the seat-back pockets were in Braille. We eventually ar-

Back at Cheltenham Town Hall over 60 years after first playing there. Neil and me at the International Jazz Festival, 2000. (Peter Symes)

rived in Cork, and I was met by a group of people who asked me if I'd like to come on a visit to a little town some distance away because there was a convention for blind people going on at the inn there. Indeed the inn made a point of catering for the blind, and when you checked in they handed you a map of your room raised on thermoform paper, so you could tell, as a blind person, where all the furniture was, and the location of the windows for fresh air. The rooms also had the phone list for room service, laundry, and so on printed in Braille.

This seemed rather extraordinary, and I very much enjoyed going up to meet everyone there, to address them briefly, and to play a little on the upright piano in the inn. As I was leaving, I told them how impressed I was that they made such a point of catering to blind customers, and asked where they got the maps, phone lists, and so forth from.

"At Arbor Hill Prison, in Dublin" they told me. And I discovered that one of the rehabilitation programs for offenders is to learn to manufacture goods in Braille. Another program is to study woodwork, and I understand the prison supplies much of the furniture for the local children's hospital. But then, to my surprise, when I investigated a little further, I found out that I'd actually had a part to play in the success of the Braille program. Apparently, a group of offenders were watching an interview I did on English television with Michael Parkinson, in which I had happened to mention that airline safety cards were never available in Braille, and they went to their Governor and said, "We don't want Mr. Shearing to be able to say this about Ireland." And with some lobbying on their behalf, Aer Lingus was persuaded to act on the suggestion. The offenders made the cards, and I came upon them for the first time on that same flight over to Cork.

I was so impressed by what I found out about this prison that I said to Ellie, "I'd like to go and play for them sometime."

Two or three years later, we managed to work it out, and I went over to Dublin to give the concert. I still remember the sinister sound of the outer gate slamming behind us as we were driven into the prison yard. In their library they had a lot of Braille books and I was given a guided tour of those. Then we came down to the site of the concert, which was a point at which the four cell blocks met at a central atrium. The tuner told me he'd had a high old time trying to tune the piano in such an echoey environment.

"Like shooting ducks in fog," he put it.

Ellie told me that all the offenders, guards, and priests in the audience were dressed in civilian clothes. So there was a very relaxed atmosphere, given that we were inside a jail. One of the offenders came up before I began and presented me with an edition of Irish folk tales that he had put into Braille, in honor of my visit.

After Neil and I had played the concert, the two of us and Ellie were taken to tea with the Governor, via an impromptu visit to the kitchen. At the tea party we met another offender who specialized in Braille music. He showed me some of his work, and I said, "The next time I come, I'd love to see more of your handiwork."

"Mr. Shearing," he said, "I won't be here. I'm getting out in a fortnight, and I have a job to go to as a music Brailler."

I was really heartened to hear this, and I wondered to myself why more prison education programs, particularly in the United States, don't do such useful work in training and rehabilitation. Arbor Hill is a model prison, with individual cells for all the offenders. As I was leaving, the Governor said, "Well, Mr. Shearing, if ever you're back in Dublin and stuck for somewhere to stay, don't hesitate to give me a call!"

I'm proud to say that following the example of Aer Lingus, nearly all the major airlines have followed their lead and now have Braille safety cards. So I think I may have played a minor role in making the world a safer place for the blind!

Coming back to the subject of our summers in the Cotswolds in England, there's another British venue with which I was glad to be associated. John Dankworth and Cleo Laine redesigned the old stables in their Buckinghamshire garden and built a lovely theater. The original venue, which they opened in the 1960s, was tiny. The stage and about a hundred seats were squeezed into the old stables building itself. But in 2001, with help from the National Lottery, they opened a marvelous new theater on the site, and what had once been the auditorium became the foyer of the new building. I played one of the opening concerts on the new stage, and as I walked out to play, there was a standing ovation. I turned to the audience and said, "Where were you when I played Wigan?" That got a huge laugh and we started the concert in high spirits.

I've been a fan of John and Cleo ever since they first got together as a double act during the 1950s in the days of the Johnny Dankworth Seven, with Cleo as the vocalist. I'd heard John well before that because he was coming up as a teenage prodigy on the British jazz scene during the war. He began the partnership with Cleo as her arranger and musical director. John has very skillfully pulled out every stop of her musical capabilities, from her enormous range to her tremendous ear. The result is a marvelous partnership. I've worked on the same bill with the two of them many times, and enjoyed it immensely every time.

It was during another of my summers in England that I got an announcement from the office of the Queen that I had been nominated for the O.B.E. (Officer of [the Order of] the British Empire), and I replied that I would be honored to accept. A few months later, I attended an investiture at Buckingham Palace. I was also rather pleased to be able to reflect that I had been able to play for three U.S. presidents. Now I was being honored by the Queen of the country where I was born. I have received a number of other awards, including three honorary doctorates in music. One of these came from Ellie's alma mater, DePauw University in Greencastle, Indiana, another from Hamilton College, in upstate New York, and the third from Westminster College in Salt Lake City, Utah. I am extremely proud of these honors, but in the quiet moments when I reflect on all this, I can't help thinking, "Not bad for a kid from Battersea!"

I'm beginning to feel that it's time to stop writing. But I ought to finish on a lighthearted note. I've been asked a number of very inappropriate questions from time to time. Inappropriate because they're asked at the wrong time or addressed to the wrong person. For example, ask me about cricket, not football. Or bridge, not pinochle. Or tennis, not hockey.

I started this book with three questions. The first two I have been asked over and over in my professional life. I hope you've figured out the answer to the third, but I'd like to close by adding a fourth. That is, "Have you been blind all your life?"

To which I must joyfully and resoundingly answer, "Not yet!"

RECOMMENDED RECORDINGS
(compiled by Alyn Shipton)

There is no space in this book for a full listing of George Shearing's many recordings, but this is a short list of discs that together give a cross section of his work, and were currently available at the time the book went to press.

Midnight on Cloud 69 (Savoy)
All the tracks recorded by the original Quintet for the Discovery label in 1949, before George signed with MGM, including 'Life with Feather' and 'Bebop's Fables'. Four additional tracks by Red Norvo are also included.

The Definitive George Shearing (Verve)
A 21-track anthology of the best of the Quintet's early recordings, from both the MGM and Capitol periods, 1949–1963. As well as 'September in the Rain' and other hits by the original line-up, this also contains pieces recorded by later versions of the group featuring Joe Roland, Cal Tjader, Toots Thielemans, Al McKibbon, and Gary Burton. Featured vocalists include Peggy Lee, Billy Eckstine, and Nancy Wilson.

Nat King Cole and George Shearing: Essential Cole and Shearing (EMI)
A classic album containing the famous hit version of 'Let There Be Love' as well as the infectiously swinging 'Pick Yourself Up', plus thirteen other examples of this acclaimed collaboration.

George Shearing and the Montgomery Brothers (Original Jazz Classics)
Fourteen tracks from the 1961 studio partnership between George and the brothers Montgomery—Wes, Buddy, and Monk—that offer a rather different take on the Shearing sound, plus a selection of ballad and Latin tracks.

The Heart and Soul of Joe Williams and George Shearing (Koch)
In another masterly partnership with a singer, this captures the warmth and affection of the musical relationship between Joe Williams and George Shearing. It features over a dozen tunes that are linked by their titles to the name of the album, ranging from 'Body and Soul' to 'I Let a Song Go Out of My Heart'.

Mel Tormé and George Shearing: The Complete Concord Recordings (Concord)
This is a 7-CD set, but it captures in one place the full discography of the "two bodies with one musical mind" partnership of George and Mel. All their classic albums are included, together with a bonus CD of additional material.

George Shearing and Barry Tuckwell: Play the Music of Cole Porter (Concord)
A highly successful pairing of the top classical French horn player and the Shearing piano, playing eleven Cole Porter standards, beautifully arranged by George for duo, Quintet, and orchestra.

Duets (Concord)
A cross section of partnerships from the 1980s, including guitarist Jim Hall, and singers Ernestine Anderson and Carmen McRae, as

well as George's two-piano sessions with his mentor Hank Jones and fellow British expatriate Marian McPartland.

How Beautiful is Night (Telarc)
George Shearing meets the Robert Farnon Orchestra in his second recorded collaboration with the great arranger, cut in London in 1993, and featuring a dozen exceptional tracks drawn from various stage musicals including *Bandwagon* and *Oklahoma!*

Back to Birdland (Telarc)
The re-formed Quintet recorded live at the new Birdland club in the fall of 2000 revisits the group's classic repertoire, plus some surprise new additions, in a lively and infectiously swinging package.

George Shearing and John Pizzarelli: The Rare Delight of You (Telarc)
Highly successful 2002 teaming of George with the singer/guitarist who is a member of one of the most distinguished families of jazz musicians, that includes fifteen songs played as duos or with the Shearing Quintet.

INDEX